The Hoover Report *1953–1955*

THE MACMILLAN COMPANY
NEW YORK • CHICAGO
DALLAS • ATLANTA • SAN FRANCISCO
LONDON • MANILA
THE MACMILLAN COMPANY
OF CANADA, LIMITED
TORONTO

The Hoover Report *1953-1955*

WHAT IT MEANS TO YOU AS CITIZEN AND TAXPAYER

NEIL MACNEIL

AND

HAROLD W. METZ

Introduction by

HERBERT HOOVER

35637

New York 1956

THE MACMILLAN COMPANY

JK
643
.C53
M3

© Neil MacNeil and Harold W. Metz 1956
Published simultaneously in Canada

All rights reserved—no part of this book may be reproduced in any form without permission in writing from the publisher, except by a reviewer who wishes to quote brief passages in connection with a review written for inclusion in magazine or newspaper.

First Printing

Printed in the United States of America

Library of Congress catalog card number: 56-7319

Introduction

To write a readable and interesting book on the extraordinarily complicated problems of reorganization of some 1,900 Federal Government agencies is an accomplishment in itself.

This book does two things:

First, it presents the philosophic background enunciated by the Commission in approaching its problems. These philosophic backgrounds are indeed the backgrounds of our form of government and our way of life. Unless every recommendation of change had been tested by these touchstones, they would lead only to confusion both in concept and in administration.

Second, the authors have done an amazing job in condensation and lucidity of presentation of the Commission findings and recommendations. About 3,300,000 words giving the facts, findings, and recommendations were presented to the Commission by its task forces and research staff. The Commission, in giving their majority views in reports to the Congress, condensed these to about 600,000 words. The authors of this book further condense them to about 100,000 words, and in so doing cover the major issues. If the reader wants to know more, he can go back to the Commission reports and thence to the Task Force reports, each of which can be had from the Public Printer.

One of the important purposes of the Commission was to open the doors of understanding of the functions of our government to our people at large. They are a lesson on civil government of significant educational value. And this book is a condensation of those lessons and the arguments over them.

One reason for the high standards of this presentation is the men who did it. Mr. Neil MacNeil, with a life background in editorial work on most important journals, was the Commission's editor in chief over its entire life. In that capacity every report passed through his hands not once, but often two or three times. Dr. Harold Metz, with a background of twenty years of research into problems of government, was the chief of the Commission's research staff during its entire life, and his duty was to check every statement of fact in the reports.

In addition to their contacts with documents, the two of them attended every one of scores of Commission meetings and many Task Force meetings. They know more about the work of the Commission than any other mortal. They are both men dedicated to the service of the American people.

Herbert Hoover

Contents

1.

Servant or Master?

CHAPTER 1

The Ever Present Government

Whether he realizes it or not, Government in one form or another accompanies the American citizen as an uninvited guest almost everywhere he goes and in almost everything he does. It puts its long finger into his pay envelope and extracts what it wants before he takes that pay envelope home to his family. If he goes into business it becomes his silent partner and takes a large share of the profits while refusing to share in the losses, except in a minor degree. If he buys a package of cigarettes, a washing machine, a coat or a car or anything else for himself or for his family, it imposes its toll in the form of taxes of one sort or another. Not content with all this, it also persists in issuing directives that tell him what he can do and how, and that are always a dilution of his liberties.

The result is that today the American voter and taxpayer counts for less as an individual, as a free citizen, than ever before in American history. Often he feels more like a cog in a huge wheel than he does as a person with God-given "unalienable" rights. In fact, he feels so impotent as one individual among 165,000,000 to deal with his huge, all-pervading Government and the colossal and complex economic system in which he must make a livelihood for himself and his family that he strives to align himself with some group or organization, such as a labor union or farm union, that will advance his interests and protect his rights. He dreads bureaucrats. He thinks of them as milkers and he knows he is the one being milked.

Nor does the businessman escape, whether he be big or little. He is daily in contact with the regulations of Government bureaus and departments. Often he must face the unfair competition of Government-financed and tax-free business. The very taxes he himself pays, supposedly to support that Government, are used by it to set up rival businesses that make it more difficult for him to pay those taxes or to make a profit on his investment of capital and labor. At the same time he must make numerous expensive and time-consuming reports to Federal agencies and obey scores of petty regulations. So he too feels that he must belong to some organization to advance his interests and to protect his rights.

It is the little man, whether as worker, farmer, or businessman, that suffers most under this system. It is he who feels insecure. Only Big Business can cope with Big Government. This has tended to stifle American enterprise. Less and less can the American start his own business, and more and more must he work for wages. Meanwhile, Big Business has been getting bigger, and Big Government is becoming a Frankenstein's monster that turns upon its creators.

These are some of the reasons why the Commission on Organization of the Executive Branch of the Government, under the chairmanship of the Honorable Herbert Hoover, thirty-first President of the United States, made its extensive study of the functions of the American Government. In its examination it found extravagance and waste in the expenditure of the taxpayer's money, inefficiency and duplication in many operations, and numerous instances of bureaucrats pushing the people about. The implementation of its findings and recommendations will go far to determine whether the American Government will be your servant or your master.

THE PROBLEMS OF BIGNESS

Most Americans would agree that the best Government is the Government that governs least. They do not like regimentation. They do not like to be tyrannized over by bureaucrats. They do not like Big Government and what it means.

As a people, Americans have always cherished personal liberty. We have exalted the dignity of the individual and the sacredness of the human being. Each American considers himself as good as any other American, and before the law he is. The American firmly believes that it is his inherent right to do what he pleases, to go where he wishes, to say what he wants to say, and to earn his livelihood in the way that suits him best, as long as he does not impinge on the right of his neighbor to do the same. At one time he took political liberty and economic liberty for granted as he did the air he breathed.

Despite certain modern thinkers who deny the validity of natural law, and the proponents of alien ideologies, the average American still believes in the precepts of the Declaration of Independence. He is convinced that as a citizen of the United States he is endowed with certain "unalienable Rights" and that "among these are Life, Liberty and the pursuit of Happiness." Moreover, he believes that these rights are based on "the laws of nature and of nature's God." He repudiates the idea that rights come from Government, for he knows that Government can grant only what it has previously taken from the people.

Every American, old and young, knows that his Federal Government had its origin in the Constitutional Convention in Philadelphia and he also knows that his rights existed before that Convention ever was held. He knows that his Government was set up not to confer rights on him, but to protect rights that were already his. The Fascist or the Communist or the Socialist theories of the all-powerful Government, the Big Government, have never had any appeal for him, for he wants the Government to be his servant and not his master. He has always distrusted the bureaucrat who grasped for power and still more power. The objective in drafting the Constitution was to protect the individual through the formation of a Government with limited powers.

The very form and structure of the Government were designed to promote this goal. The Constitution itself as the supreme law of the land gives protection to these rights. There are the three branches of the Federal Government, the legislative, the executive, and the judicial, each independent of the others and each a check on the activities of the others. Then there is the division of power between the Federal Government and the State governments so that each will limit the authority of the other. Finally there are the numerous local governments, county, city, and village, that bring government down to the level of the citizen no matter how remote he may be from the national or State capital. There he sees government in actual operation and can make his desires known and get results. All this elaborate structure of government has had one primary purpose: to protect the individual from domination by a transitory majority while yet ministering to those needs of the people which cannot be met through their individual endeavors. Meanwhile it has also served to keep control of government in the hands of the governed. It has also tended to prevent any one Government from becoming too big.

This system of government worked well in the United States for more than a century, and in that century the United States laid the foundations of the mighty nation it is today. It would have continued indefinitely to serve that purpose except for conditions beyond the control of the American people. First of all, the United States itself became big. It spread across the continent from the Atlantic to the Pacific, and its population increased from 5,000,000 in 1800 to 165,000,000. It also developed a tremendous industrial output with mass production, mass distribution, a vast and intricate maze of factories and communications with more than 60,000,000 workers. Finally came the military crises of the two world wars and of the Korean War. Similarly, the economic crisis of the big depression was upsetting.

Conditions resulting from these emergencies served to enlarge the Federal Government, often at the expense of State and local governments. The needs for interstate regulations, for antitrust controls, for order in a vast and speedy communication system, for supervision of huge financial operations, made many new agencies of our Government necessary and added to the size of many existing departments and bureaus. The insistent demands of national defense, especially in the two world wars, which had to be met quickly regardless of cost, served further to expand the Government. Moreover, pressure groups, corporations, labor unions, and even the States, got into the habit of turning to Washington to solve their problems.

The tendency for more than two decades has been to set up a new agency of Government to meet each new demand, and these have in turn tended to become little empires with their own budget, their own bureaucracy and their own self-serving pressure group. Often they continue long after the purpose for which they were created ceases to exist. The Federal Government has gone far afield, often into Socialist experiments. It has entered into competition with private enterprise in many areas, using the national credit to serve one segment of the people at the cost of the whole people. It has imposed one control after another on business, on agriculture, on the activities of citizens, until all but a few phases of life feel the heavy hand of the Federal Government. At the same time it has also imposed a burdensome load of debt and taxes on the American taxpayer and the national economy.

Some idea of the colossal size of the National Government may be gained from the fact that in 1954 it embraced 2,133 different functioning agencies, bureaus, departments, and divisions. From 1800 to 1953 Federal expenditures rose from $5,776,000 to $74,607,-420,000. In the same time the number of Federal employees increased from about 5,000 to 2,345,000. The fastest growth came, of course, in the period from the beginning of World War I to the end of the Korean War, when Federal expenditures multiplied fourteen times. In these years the public debt grew even faster, going from $1,191,264,000 in 1915 to $266,071,061,639 in 1953.

This vast and rapid expansion of Government naturally made for waste and extravagance. Especially it strengthened and expanded the executive branch of the Federal Government and weakened the others. It encouraged the trend toward collectivism, which for the first time made its appearance in the United States, and it went far to discourage and weaken the free enterprise system. It has greatly weakened the position of the individual in relation to his Government. Thus there long has been a crying need for a group of competent public men to resurvey the Government's activities for the purpose of bringing them back into conformity with the principles of the American Constitution.

MORE THAN DOLLARS INVOLVED

This sprawling and amorphous mass of overlapping and extravagant agencies of our Government is difficult to supervise and almost impossible to control. Its sheer size and the variety of its impact make it easy to evade responsibility. As it multiplied its services it also expanded its propaganda, and seized every opportunity to direct the thinking of the people. The result is that while bureaucrats still speak in terms of serving the public, more and more they have been telling citizens what to do and how to do it.

There is more need of control of Government today by the people than ever before in the United States because the ramifications of Government are broader.

For instance, because Congress has often found it difficult to legislate adequately concerning new and important functions that demanded regulation, it has given legislative authority to a dozen or more regulatory agencies. Such agencies make their own regulations, interpret them, bring charges under them and, acting both as prosecutor and as judge, impose fines or other penalties on citizens, so that in fact the servant has become the master. All too often adequate judicial review of their decisions is not available to the citizen. The growth of Federal agencies has thus been accompanied by a steady erosion of liberty.

The cost of this huge American Government must be met in dollars that must be collected in taxes which must be paid for in the work of the people. But what is even more important than its inefficiency and cost is that this all-powerful Government is controlling our lives in every possible way in a manner incompatible with individual liberty.

Thus today the gravest internal problem we have is whether the people run the Federal Government or the Federal Government runs the people.

ATTEMPTS AT REORGANIZATION

The steady growth in the mere size of the Federal Government, along with the steady expansion of its activities, has long disturbed students of government and American statesmen. Presidents as well as members of Congress have tried at various times to halt that growth or at least to make the colossal machine Government had become more efficient and more economical. Other observers have been disturbed over the continuing erosion of American liberties, especially in the area of free enterprise, as the Government has competed more and more with private industry.

The earliest of the modern attempts to reorganize the American Government was undertaken by the Cockrell Committee, which was created by the Senate, and which from 1887 to 1889 investigated business methods in the executive departments. Next, in 1893–1895, came the Dockery-Cockrell Commission, set up by the House of Representatives and the Senate, to look into the functioning of the executive departments, other Federal organizations and laws. Then came the Keep Commission, acting for the President, which from 1905 to 1909 made a study of departmental methods. Again, in 1910, the President, this time acting with congressional authorization, created the President's Commission on Economy and Efficiency, and it functioned until 1913. In 1921 the House and the Senate sponsored the Joint Committee on Reorganization of Government Departments. And again in 1936–1937 two committees operated in the same area, the Byrd Committee for the Senate and the President's Committee on Administrative Management headed by Louis Brownlow.

All of these bodies made serious studies, and most of them made important reports to the Congress or to the President. Yet for the most part they were ineffectual. They did not get public support. Little or nothing was done about their recommendations, and the reforms they proposed died a-borning.

Since World War II we have had the two Commissions on Organization of the Executive Branch of the Government, each headed by Mr. Hoover, and each popularly known as the Hoover Commission. Both of these were created by unanimous votes of both houses of Congress. The first functioned in 1947–1949 and the second in 1953–1955.

The method of selecting members of each Commission was identical. Each was composed of twelve members. Four of these were named by the President, four by the Vice President, and four by the Speaker of the House of Representatives. Each of these was to name two men from public and two men from private life. In each case the Commission, when named, was authorized to select its own chairman, and each chose Mr. Hoover. The first Commission included six Republicans and six Democrats, and the second, seven Republicans and five Democrats. It should be added here that neither Commission ever divided on partisan lines.

The two Hoover Commissions differed widely in the scope of their authority and in their approach to the problems of Government.

The first Commission was given authority to "study and investigate the present organization and method of operation of all departments, bureaus, agencies, boards, commissions, offices, independent establishments and instrumentalities of the Executive Branch of the Government." Concerning objectives of the Commission the Act was vague, and this resulted in some confusion. Consequently the Commission decided to confine its recommendations to the organization and structure of the various agencies under inquiry in an effort to promote greater efficiency and to effect economies.

Concerning the Commission's approach to Government activities, Mr. Hoover himself emphasized: "It is not our function to say whether it should exist or not, but it is our function to see if we can make it work better."

The first Commission set up twenty-four studies of various phases of Government activities. Some of these were done by contract with research institutions. Others were performed by Task Forces. These latter were made up of distinguished Americans like Henry L. Stimson, former Governor Leslie Miller, of Wyoming; Robert Moses, of New York; and other public leaders with special competence in the field under review. The Commission itself had only a small staff. Each Task Force had only one order from the Chairman: get the facts. The Commission in its turn based its recommendations to the Congress on those facts and its own knowledge. The Commission's reports and the Task Forces' reports totaled about 2,000,000 words.

In all, the first Commission made 273 recommendations for reorganization of the Government. These sought to establish a clear line of command in most of the important agencies of Government. They suggested improved budgeting methods, records management, procurement practices, the creation of the General Services Administration to handle operation and management of public buildings, and many other ways of getting efficiency in operations or in effecting savings. If carried out, the 273 recommendations would have saved the taxpayer between two and three billion dollars.

The latest available box score on the first Commission's recommendations indicates that better than 72 per cent of them have been implemented either by administrative action or by legislation. This is by far the best record on any attempt to reorganize a republican form of government. How substantial the savings were will never be known for the simple reason that soon after the termination of the Commission's activities the Korean War broke out and the Federal budget leaped from $40 billions into the $70 billions. There is no doubt, however, that the savings were large.

The success of the first Commission made the second Commission inevitable. With the further growth of the Government, and especially of the Defense Department, resulting from the Korean War, and the consequent crushing burden of taxes, many thoughtful citizens, both in and out of Congress, felt that another Hoover Commission should take a good look at the executive branch of the

Government, and it was emphasized that this time the Commission be given wider powers to investigate the wisdom of the policies of the Government as well as the appropriateness of its structure. The Congress did this in 1953, and President Eisenhower signed the law on July 10, 1953. Under that law the second Hoover Commission was charged by Congress with the duty "to promote economy, efficiency, and improved service in the transaction of the public business" in all the executive agencies by:

1. Recommending methods and procedures for reducing expenditures to the lowest amount consistent with the efficient performance of essential services, activities, and functions;
2. Eliminating duplication and overlapping of services, activities, and functions;
3. Consolidating services, activities, and functions of a similar nature;
4. Abolishing services, activities, and functions not necessary to the efficient conduct of government;
5. Eliminating nonessential services, functions, and activities which are competitive with private enterprise;
6. Defining responsibilities of officials; and
7. Relocating agencies now responsible directly to the President in departments or other agencies.

This Act thus provided sweeping authority for the Commission. Moreover, the Act also provided that the Commission in its final report might propose "such constitutional amendments, legislative enactments, and administrative actions as in its judgment are necessary to carry out its recommendations." With explicit authority to recommend changes in the Constitution itself, one would not expect its right to deal with policy matters to be questioned. Yet this has happened. So, to end any doubt about the intent of Congress, it might be well to quote here from the sponsors of the Act before its enactment in the Congress.

AUTHORITY ON POLICY MATTERS

Hearings held by the Senate and House Committees on Government Operations on the bills sponsored by the then Senator Homer Ferguson and Representative Clarence Brown indicate clearly that the sponsors intended that the Commission should have this authority.

In the Senate hearing (on S. 106, 83d Congress, First Session, April 14, 1953, p. 49) Senator Ferguson said:

> The most important difference between this bill and the first Hoover Commission statute is found in paragraphs 7 through 10 of section 1, the Declaration of Policy section. These paragraphs are intended to make certain that this Commission has full power to look into the activities of the Federal Government from the standpoint of *policy* and to inquire "Should the Federal Government be performing this activity or service and if so, to what extent?" This Commission must ask questions of this nature which the original Hoover Commission did not ask.

In the House hearings Representative Brown expressed the same view:

> I learned, as a member of the original Hoover Commission—as did the other members of that Commission—that the greatest opportunities for savings in the conduct of the public business were to be found in the field of governmental *functions* and *policies,* rather than in the more strait-jacketed field of operational procedure only. . . .
>
> It is my thought that the new Commission, if created, would go into matters of Government functions and policies, and would recommend to the Congress how additional savings could be made by the proper adoption, elimination, or changing of Government functions and *policies.* In other words, the Commission would not only go into how we can get greater economy and efficiency in the actual operation of the executive branch of our Government but whether or not the Federal Government should engage in certain functions or follow certain policies—and if so, under what limitations and restrictions.

The Senate Committee on Government Operations, in reporting out S. 106 (the Senate version of Public Law 108), stated in Senate Report No. 216, page 1:

> Although the proposed Commission would be similar in composition to the earlier Commission on Organization of the Executive Branch of the Government . . . it would have added authority to study all activities of the Federal Government, and to make recommendations to the Congress and the President relative to changes in Federal programs and *policies.*

And a little further on it declared that

the Commission should have adequate authority as proposed in the bill, to examine not only all of the governmental operations previously examined by the Hoover Commission, but also Federal functions, programs *and policies* as well.

The House Committee on Government Operations, in reporting out H.R. 992 (later P.L. 108), emphasized the same points (H.R. No. 505, page 2):

> The proposed Commission would have the purposes and duties of the Commission on Organization of the Executive Branch of the Government established under Public Law 162, 80th Congress, generally referred to as the Hoover Commission, with some very important additions. . . . The scope of the activities of the proposed Commission under the Ferguson-Brown bills (S. 106 and H.R. 992) would thus be significantly broadened. . . . In this connection former President Hoover has commented as follows:
>
> > "The Ferguson-Brown bill looks to the reestablishment of such a Commission on Organization of the Executive Branch of the Government as that over which I presided from 1947 to 1950 with powers to investigate and recommend policies as well as administrative methods. That former Commission was unable to report on *policy questions*."

A SERIES OF GOALS

In making its appraisals of the need for organizational and policy changes throughout the executive agencies, a series of standards, tests, or goals were applied by the Commission. Although these tests were more implicit than explicit in the Commission's deliberations, nevertheless they ran as consistent threads through its analyses and recommendations. The more significant of these tests were:

1. Is the activity so conducted as to maintain the separation of powers and to preserve the rule of law?

   In a responsible constitutional republic the maintenance of the rule of law is of preeminent importance in the protection of the individual against the bureaucracy. All activities of the Government must conform to existing law. The preservation of the separation of powers between the legislative, executive, and judicial branches of the Government is of transcendent importance under our American system in preserving the rule of law.

2. Does the present method of conducting the activity impair congressional control over the purse?

The history of Anglo-American countries has demonstrated over and over again that the legislative branch, consisting of responsible representatives of the people, must control the purse to ensure that the functions of Government are limited and that the executive does not waste public funds.

3. Is the activity so conducted as to transgress upon civilian control of the Government?

Civilians must be responsible for the Government as a whole, and especially for the armed services. The armed services should not run ordinary civilian functions of the Government, and the armed services themselves must at all times be kept under civilian control. Military personnel, despite good intentions, have one objective in mind: the protection of the country against a foreign enemy. The military officer, in his zeal to carry out his task, tends to forget other objectives of Government. In his mind the need for preserving the liberty of the individual is much less significant than the protection of the country against a potential aggressor.

4. Does the activity as organized and operated interfere with or transgress upon the private enterprise system?

Especially in the United States it has been demonstrated that the free private enterprise system is the best way to organize the economic activity of the people so as to allow maximum individual liberty and initiative and at the same time to produce large amounts of goods and services with minimum effort. The significance of the free private enterprise system is far more important than its economic aspects because that system is the best way of organizing production so as to protect the individual and his rights. From the standpoint of Government, the private enterprise system is a source of revenue out of which public services are financed. The more Government competes with private enterprise by producing goods and services itself, the less will private enterprise produce out of which taxes can be paid to support the Government. The smaller the sector of private enterprise that can be taxed, the greater must be the amount of taxes imposed upon the enterprises that remain and the individuals connected with them. The higher the burden of taxes on the individual, the less is his liberty to spend his income as he desires, or to conduct his affairs as he sees fit.

In the Preface to its report on Business Enterprises the Commission said:

The genius of the private enterprise system is that it generates initiative, ingenuity, inventiveness and unparalleled productivity. With the normal rigidities that are a part of Government, obviously, the same forces that produce excellent results in private industry do not develop to the same degree in Government business enterprises.

Because of vested interests, misleading or incomplete accounts, or other reasons, it added, some of these enterprises set up to meet war or economic crises "established an astonishing longevity."

5. Is the activity conducted in the most efficient and economical manner?

Do we get the services or regulation required of Government with the minimum of expenditure of money, personnel, and goods and services? This last criterion is generally taken for granted in any study of Government reorganization.

From the findings of the first Hoover Commission the second Hoover Commission started with the knowledge that there was colossal waste, duplication, extravagance and inefficiency right through the Federal Government. It knew that with more than 2,000 agencies functioning in Washington there could not be adequate supervision of their activities and efficient control of their expenditures. It also knew that great savings could be effected along with better administration, and thus relieve some of the burden on the taxpayer.

These five objectives, of course, are not inclusive. The Commission did not limit its investigations to them, nor its findings. As early as 1925 Mr. Hoover himself had pointed out that there was serious confusion concerning the separation of powers in Government in contravention of the Constitution. He declared then that he had observed many agencies of the executive branch of the Government performing legislative and judicial functions. Among the worst offenders at that time he named the Department of Agriculture, and the Department of Commerce, which he himself headed. The Commission re-explored all these problems. It also looked into such matters as invasion or vitiation of States' rights by the Federal Government, especially in the area of public power.

The second Hoover Commission had full authority to investigate all functions of the Executive Branch of the Government. It did just that.

With such objectives in mind, it is clear that any study of Government activities cannot be merely in terms of efficiency and economy and of the organization of the structure of the Government. It must go to the heart of the problem if it desires results. It must consider:

What functions does the Government perform and which of these are necessary and desirable for the advancement and protection of the individual and his rights?

Which of the functions now performed impede or transgress upon the individual's liberties or his opportunity for self-government?

THE COMMISSION

The second Hoover Commission as sworn in at the White House on September 29, 1953, was a distinguished group of American citizens. Named by the President were: Herbert Brownell, Jr., Attorney General; Arthur S. Flemming, Director of the Office of Defense Mobilization; James A. Farley, former Postmaster General; and Mr. Hoover. Named by the Vice President were: Senator Homer Ferguson, who resigned on April 4, 1955, to become Ambassador to the Philippines and was succeeded by Senator Styles Bridges; Senator John L. McClellan, Solomon C. Hollister, Dean of the College of Engineering, Cornell University; and Robert G. Storey, Dean of the School of Law, Southern Methodist University. Named by the Speaker of the House were: Representative Clarence J. Brown, Representative Chet Holifield, Joseph P. Kennedy, former Ambassador to Great Britain; and Sidney A. Mitchell, Executive Director of the first Hoover Commission. The first act of the Commission was to elect Mr. Hoover as chairman.

The Commission decided to make a broad study of important functions of Government, right across the face of the executive branch, and in doing so to consider policy as well as organization. With the experience of the first Hoover Commission before it—five of the members had served with the first Commission—the Commission

ERRATUM

On page 17 in the list of Task Forces or Committees that served the Commission and their chairman one Committee was omitted and its chairman's name used in place of the name of the chairman of the Committee on Business Organization of the Department of Defense. Following "Water Resources and Power" the list should read:

Committee on Business Organization of the Department of Defense	Charles R. Hook
Subcommittee on Business Enterprises in the Department of Defense	Joseph B. Hall

decided to use the Task Force method of study. So over the next few months Task Forces to study each major problem were set up and the work was under way. These were composed of men of proven competence in the field involved. In all, nineteen Task Forces or Committees served the Commission. They and their chairmen were:

Budget and Accounting	J. Harold Stewart
Intelligence Activities	General Mark W. Clark
Legal Services and Procedure	James Marsh Douglas
Lending Agencies	Paul Grady
Medical Services	Dr. Theodore George Klumpp [1]
Overseas Economic Operations	Henning W. Prentis, Jr.
Paperwork Management	Emmett J. Leahy
Personnel and Civil Service	Harold W. Dodds
Procurement	Robert Wilson Wolcott
Real Property	John R. Lotz
Subsistence Services (Food and Clothing)	Joseph P. Binns
Depot Utilization	Clifford E. Hicks
Use and Disposal of Surplus Property	General Robert E. Wood
Water Resources and Power	Admiral Ben Moreell
Committee on Business Organization of the Department of Defense	Joseph B. Hall
Research Activities	Mervin J. Kelly
Special Personnel Problems in the Department of Defense	Thomas R. Reid
Transportation	Perry M. Shoemaker

In all, close to 200 men served on the Task Forces and Committees of the Commission. Many of them were busy men who had to make large personal sacrifices to do so. It is interesting to note that only two men declined Mr. Hoover's invitation to serve. One of them had just had a heart attack, and the other had important commitments which would take him abroad. Almost all of them served without compensation, and many of them paid their own expenses.

The roster of the Commission's investigators made one of the most distinguished groups ever assembled for one job in the United States. The members included men with outstanding talent in educa-

[1] Appointed September 26, 1954, succeeding Chauncey McCormick, deceased.

tion, in medicine, in engineering, in accounting, in administration, and in law, and many of them had had previous experiences in the areas of Government on which they were required to pass judgment.

They included seven college presidents (those of Princeton, Northwestern, Montana, Purdue, South Carolina, Long Island University, and The Citadel); and five deans or former deans of law schools, including Harvard (two), Illinois, New York University, and Michigan; and the former dean of the Yale Medical School and the dean of the School of Dentistry at Washington University; and hospital administrators. Others were an assistant attorney general, a deputy attorney general, an undersecretary of the army, and an assistant secretary of the navy, as well as a former secretary of commerce and an assistant secretary of commerce. Still others were an associate justice of the United States Supreme Court, the chief justice of the Supreme Court of New Jersey, two judges of the United States Circuit Courts of Appeals, a former chief justice of the Supreme Court of Missouri, and a judge of the Appellate Division of the Supreme Court of New York.

There were three governors or former governors of States (New Jersey, Utah, and Wyoming), one lieutenant governor (South Carolina) on Task Forces. A number of members had had brilliant careers in the armed forces. These include two admirals, one general of the army, one rear admiral, a lieutenant general, a major general, and a brigadier general. A number of others had extensive experience in public office. These include a deputy administrator of the Economic Cooperation Administration, a vice chairman of the War Production Board, director of the United States Employment Service, vice chairman of the National Security Resources Board, assistant director of the Office of Defense Mobilization, medical director of the Veterans' Administration, several presidents of Home Loan banks, of a Bank for Intermediate Credit, and of Federal Land banks; two former members of the Civil Service Commission, members of the Federal Trade Commission, Securities and Exchange Commission, and the Civil Aeronautics Board. Two served in the House of Representatives. Another member was director general of the United Nations International Refugee Organization.

Many of the members had been presidents of professional and trade groups of significance, including the American Bar Association, the American Association of Law Schools, the American Society of

Civil Engineers (two), the American Institute of Accountants (two), the National Association of Cost Accountants, the Comptroller Institute of America, the American Society of Business Budgeters, American Society of Appraisers, National Security Industrial Association, the Junior Chamber of Commerce, the National Association of Manufacturers (three), the president of the Board of Governors of the Aircraft Industries, the National Reclamation Association (two), Air Transport Association (two), and the National Restaurant Association. Members had been presidents of the American Medical Association, the American College of Surgeons, and the American Board of Psychiatry and Neurology.

On the Task Forces there were sixteen doctors of medicine, five dentists, forty lawyers, thirty-seven engineers, eight certified public accountants, two economists, six judges, eight bankers, five publishers, three insurance executives, sixty-five business executives, and six Government administrators.[2]

HOW THE TASK FORCES WORKED

The Task Forces had a completely free hand from the Hoover Commission. Each was simply instructed to find the facts and make such recommendations as it believed were required in the light of the facts. Never was one told what to find or what to recommend. Neither was one ever told what not to investigate. Each was given a function of Government to examine in the interest of efficiency and economy and then left to its own devices to do the best possible job. In a few instances Task Forces found that the areas they were investigating were wider than they or the Commission had expected, and wandered from their original assignments, but never was one ordered to halt.

The Task Forces gathered their information any place that they were able to find it. They took advantage of the material already available in each area, such as information gathered by previous official or congressional bodies. Since the objective was not to make an exposé or merely to uncover dirt, there was no place for the snooper or the confidential agent. While the Commission was authorized by law to subpoena persons or documents, it never did so. On the contrary, for the most part it got the cooperation of

[2] These categories are not exclusive. A given person might fall in several.

Government officials, many of whom realized that reforms were needed and welcomed the study of the Commission as a means of doing what they themselves could not do. Only one Task Force, that on Water Resources and Power, held public hearings.

Many of the Task Forces broke up into special study groups or subcommittees, each made up of members with specialized knowledge of the field, to gather data or to study special aspects of the function under inquiry. In all cases members of the Task Forces interviewed responsible people in the agencies of Government involved, and visited the sites or the factories or the plants or the functions being studied. Nothing was left to hearsay evidence. Nothing was left to chance.

All of the Task Forces hired professional experts to help them in their work, and these devoted full time to their inquiries.

Once the investigation was well in hand the Task Force would begin holding meetings to get reports from individual members, from study groups or subcommittees, or from staff experts. The Task Force had to evaluate the information, to correlate it, to focus it on the group's major objectives, and finally to decide what improvements in Government organization or policy should be recommended. Mr. Hoover might be invited, and usually was, to give the members an inspirational talk or to discuss their problems with them. He was always available, and he gave of his time and his experience without stint.

After the Task Force had finally gathered and digested its material and decided on its recommendations, it drafted its report to the Commission. Again it had a free hand. It wrote its report as it felt it should be written, made its own choice of language, and put into the report what it wanted to have there. The Task Force reports varied widely in literary flavor. The duty of the Task Force was to make a thorough study and present its findings and recommendations as simply as it could. That done, its job was finished and it turned the report over to the Commission.

HOW THE COMMISSION WORKED

Only then did the real job of the Commission begin. Chairman Hoover usually named a committee of three of the Commissioners to study the Task Force report and to draft a *pro forma* report for all the Commissioners to study. This Committee would work in close cooperation with Mr. Hoover. Always these committees were composed of men with special competence to deal with the report in hand. They, of course, were not under any obligation to accept the recommendations of the Task Force, and in fact only one such report, that of the Hook Committee on the Business Organization of the Department of Defense, was accepted by the Commission exactly as it was submitted by the Task Force. In all other instances, including Intelligence Activities, the Commission in its reports modified or rejected the Task Force's recommendations as it found necessary.

The preliminary or *pro forma* draft of a Commission report would be circulated among the Commissioners and the staff members for comment and revision in advance of its consideration by the Commission in a full meeting. The textual material in the report, as well as the recommendations, would be discussed, alternatives considered, the facts rechecked, and changes suggested. As many as eight drafts were prepared of some proposed reports before the Commission considered them in formal session to take final action.

When the Commission did act as a body on the reports, it took them up recommendation by recommendation, approving or rejecting or modifying each before it moved to the next. A wide range of talent and experience was represented around the Commission table, and each Commissioner was encouraged by the Chairman to express his views freely. Naturally there were differences of opinion. The discussions, while quiet and friendly and nonpartisan, were frequently lively. The result was that each report of the Commission as finally passed represented not only the data gathered by the Task Force and the best opinion of its members and staff, but also the best opinion and experience of each of the twelve Commissioners.

When the Commissioners had finished with the report, it was re-edited by the Committee of Commissioners and the staff to incorporate the final changes made at the meeting, and then it was sent to the Government printer. When printed and bound it was sent to the President of the Senate and the Speaker of the House of Representatives.

Most of the Commission reports carried dissents, some of these to one or more recommendations, and some general; and in some cases, there were also explanatory statements. This was to be expected in a free Commission in a free country. Majority rule prevailed in the Commission, and it was the majority opinion that made the final Commission report. In this book we are considering only the action of the Commission.

MR. HOOVER'S CONTRIBUTION

Why have the Hoover Commissions been so successful when other attempts to reform the Federal Government have met with indifference and even outright failure? This question has been asked frequently by students of government. The answer is Herbert Hoover. His prestige and his genius assured each of the Commissions of success. As the most distinguished of our elder statesmen, Mr. Hoover has been above politics and in a position to inspire and direct a nonpartisan effort to give the American people better government.

Mr. Hoover's gift for organization is unparalleled. He devised the Task Force method of study, and it proved both effective and economical. It made it possible for him to obtain the services of men of great ability and unusual talent to serve the Commission for just the time needed to do a study in a given area. It also permitted the Commission to function with the minimum of staff. Moreover, Mr. Hoover's wide acquaintanceship made it possible for him to gather around the Commission an array of talent and of loyalty that assured the Commission of outstanding work and that also favorably impressed the White House, the Congress, the agencies of Government, and the American people. All of them felt that the resulting effort was so important that it could not be ignored. The vast majority of them felt that the Commission's recommendations should have a fair trial.

Mr. Hoover also brought to the Commission a knowledge of American Government and of public affairs that is both extensive and sure. In relieving distress all over the world and as food administrator of the United States he had first-hand information that no other American ever had had. As secretary of commerce he initiated developments in radio, in aviation, and in numerous other fields of activity that we today take for granted. As President he had to deal with the worst depression of modern times. Finally, as a student of American Government for many decades, with the benefit of work and travel all over the globe, he had a store of wisdom and experience that was both unique and invaluable.

Mr. Hoover's own efforts were prodigious and inspiring. He worked seven days a week. Often he had visitors for breakfast, office conferences at luncheon, and important guests to consult for dinner. He lived with the Commission's work from early morning until late at night. He presided at all the numerous sessions of the Commission. He also attended many of the sessions of the Task Forces. He read all reports, including all the versions of them, and knew more of their contents than did anyone else. Often he would amaze members of Task Forces by citing data that many of them did not know they had in their reports. He was always available for consultation. Working with a stack of sharp lead pencils on foolscap paper, he labored to condense the long Task Force reports into the brief Commission reports. He was always shortening and clarifying. He wanted his reports read and understood. He kept a battery of secretaries occupied. No one could complain of overwork when he or she could observe the eighty-year-old former President of the United States eternally on the job.

Perhaps, however, Mr. Hoover's leadership was his biggest contribution. Nothing dismayed him. He was always hopeful. He was always convinced that a way could be found to solve the numerous problems, some of them intricate in the extreme, that came before the Commission. Almost always when a deadlock threatened in a Commission session it was he who came up with the new solution or the compromise that could be accepted. At all times he was patient, kind, and considerate. He listened with respect to the opinions of his colleagues. He never appeared hurried. His very confidence made success certain.

An important contribution to the success of the Hoover Commissions was also made by the Citizens Committee for the Hoover Report, which was organized by Mr. Hoover after the first Commission and is still functioning for the benefit of the second Commission, now under the leadership of Clarence Francis, former chairman of General Foods Corporation. Here is another evidence of Mr. Hoover's genius for organization. Other attempts to reform the Government did not have such support. Mr. Hoover knew that his work had the support of good citizens throughout the nation, and these he organized on a national basis to support the Hoover reports and to spread information about them. The Citizens Committee has done and is doing much to muster public opinion behind the Hoover recommendations for better government.

How his fellow Commissioners felt about Mr. Hoover and his leadership was expressed in a resolution, signed by all eleven of the other Commissioners, and presented to him at the final session. It reads:

RESOLUTION
IN APPRECIATION TO HONORABLE HERBERT HOOVER

We, the Members of the Commission on Organization of the Executive Branch of the Government, hereby express to our distinguished Chairman, Honorable Herbert Hoover, our very great appreciation for his able, fair, and patient leadership in the conduct of the work of this Commission and for the particularly outstanding contribution made by him to the successful completion of the complex tasks assigned to us by the Congress.

We fully recognize the immense store of knowledge and experience which he possesses and which he utilized in his capacity as Chairman.

We know and appreciate the fact that his accomplishments in analyzing data and drafting reports were greater than those of any other one person.

We will always cherish the privilege and pleasure we have had of working with him as Members of the Commission.

The presentation on behalf of the Commission was made by the Honorable James A. Farley, postmaster general in the Administration of President Franklin D. Roosevelt and former chairman of the Democratic National Committee. Mr. Farley spoke with deep emotion. His words follow:

I have been highly complimented in being permitted to serve on this Commission. The President of the United States and the country were fortunate in having the services of Mr. Hoover in directing the work of this Commission. He has worked untiringly and unselfishly, twelve to fifteen hours a day, for nearly two years.

He was patient, and considerate at all times, of all the members of the Commission, fully respecting their views and their rights to their individual opinions on all recommendations that came before the Commission. At no time did politics enter into the deliberations of the Commission. Where we differed, they were honest differences of opinion, and

Mr. Hoover recognized the right of each member to give free expression of his views.

I know of no American alive today who could have made the same contribution as Mr. Hoover has. His patriotic service will long be remembered by generations yet unborn. It is my sincere wish that the recommendations of the Commission will be given serious consideration by the Congress, so that the work he has directed so well will bring about efficiency in the operation of our Government, vast savings, and go a long way toward balancing the budget and eliminating unnecessary taxes. I pray God will continue to give Mr. Hoover the health and strength to enable him to render service to the country for many years to come. He is truly a great American and a great patriot.

RECOMMENDATIONS AND REPORTS

In all, the Commission made 314 recommendations. While there is inevitable overlapping, 145 of them can probably be carried out by administrative action in the departments and agencies of Government; 167 will probably require legislative action; and finally, about 50 might be presented to the Congress by the President under the Reorganization Act of 1949, as amended, or might be implemented by presidential action. Some of the second Commission's recommendations are more controversial than were those of the first Commission, but the second Commission is hopeful that it will match or better the success of the first Commission.

The reports of the second Commission and its Task Forces are also more voluminous than were those of the first Commission. They are estimated to contain 3,300,000 words. Never before in the history of the United States has so thorough and so wide an inquiry been made into the activities of Government. The reports are in fact an encyclopedia of American governmental practices.

In attempting to condense this vast mass of material into the pages of one normal-sized book, the authors found that the reports made a pattern, and they have divided this book accordingly into four major divisions: The Tools of Government, Big Government, The Big Spender, and Overseas Economic Operations. The chapters that follow give one after the other the functions of Government that the Commission studied, with an analysis of the problems it found and the major recommendations that it made to solve them.

2.

The Tools of Government

CHAPTER 2

Personnel and Civil Service

In the final days of the Commission a newspaper reporter asked Mr. Hoover this question:

The Commission has made 314 recommendations. If you were granted the right to have one accepted, and only one, which one would you pick?

Without hesitation Mr. Hoover replied:

"I would pick the recommendation for the setting up of a senior civil service.

"Government," he went on to explain, "cannot be any better than the men and women who make it function. Our greatest problem is to get the kind of men and women the Government needs and to keep them in Government. Right now we have a turnover of about 25 per cent yearly. We need civil servants of great ability, but as soon as they show ability they are grabbed by private business. We lose the best and keep the second best. We must make civil service so attractive, so secure, so free from frustrations, so dignified, that the right kind of men and women will make it a career. Then we can have the kind of Government that the United States needs and should have.

"That is why our Report on Personnel and Civil Service is the nearest to my heart."

The United States has about 2,300,000 Federal employees. The annual payroll is more than $9,000,000,000. The Commission's Report on Personnel and Civil Service aims to make them better public servants. It recognizes that ours is a government of laws but that human beings implement those laws. It recognizes also that the more competent the public servants, the better will be the administration of Government and the cheaper. The Commission realized that a capable civil service is fundamental in a republic like ours that is responsible to the people and operates under the two-party system.

THE NATURE OF THE PROBLEM

During the more than 160 years of party government in the United States, the American people have sought to achieve a workable balance in the Federal Government between two vital requirements.

One is that the public officials who are responsible for establishing and defending Government policies and programs should be selected by and represent the political party in power. This requirement arises out of the rotation of the political parties in the control of the Government. If the party that wins at the polls is really to be accountable to the people, if it is to carry out the promises upon which it won public office, it must have control over the policy-making executives in the Government. Otherwise the will of the people would be defeated.

The other requirement is that there must be trained, skilled, and nonpartisan employees in the public service to provide continuity, "know how," and efficiency for its operations.

As the United States has grown in population and in wealth, in production and in commerce, in scientific achievement and in fast communications, the need for governmental supervision of American activities has also grown. This has imposed new duties on civil servants and has demanded wide knowledge of many intricate problems in Federal bureaus. Consider, for instance, the problems with which the Atomic Energy Commission, the Federal Reserve Board, and the Interstate Commerce Commission, must deal. These and scores of other Federal agencies require highly trained specialists for their staffs to make them function effectively for the American people.

The Government itself in the past century has grown from a small, simple organization with few functions, into a huge, elaborate, amorphous grouping of more than two thousand separate agencies, each with complex problems and difficult operations, all of them combining to make the biggest business on earth, the most complex, and the most difficult to run efficiently and economically.

A workable balance between policy-making employees and career employees is not easy to attain. Both extremes, a Government composed of political employees, and one with practically no political appointees in high policy positions, have been tried in the last century. The Federal Government has moved from extreme turnover of personnel under the spoils system toward the practice of granting special career rights even to employees who actively engage in public debate and defend the policies and programs of the Administration in power. Both extremes have proved unworkable, under our republican form of government.

The Commission found that in recent decades the Government failed to realize a clear division of function between career and non-policy-making employees. It also found that it failed to attract or to train sufficient numbers of experienced and able personnel in either group.

As a result, the primary objective of the Commission's Report on Personnel and Civil Service is to develop an effectively workable system and thus balance the needs for career employees with the equally important requirement for an adequate force of competent non-career, politically responsible executives.

In order to understand this problem better, and to furnish a factual background for the Commission's analysis and recommendations, an understanding of the operation of the present civil service system of the Federal Government is necessary.

THE PRESENT CIVIL SERVICE SYSTEM

The 2,350,000 persons working for the Federal Government on June 30, 1954, were employed under a diversity of employment systems, and more than 84 per cent of them were employed under a single program—the civil service system. The basic idea underlying the civil service system is that all positions should be filled on the basis of merit as determined by open competitive examinations or by other procedures fixed by regulation.

The remaining 16 per cent of the positions are filled under other special recruitment programs, or are exempted from the civil service.

The present civil service system has grown by legislative and executive action through slow stages in the past seven decades. The original law creating the system, passed in 1883, provided for inclusion within the system of certain specified clerical positions. The statute authorized the President to extend the coverage to such other classes as he might see fit. Originally, fewer than 10 per cent of all employees were under it. By executive and congressional action the civil service has been steadily extended and widened. This growth unfortunately has not always resulted from rigid adherence to the merit principle.

In general, the civil service system has grown from the bottom up. It was originally intended to protect primarily the lower grade clerical positions; but by successive steps Congress and the President have brought in other groups or classes until today the system embraces even those close to the top levels of management and policy development. This final extension to the top positions was made mainly during the last fifteen years. The strains resulting from the extension of the system and the efforts to apply uniform personnel techniques to widely dissimilar positions have resulted in many infirmities in the system.

To protect and administer the merit system, Congress, in the original Act of 1883, provided for a Civil Service Commission of three members appointed by the President. The major work of the Commission consisted of the development of rules and regulations, the prevention of pernicious political activities, and the hearing of appeals. As the result of a recommendation of the first Commission on Organization of the Executive Branch, the Chairman of the Civil Service Commission was made responsible in 1949 for the direction of the executive and administrative work of the Commission, which had meanwhile vastly expanded.

The work of the Civil Service Commission also has shifted. Originally it operated the system completely, but now it merely sets standards and provides guides under which the separate Federal agencies can administer their own personnel programs. Thus in the beginning the Civil Service Commission was an examining agency; today it has changed into a central personnel agency supervising the executive branch. Its operations have been largely decentralized to the different Federal departments and agencies. These include such tasks as examining employees and classifying positions. At present, a large portion of the work of examining employees is done by decentralized boards of examiners within the separate agencies.

After an employee has been appointed under the civil service system, the head of the agency concerned may at his discretion assign such person to fill any vacancy for which he is qualified. Once an employee has gained admission to the public service he can, by demonstrating his competence, be promoted or transferred. However, methods of promotion within the Government differ widely between agencies. Some have detailed programs, while others have practically no programs at all.

Under existing law, veterans receive preference in obtaining and retaining employment in the civil service system. Approximately 1,000,000 of the 20,000,000 veterans of the American armed forces are on the Federal payroll. Approximately 50 per cent of all employees and 60 per cent of the male employees are veterans. In selecting prospective civil service employees, veterans are placed ahead of other equally qualified eligibles "and in no case can a qualified veteran be passed over in selection without good cause." They also receive special protection in case of lay-offs; and in the case of disciplinary action they have special privileges.

The civil service system provides safeguards against dismissal. When a civil service employee is dismissed for cause, he must get a written notice and have an opportunity to reply to the agency's charges. In certain circumstances all employees have the right to appeal a dismissal to the Civil Service Commission. Veterans must get thirty days' notice before they can be dismissed, and in all cases they have a direct appeal in person to the Civil Service Commission. With so many veterans in Government service these procedures for their protection dominate removal procedures.

On the whole, the Commission found that Government personnel is competent, faithful, "and in numerous specialties, distinguished." The greatest weakness was disclosed in the area of expert management. Chairman Hoover pointed out that the great trouble with the present system is that the men in the top civil service jobs just "are not good enough—they are there by seniority and red tape." He hastened to add that this does not mean that they should be eliminated, but that they should be transferred to posts in keeping with their ability.

The first Commission on Organization of the Executive Branch, in its Report on Veterans' Affairs, presented an illustration of the ineptitude of Government service. The Veterans' Administration, it said, had more than 9,000,000 life insurance policies. This phase of its work closely paralleled the operations of privately owned insurance companies. However, the Veterans' Administration, in its section handling policies, had one employee for each 450 policies, while the Metropolitan Life Insurance Company had only one for each 1,706 policies. Thus it took almost four workers in Government to do what one did in private enterprise. As a result of the first Commission's criticism and recommendation, the situation has improved.

The second Commission has addressed itself particularly to the problem of improving managerial direction by proposing remedies for the defects revealed by its investigation. Its approach to the task has been threefold. It has sought to improve the effectiveness of the non-career political employees. It has sought to improve the position of employees from the level of the top career administrators down to the level of first-line supervisors. Finally, it has offered proposals for managerial development at the lower levels.

THE PROBLEM OF POLICY-MAKING EXECUTIVES

It is widely realized that the Government requires non-career executives functioning near the top levels to represent the political party in power and to support the measures to which that party is committed. Obviously, such employees must serve at the pleasure of the President, or of his agency heads. The Commission has found that policy-making executives at present are too few to perform the tasks imposed on them.

There have been two major difficulties in obtaining an adequate supply of competent policy-making political executives.

First, persons appointed to such posts tend to serve for only short periods. The average secretary of a department, for instance, serves less than four years, undersecretaries less than two years, and assistant secretaries only slightly more than two years.

The second difficulty is that the average policy-making executive usually comes to his position unprepared for the political environment in which he finds himself. Executives in industry are recruited from among men experienced in their tasks who have risen from lower positions to the top. Policy-making executives in the Government are usually brought in from the outside and are expected to direct experienced employees in long-standing activities about which such executives have only limited knowledge.

As a consequence, policy-making employees have often been overwhelmed by the task of developing policies and programs and of defending them in the political arena and before congressional committees. Because of their lack of experience, these executives have increasingly tended to rely on career administrators to help carry their load. Thus nonpolitical career administrators have been drawn out of their proper sphere and have had imposed on them the task of defending the Administration or party policies. The Commission finds that once civil service employees have done this they inevitably become vulnerable to political attack, and that their further usefulness in the public service is directly threatened. If these employees are to merit the safeguards of the civil service system, it asserts, they must abstain from all participation in political activities.

For these reasons, the Commission recommended that career administrators should be relieved of the responsibility of advocating or defending Administration policies and programs and should be kept out of participation in political controversy. To make this possible, the Commission believes that additional competent, non-career executives "should be worked into management organization at the departmental level to help carry the workload . . . and to take over the political tasks formerly handled by many career administrators." Policy-making officials should fill all positions that involve advocating new policies or developing or defending the basic policies of the Administration or of the political party in power. Such appointees should also fill most positions of a personal and confidential nature.

At present there are only seven hundred to eight hundred of these political executive positions in the Government. The Commission recommends that there be about 5,000. So few among so many employees would not mean a revival of the "Spoils System."

There are other reasons also why it has been difficult to recruit an adequate supply of competent policy-making employees. One of these has been low salaries. To correct this, the Commission recommends that Congress authorize salary increases for the Government's top managers, both career and policy-making.

Still another obstacle is the "conflict of interest" laws requiring Government officials to divest themselves of personal investments and rights that might conflict with the discharge of their public duties. Too often prospective employees have been reluctant to give up their lifetime accumulation of investments and pensions in order to take a short-term position in Government.

To remedy this situation the Commission recommends that Congress make a study of the "conflict of interest" laws to determine whether their intent can be better achieved by other means which would encourage rather than deter the entry of competent people into public service.

A SENIOR CIVIL SERVICE

There are glaring defects in the civil service system for the development of the men and women capable of filling high managerial positions in Government. These shortcomings spring from the failure of the Government to evolve a method of identifying such men and women. The Commission found that "the Civil Service System emphasizes positions, not people." It pointed out that jobs are classified and rated and their compensation determined ". . . on the bland assumption that they can always be filled like so many jugs, merely by turning the tap."

To supply career executives at the higher levels it found that new concepts, new policies, and new procedures are imperative. The civil service system, designed to combat the spoils system, is adapted to the large-scale employment problem of large government, and that only. Devices designed for a large number of standardized positions at a low level of responsibility, the Commission said, do not work effectively for high-level executives "because such concepts disregard so completely both the personalities and the careers of individual men." The civil service system has not been geared to develop the competence of professional administrators at the higher levels.

To correct this situation the Commission proposes that the Government establish a senior civil service consisting of career administrators selected from all agencies of the Government solely on the basis of demonstrated competence to fill positions requiring a high degree of managerial competence. The members of this new service would be nominated by agency heads and appointed by a senior civil service board. The members of the new service should have status, rank, and salary as individuals. They should be employed in positions calling for outstanding administrative talent.

The primary objective of the senior civil service is to have in the Government a group of highly qualified administrators of demonstrated competence, integrity, and faithfulness. The existence of such a group of employees would make it easier for non-career executives to discharge their responsibilities. Furthermore, the development of such a senior civil service would make a career of public service more attractive. The Commission felt that initially there would be about 1,500 persons in the senior civil service, and that later the number would increase to 3,000, or more.

The granting of personal rank would be one of the most significant distinguishing characteristics of this senior civil service, and would differentiate it from the ordinary civil service. Normally in the public service, rank and salary are attached to the job and not to the person filling it at any time. The rank and pay of the individual in the senior civil service would attach to him and not to the job.

The senior civil service would differ from the ordinary civil service in a number of other important respects. Personal rank would make it possible for its members to move from position to position without the danger of suffering a loss in basic pay or status. At the same time there would be an obligation on the part of the members to serve where needed most. Its members would of necessity have to refrain from political activities in Government and out of it that would adversely affect their ability to perform their duties. They would not be permitted to make public statements except of a factual nature. Their pay would be above that of most ordinary civil service employees, ranging from about $11,000 to $17,000. Increases in compensation should be awarded periodically in recognition of continued growth and satisfactory performance.

Members would have tenure resembling that of general or flag officers in the armed service in that they would have rank, status, and salary as individuals and regardless of assignment. In addition, they would be completely neutral politically and prepared to serve any administration in office faithfully, regardless of position or of political controversies.

Should a member of the senior civil service be temporarily unassigned, he would continue to draw his basic pay for a limited period. During such time he could be utilized for temporary assignments throughout the Government. Should no permanent position be worked out for him at the end of a six-month period, the senior civil service board should have authority to continue him in a temporary position at regular pay for an additional six months, or put him on half-salary in a temporary position for six months or, as a last resort, it could retire him.

A bipartisan senior civil service board composed of five members appointed by the President is proposed by the Commission to supervise the senior civil service. The members would serve on a full-time basis, and for administrative purposes the board would be under the authority and jurisdiction of the Civil Service Commission. This new board would select the members of the senior civil service from among those candidates nominated by the heads of agencies. It would regularly appraise the work of the senior civil servants and give promotions on the basis of demonstrated competence. It should also have the right to "select out" employees who are repeatedly passed over for increases in pay.

Both the Army and the Navy provide precedents for the selection of the senior civil service. In the armed services promotions beyond a certain rank are on the basis of demonstrated competence and leadership. The value of such a system was proved in both world wars. For instance, Dwight D. Eisenhower was jumped from the rank of lieutenant colonel to that of major general, over the heads of scores of senior officers, when he was sent to command American troops in Europe. Similar promotions were numerous in all the armed services then, and still are.

"This simple fact," Mr. Hoover has said, "saved us in both wars. Otherwise we would have been commanded by a lot of old codgers or dodoes who got their commands by seniority—by the simple fact that they had lived long enough."

The Commission wants this proved system applied to the civil service. The Hoover Commission believes that this fresh approach to the problem of top management in the career public service would strengthen these significant positions and thereby improve the entire operation of the executive branch of the Government. This, the Commission feels, would result in monetary savings that would far exceed the higher salaries and other costs involved.

TRAINING AND MANAGERIAL DEVELOPMENT AT LOWER LEVELS

For the senior civil service system to be successful, there must exist a large reservoir of talent out of which unusually qualified persons may be selected. This reservoir should consist of the middle and lower grades of employees in the regular Civil Service. These would provide the proving grounds for potential senior civil servants.

Up to the present, little has been done to train and equip middle and lower management personnel to perform their duties. Yet training of these employees is of fundamental importance both for better functioning of the Government in the immediate future and for the long-run development of a senior civil service.

The civil service system was designed to keep politics out of the large mass of routine low-level positions, but in doing so it has not been effective in developing managerial talent. It has operated mostly as a wholesale supply system. As previously pointed out, it inventories jobs carefully through a classification system, and it supplies manpower for them in large numbers. In its task of filling round holes with relatively round pegs it has operated in a deliberately impersonal manner.

The Commission found that "the system is job-oriented, not people-oriented," and that "it assumes an available supply of talent to be sorted and fitted into jobs."

For the development of managerial skill among the general run of civil servants, some form of training needs to be developed. Employees must prepare themselves by education to meet the ordinary normal requirements of their employment. They must provide their own basic training requirements for their jobs. But because the duties of many occupations are changing rapidly and because modern management and production methods are in a state of flux, further training is imperative, especially for development of managerial competence. As a consequence, job training "is a necessary corollary of continuous technological change." Much of this must be supplied by the Government for ordinary civil servants.

The personnel offices of Government agencies have been so occupied with routine tasks that they have done little to develop managerial competence. These offices have been absorbed in problems of mass employment, the Commission found. They have been so burdened with the mechanics of administering statutes, rules, and regulations that they have had little time and energy for the development of positive, forward-looking personnel programs.

Training in the public service is needed, the Commission declares, both to improve job skills of workers and to develop employees who can move forward in a career of public service. Although career training benefits the employee, it is also essential to the efficient continuity of government, the Commission points out. Such training should be more than the mere building of employee skills. Training beyond the entrance level should be a reward for competence, it asserts, an incentive to increased production, and a sign to employees that their talents and capabilities have been recognized. Through building up the employee's skill and morale, the public will also be benefited, the Commission adds.

There are at least three points in the career of Federal employees, according to the Commission, where training at the public expense is necessary.

First, when the worker enters an agency the civil service should make certain that he has an understanding of the fundamental needs and requirements of American public service. He must know the importance of high standards of honesty, fair dealing, and impartiality. He must be informed concerning the policies and operations of the agency. Such training is almost non-existent in Federal service today.

Second, when the employee advances in the service there is ultimately a time when he needs advanced skill in a special occupation, or in the supervising of others. The agency should provide him with opportunities and positive encouragement to acquire such skills. Doubts as to the existence of authority to provide such training, and the preoccupation of personnel officers with daily tasks, have completely stultified the development of this type of activity.

Third, as an employee enters higher executive positions, he needs a knowledge of Government programs and policies outside his specialized area. He needs further insight into public attitudes and a more comprehensive view of the techniques of management. Although there is an increasing awareness of the need for this kind of training, there is still no integrated, Government-wide career executive development program. Except in a few instances, agency executive development programs have not been effective.

The training needed at these three levels should be provided by the Government, and much of it should be made an integral part of the employee's work and not be provided at a remote educational institution. Emphasis must be placed upon building a systematic Government-wide executive development program which will improve the quality of first-line supervisors and junior executives, the Commission asserts, and efforts should also be made to increase the supply of experienced and competent senior civil servants for top management posts.

IMPROVEMENT OF THE EMPLOYMENT PRACTICES FOR THE MASS OF EMPLOYEES

In many respects the civil service system has done well in handling problems of large-scale employment. To a significant extent this is a consequence of the implementation of the recommendations of the first Commission on Organization of the Executive Branch. Despite this, there are personnel practices which should be reviewed, revised, and improved in the light of changed needs and conditions.

CLASSIFICATION AND PAY

The classification of positions and the determination of wages are major areas where the present personnel system is capable of improvement, according to the Commission. Within the National Government there are a number of classification and compensation systems; but by far the great majority of Federal employees are paid according to one of three systems.

First, 1,000,000 employees are subject to the Classification Act of 1949.

Second, about 500,000 workers are under the Postal Pay Act of 1945.

Third, about 750,000 are under a multiplicity of wage boards that fix wages according to local labor market conditions.

Although their basic objective of equal pay for equal work is a most commendable goal, there are a number of weaknesses in these several systems that need to be remedied, the Commission found.

Generally the procedure for classifying positions for the purpose of compensation has become overly elaborate. With the great increase in grades (18 under the Classification Act and 92 under the Postal Pay Act) the distinction between grades both as to pay and as to duties has become blurred.

Second, the range of pay between low-rank and high-rank positions has been so narrowed as to destroy incentives. The Commission has found that "the general trend under all pay systems has been toward a compression of the difference between the lowest and the highest salaries in the system." This is a result of periodic pay increases involving across-the-board raises for lower paid employees with little or no increase for those in higher grades.

Third, the pay scales generally lack adequate flexibility to provide for the adjustment of pay to local conditions.

Fourth, there is no central coordination or review authority for those systems where remuneration is based on prevailing rates of pay.

To remedy these defects the Commission has recommended: First, that the number of grades in the so-called classified service established under the Classification Act of 1949 be reduced from fifteen to ten.

Second, that a genuine classification of postal employees should replace the misleading system that has existed for years. Congress has recently provided for this.

Third, that Congress should provide a statutory basis for the multiplicity of systems for determining the prevailing rates of pay by a multiplicity of wage boards. The Civil Service Commission, it recommends, should receive authority to issue rules and regulations for the operation of these systems.

Fourth, that the Civil Service Commission and congressional committees should determine whether additional positions should be compensated for under local wage board arrangements in order to promote economy and efficiency.

This last proposal involves the possibility of large savings to the Government. The pay for many positions as determined on a nationwide basis by the Classification Act is frequently far above the rates paid for comparable work in the locality where the workers are employed. This means that the Government is paying more than necessary to get competent employees. By paying such rates it also disrupts the local labor market.

RECRUITMENT AND EXAMINATION

In the recruitment, examination, and appointment of employees, many of the procedures of the civil service system are obsolete. The Civil Service Commission's program for recruiting is based on the assumption that sufficient people will seek Federal employment to fill all needs of the Government. Experience in the past two decades has demonstrated that this is not always true. The remedy is for the Government to develop a continuous recruiting program. Further, most Federal recruiting at present is done in large cities close to Federal agencies. The Hoover Commission believes that if the Federal service is to be truly competitive, its personnel needs should be made known to qualified persons in all parts of the nation. This requires a more extensive recruiting system.

Procedures for conducting examinations and for making appointments also need improvement, the Commission found. The scores resulting from the grading of examination papers are too often treated as though they were precise measurements of the candidate's qualifications. Actually, tests frequently are not so constructed as to measure exact mentality and exact differences in competence. As a consequence, the Hoover Commission believes that in many instances it would be more appropriate for candidates to be graded on their examinations as being merely in one of four groups, "outstanding," "well qualified," "qualified," or "not qualified."

The present long-standing practice of filling vacancies from the first three names on the civil service list should be revised, the Commission recommends, so as to permit the appointing officer to make the selection from at least the first five eligibles. This would permit more latitude, and it would enable the agency to get an employee who would more nearly fit the special needs of the position.

EFFICIENCY RATINGS

In a large organization some form of rating the performance of employees is imperative, especially to prevent individuals from feeling they are lost in the large mass of workers. But the Hoover Commission has found that the present civil service rating system "takes more out of the organization in effort than it puts back in efficiency and morale." At present, an employee who is rated "unsatisfactory" by a conscientious supervisor is placed at a disadvantage as compared with many other workers with less conscientious supervisors. Under existing methods approximately 98 per cent of all employees are considered to be "satisfactory." The remaining 2 per cent fall into the "outstanding" or "unsatisfactory" categories. Only the most perfunctory judgments are made under the system; consequently it falls short of its objectives. The procedural safeguards designed to protect an employee from an "unsatisfactory" rating are overly complicated. As a consequence, it is often simpler and more effective to remove an "unsatisfactory" employee for cause than to give him the appropriate rating.

As a result, the Commission recommends that in place of the present performance rating system supervisors report once a year on all employees, indicating those with capacity for further development and deserving meritorious awards, those miscast in their present assignments, those undeserving of pay increases and, finally, employees who should be dismissed. Appeals from the original agency decision, it declares, should be limited to one appeal to higher authority within the agency itself.

REMOVAL

Present procedures for removing incompetent or undesirable civil service employees from the public service are complex. Although existing law provides a simplified removal system, the agencies have made it unnecessarily elaborate by their regulations. Existing law requires that a statement of charges in writing be made to the employee, that he must have a reasonable opportunity to reply, and that the agency must consider his reply. A non-veteran employee can appeal to the Civil Service Commission from an agency decision only if he believes that he has been subjected to political, religious, or racial discrimination. Veterans, whether in the civil service or not, are entitled to an appeal to the Civil Service Commission after exhausting these procedures.

Here again unnecessarily elaborate requirements have been developed by the agencies. The Commission found that these procedures result in contests of strength between the employee and his supervisor "which the other employees watch closely and [which] in some cases even become a public spectacle." This produces bad morale.

The Commission believes that the granting of special employment privileges to any group runs contrary to the basic principles of the Federal merit system. But it believes that veterans should have preference in Federal employment during the early years of their readjustment to civilian life at the end of their military service. Therefore, the Commission recommended that a veteran's special right of appeal to the Civil Service Commission be limited to the first five years after appointment to the public service. It further recommends that when the Civil Service Commission considers any appeal it should restrict itself to determining whether the procedural safeguards of the law have been complied with and whether there was some evidence to support the agency's decision.

REDUCTIONS IN FORCE

When it becomes necessary to reduce the number of Government employees, either because their mission has been completed or because Congress has reduced appropriations, the priorities used produce many difficulties. First, career employees get preference over so-called "career conditional," or employees with indefinite appointments. Second, veterans are laid off only after all non-veterans in the same tenure groups have been separated. Finally, seniority is a factor in determining who is to be retained and who is to be laid off. In practice seniority is subordinated to tenure and to veterans' preference in fixing retention rights.

In operation these three principles have had a disrupting effect on the whole public service. This is because a career employee who cannot be retained in his present position must be changed to a different place in the competitive service in the agency if it is possible to find a position for which he is qualified and which is occupied by an employee of a lower retention group. Thus the reduction of force of a single employee may cause a chain reaction producing a long series of personnel shifts throughout an agency.

Also as a result of the operation of these principles the Government often loses its experienced and skilled career employees because the performance and ability of employees are almost irrelevant considerations in determining who is to be retained and who is to be laid off.

Because the Commission believed that the system of veterans' preference works severely against non-veteran employees of long service, it recommended that in any reduction in forces employees be divided into three categories. The first should consist of veterans with compensable service-connected disabilities. The second should consist of all other veterans and non-veterans of fifteen or more years of service. The third should consist of all other employees. In any lay-off it recommended that veterans with compensable service-connected disabilities should receive first preference. Then those other veterans and non-veterans with fifteen years or more of service should be considered as a group. Non-veteran employees with competitive status should constitute a low group only having preference over all other employees without status. Finally, no employee, except veterans with compensable service-connected disabilities and with less than five years of Government service, should have the right to be reassigned to other positions in the case of a reduction in force.

EXTENSION OF MERIT SYSTEM

There is a large group of employees not under civil service. A number of agencies outside the system have developed their own career merit systems. Such agencies are the Tennessee Valley Authority, the Atomic Energy Commission, the Federal Bureau of

Investigation, the Public Health Service, and the Foreign Service of the State Department. The Commission found that no over-all Government standards exist for measuring quality and merit in these independent personnel systems. Further, it pointed out that persons under one of these merit systems do not have the right to transfer to the civil service or to another independent merit system.

The Commission proposes that the President's adviser on personnel management should be empowered to study the personnel systems outside the regular civil service and to report on them to the President. It also recommends that persons who have served satisfactorily in a recognized Federal merit system outside the civil service should be eligible for transfer to a competitive position under the Civil Service Act.

In addition, there are about 200,000 employees excepted from the regular civil service under various schedules in the civil service rules. A person holding such an exempted position cannot move freely from that position to another position in the competitive civil service. The Commission recommends that positions which presently are exempted from the competitive civil service, such as those in the territories, should be brought into the competitive civil service to the greatest extent possible, or that a merit system should be developed for these posts designed to meet their special problems.

CONCLUSIONS

These proposals of the Hoover Commission to improve the public service have three major objectives.

One is to make the public service more responsible to the voters. The development of a definite program for non-career top management employees would do this.

The second is to improve the efficiency of the public service. This would be promoted through the establishment of the senior civil service and of managerial training at lower levels.

The third is to improve employment practices for the mass of employees.

All should result in economy.

The Commission believes that greater prestige attached to Government employment is the most important intangible that can be used to attract the type of persons so badly needed in the public service. Prestige is of particular importance, it feels, because the

Government cannot offer the same financial rewards to persons in the top grades of the civil service that are offered in private business.

It is impossible to measure exactly the savings that would result from the implementation of the personnel recommendations of the Commission. These proposals are designed to simplify and expedite Federal personnel management, to contribute to higher employee morale and efficiency, and thereby generally to raise the level of service to the people. The benefits and economies that will result, while not reducible to terms of dollars, are certainly substantial. They would much more than offset any increases in cost which might result from their implementation. The recommendations for improved management and for the training of middle-level employees would renew incentives for improved service and would result in lower turnover throughout the Government.

At present, turnover in the Federal service is at the rate of about 25 per cent a year. This is far above the turnover rate of private industry. Because it costs the Government about $500 to replace a single employee, turnover cost the taxpayers about $278,500,000 in 1954. If this turnover rate could be reduced to 23 per cent, a saving of $14,000,000 would result, or if it could be reduced to 20 per cent the saving would be $48,500,000.

An over-all estimate of savings is not feasible; besides, the Commission believes that the savings would be dwarfed by the gains that improved personnel management could bring to the public service. Every segment of the nation would benefit from improved management of public affairs.

This report of the Commission and the recommendations contained in it are of transcendent importance because all functions of Government, from the collection of revenues to national defense, social welfare, and Government business enterprises, require efficient and economic administration. Such administration depends on the people who run the Government. And above all, Government is people.

It is little wonder that Chairman Hoover, after more than forty years of public service, considers this Report on Personnel and Civil Service as being "nearest to my heart."

CHAPTER 3

Budget and Accounting

Financial management of the American Government raises problems that are difficult to understand and still more difficult to solve. Neither the complexity of these problems nor the lack of public interest in them is a measure of their true significance to the Government and to the American people. Most of us know the importance of personal budgeting and account keeping in our own efforts to live within our incomes. The same is true on a national scale, but magnified tremendously because of the vast dimensions of the Government's operations and of its expenditures.

The budgeting and accounting for expenses of more than $64,000,000,000 in the more than 2,000 agencies of our Government require the services of more than 90,000 full-time workers and tens of thousands of additional man-years of the services of part-time workers.

Moreover, control of the purse, when real, could give Congress some supervision of the operations of the multiplicity of bureaus that make up the labyrinth that is the Federal Government, and again, through the Bureau of the Budget the President has his best chance of imposing proper business methods and of some degree of managerial regulation over the executive branch of the Government.

These are the two objectives the Hoover Commission sought in this area.

THE NATURE OF THE PROBLEM

The preparation of the annual budget is the most effective device available to the White House for controlling and directing executive activities of Government. It involves much more than mere estimates of proposed expenditures for the President to send to Congress for consideration and approval. It involves not only control over the expenditures of all executive departments and agencies, but also the power to shape their policies as well as the authority to insist on their efficient management.

Moreover, an effective budget system must be developed and enforced if Congress is to regain full control over the nation's purse. Congressional control over spending as provided by the Constitution is imperative if the executive is to be kept responsible to the people.

Thus, the budgeting process is vital to the proper conduct of the Government, and the safeguarding of our American liberties.

Accounting in the Federal Government is much more than the tabulation of revenues and expenditures. It is fundamental to the maintenance of our Republic for a number of important reasons.

First, proper accounting methods are required in Government, as well as in industry, to supply the financial information which is basic to effective management—that is cost data. The absence of such accurate and usable cost information is the major defect now existing in the fiscal management of the Government. Without adequate cost data no one can know whether a program is or is not worth while in terms of monetary costs.

Second, they are imperative to ensure compliance with the laws enacted by Congress governing the methods by which public funds are expended and the purposes for which such money can be used. Thus they are necessary if the rule of law is to be preserved.

Third, they are needed to ensure the honesty of the public servants charged with the task of dispensing public money.

Much has been done in the last thirty-five years to improve financial management of the Government, yet much remains to be done if it is to be on a modern business basis. The machinery of administration that was adequate for a Government with a few simple functions is far from adequate for one with thousands of functions and operating thousands of business enterprises.

Congress has enacted three fundamental laws for better financial management: the Budget and Accounting Act of 1921, the Government Corporation Control Act of 1945, and the Budget and Accounting Procedures Act of 1950.

In 1921 the Federal Government took a long step toward strengthening the authority of the President to promote efficiency and also to make possible congressional control over the purse. The 1921 law provided for an executive budget and an independent comptroller general, the latter as an arm of the Congress. Prior to this law there was no central mechanism for reviewing and appraising the requests of the agencies for the funds they would like to have during the forthcoming fiscal year. In setting up the Bureau of the Budget as an executive agent of the President, Congress made possible both presidential responsibility for financial planning throughout the Government and more effective congressional control of the purse.

Although creation of the executive budget helped in the development of an effective Government, it did not result in the efficiency of operation and in the savings its proponents believed would ensue. An independent comptroller general, however, did much to give Congress more control over the purse and advanced the rule of law in the spending of public money.

The Government Corporation Control Act of 1945 put incorporated Government business enterprises on a sound financial basis. It required them to have business-type budgets and accounts and to have those accounts audited by the General Accounting Office just as privately owned enterprises are audited by outside auditors.

The first Hoover Commission proposed reforms in this field, especially a performance budget and simplified accounting. Most of its recommendations were enacted into law by the Budget and Accounting Procedures Act of 1950.

In 1952 the Bureau of the Budget was also reorganized in the direction recommended by the first Hoover Commission. All of these improvements, although constituting steps in the right direction, have not proved as effective as that Commission hoped they would be. The executive budget is still not as successful in controlling expenditures as it should be.

As a consequence, the second Hoover Commission found it desirable to reappraise the whole budgeting process.

The primary objective of this Commission's study of financial administration was to ascertain how effective the budgetary and accounting processes were, to appraise their points of strength and weakness, and to offer proposals for the further development of the good aspects and for the correction of deficiencies. To do these, the Commission appointed a Task Force composed of men who knew at first hand the financial tools that business had used successfully. It was headed by J. Harold Stewart, a certified public accountant who had been head of the American Institute of Accountants, and on it were two other certified public accountants and four highly successful business executives.

For purposes of exposition we shall treat budgeting and accounting separately. In practice they are interrelated.

BUDGETING

Budgeting is a long-drawn-out and complicated task. Preparation of the annual budget in the departments and agencies begins anywhere from eighteen months to a year before the start of the fiscal year in which the funds are to be spent. The final document is a huge tome. For example, the budget for the fiscal year 1956 contained more than 1,200 pages and weighed more than five pounds.

It is impossible to determine the total cost of budgeting throughout the Government. It has been estimated that the budget in the Department of Defense alone costs in the neighborhood of $30,000,000. Throughout the executive branch the salaries of full-time employees engaged in budgeting, accounting, and other forms of fiscal administration are close to $316,000,000 yearly.

The operating bureaus and agencies of Government are at one and the same time the most important elements in the budgeting process and the weakest. Bureaus, agencies, and departments themselves prepare the original estimates of the funds needed by them. They always ask for more than they expect to get because they realize that their requests will be cut. In a few departments only does the secretary really review the bureau budgets and cut them. Too often the top departmental officials merely collect the bureau estimates and pass them along to the Bureau of the Budget.

Sound budget making can best be done on the bureau or departmental level, because at that level real needs and costs are known, and padding can be detected. But realistic review on the department level always has been lacking. Budgeting will only be as good as agency or departmental budgeting. This must be improved.

As already pointed out, the first Commission on Organization of the Executive Branch recommended in 1949 the adoption of a performance budget in all agencies. Such a budget is based primarily upon functions, activities, and projects undertaken by all agencies and not merely the so-called objects-of-expenditure classification. For instance, the Forest Service in its performance budget shows how much it would spend in supervising timber sales, pest control, fighting forest fires, and so on, instead of merely on such objects as personnel, transportation, rent, and so forth. The Budget and Accounting Procedures Act of 1950 provided for the use of such budgets throughout the executive branch.

Performance budgets are now generally used in most agencies, and they have resulted in some simplification of the archaic appropriation structure as well as in improvements in accounting. Nevertheless, the Hoover Commission found that "performance budgeting has encountered some difficulties and some congressional dissatisfaction with respect to program classifications and the accounting support for them."

In addition to reviewing departmental and agency budgets, the Bureau of the Budget acts as the agent of the President in other ways. In fact in many respects it is the President's best and easiest way of managing many important functions of Government. Among its duties are the evaluating of operations, the improving of management in agencies, the coordination of functions in different competing or duplicating agencies, and the reviewing and analyzing of proposed legislation. It also strives to improve the gathering of statistics.

The bureau's task of preparing the budget, however, takes precedence over its over-all management and policy functions, and in the discharging of this function it places emphasis on budget mechanics and not on the policy aspects. This function of the bureau, the Commission found, is handled in a mechanical manner and largely on a historical basis. Past expenditures are the primary standard in evaluating new requests. The estimates of the departments are reviewed primarily in terms of the amounts appropriated for them in previous years. As a consequence the desirability of programs is not reappraised or evaluated each year.

Further, although performance budgeting has been required since 1950, the most important material evaluated by the bureau in its review of estimates is the breakdown of how proposed funds will be spent on the basis of salaries, transportation, rent, and so on. These are commonly known as the objects of expenditures. On this basis, performance budgeting is only a form without substance.

The Commission recommended that the bureau be revitalized for the purpose of performing its functions properly. The Commission declared that the bureau, to make budgeting effective, must be able to discharge its management responsibilities more adequately. If these are properly discharged, the task of preparing the budget, it said, would be simplified and improved in the agencies, and the bureau would have better estimates with which to work. Especially it held that the bureau should strengthen its machinery for reviewing and promoting improved management organization and business practices. It should also organize itself so that it can carry out its over-all responsibilities for improving accounting, internal financial controls, and financial reporting throughout the Government.

The Commission recommended that the Bureau of the Budget should place one or more well qualified employees in important agencies whose duties should include continuous year-round review within each agency of its budget preparation and administration, as well as other facets of agency operations. The assignment of such personnel would greatly improve budgeting in the departments, it held, and this would of itself improve efficiency. The Commission was aware of the fact that for the proper performance of these functions additional personnel would be needed by the bureau, and it recommended that such increases in appropriations be granted for such personnel.

Because the President is responsible both for preparing an executive budget and for promoting efficiency in the executive agencies, the Bureau of the Budget, the Commission said, should make an annual review of the performance of agencies for him in terms of their programs and functions. Some reporting along these lines is now being done in connection with the budget presentations, but the present reporting is mostly directed toward justifying budgetary requests rather than toward providing information for the appraisal of the efficiency of operations and programs. The presentation of annual reports by each agency should make possible comparisons not only of costs but also of efficiency in terms of past performance.

For the performance budget to become truly effective in all agencies, however, a number of difficulties have to be eliminated, according to the Commission's report.

First, in some instances the Bureau of the Budget has found it necessary to treat as separate programs some activities for which there was not clear responsibility below the agency head, even though logically they constituted but a single program.

Second, in a number of cases it was impossible to provide adequate cost information supporting many of the programs. This is a result of inadequate cost-accounting data. Where budget activities and organizational patterns can be made consistent, and accounts developed on the basis of such patterns, these difficulties might be eliminated.

If properly implemented, the performance budget should permit congressional committees to study both the relative size of programs and the relative economy and efficiency of comparable activities in different agencies. The making of such comparisons is in fact an implicit and necessary part of the basic idea of the performance budget.

The Commission urges the continuation of performance budgeting supported by information on program costs and accomplishments. It also recommends the further review of the operation of organizational units where these fail to coincide with performance-budget classifications. Possibly, new organizational structures might be needed in some agencies to make such budgeting a reality. The Commission suggests that agencies take all steps needed to synchronize their organization structures, budget classifications, and accounting systems.

For performance budgeting to be effective the number of separate appropriation items must be reduced. The number of items in the budget has in fact been reduced in recent years, and such reductions should continue. At the beginning of World War II there were more than 2,000 appropriation items, while in the budget for 1955 there were only 375.

APPROPRIATIONS ON THE BASIS OF ACCRUED EXPENDITURES

Another difficulty in the way of the full implementation of performance budgeting is that present budgets are based on obligations and not on actual costs. Practically the entire Federal budgeting system is founded upon estimates of obligations to be incurred during the budget year. Such obligations represent orders placed, contracts awarded, services received, and similar transactions occurring during the year. Thus the obligations that have been incurred during any year "do not necessarily have any relation to costs to be incurred during the year."

Budgeting on such a basis has defects.

First, it fails to take into account inventories and working capital available for consumption during the budget year.

Second, it does not include materials which may become available out of prior years' obligations.

Third, financial information based primarily on obligations incurred does not contribute to the determination of the costs of services to be rendered or performed during the period under consideration. It does not relate planned operations to past and projected costs.

Performance budgeting cannot be meaningful when based on such figures; it must be based on valid cost data.

Cost-based budget data, the Commission reports, should generally be used in developing internal operating budgets as well as in formulating the President's budget. Although the Bureau of the Budget in 1954 issued instructions for the agencies to use cost-based data, where such information was available from integrated accounting systems, such systems still are the exception. In a few agencies, such as the Atomic Energy Commission, cost-based budgeting as used in industry has been employed successfully for a number of years.

Consequently, because of the general absence of cost-based budgeting and because it must be used in effective performance budgeting, the Commission recommended that agency budgets be formulated and administered on a cost basis. This is one of the most far-reaching proposals advanced by the Commission. It would put the Government on a sounder business basis. Without such cost data, performance budgeting will continue to be at best a meaningless form lacking vitality.

The Commission was also concerned with changing appropriations from the present obligational basis to an accrued-expenditure basis. The present method must be changed, it found, if congressional control over the purse is to be effective. One of the fundamental requirements of a constitutional republic is that Congress have control over money. Such control is vital because Congress is thereby able to exercise a veto over what the executive branch does. This control has been impaired for years, and improvements in appropriations are necessary to restore it.

At present there is no effective control of expenditures either by Congress or by the executive branch. This situation is largely the consequence of the complexity of the appropriation and accounting system and its lack of foundation on proper principles.

There are several reasons for this situation.

The first of these is Congress's practice of providing appropriations in terms of obligational authority. Thus, for 1956 Congress gave to the Bureau of Reclamation a specific amount of money to be obligated in that year. This money actually might be spent over several years.

Second, in many cases Congress has financed programs that require large expenditures over a period of years by voting lump sums at one time. Frequently the law provides that such money is to remain available until expended. This practice was prevalent during the Korean War. Because Congress did not want to be blamed for failing to vote enough money to arm the country, it handed out more than could be spent or obligated in the time available. As a consequence the balance of unexpended appropriations available to the departments rose from $11,500,000,000 in 1950 to $78,400,000,000 in 1954, and it will decline only moderately to $53,900,000,000 at the end of the fiscal year 1956.

Because of such carry-overs of unexpended funds, Congress has no control over the amount of money spent in any one year. Moreover, there is no real review of such unexpended appropriations either by the Bureau of the Budget or by the Congress. Although both review each year the new programs being considered, neither one devotes much consideration to performance under previously instituted programs.

As a result, the Hoover Commission urged that in place of basing the budget on obligational authority as at present, it should be based on annual accrued expenditures. "This contemplates that agency budgets be expressed in terms of the charges for goods and services estimated to be received during the year, i.e., the 'accrued expenditures.'"

The Commission goes on to explain that "the term 'accrued expenditures' represents the charges incurred for goods and services received and other assets acquired whether or not payment has been made and whether or not invoices have been received." Clearly, the term "accrued expenditures" is not identical with cash payments made, because charges might be incurred in one fiscal year while the cash payments to liquidate them might be made in the next year.

Where it takes several years to construct a ship or to get planes or tanks into production (so-called long lead-time programs), under the Commission's proposal the agency would submit initially a program showing the total funds required for completion of the program. Should Congress approve, it would provide an annual appropriation in terms of the estimated accrued expenditures required for the year to which the estimate is applicable. Congress also would give the agency concerned the authority to contract forward in addition to and beyond the amount appropriated.

Thus, to meet the payments due under the contracts in future years Congress would have to make appropriations in later years. Under this system the desirability of the continued operation of the program could be reviewed annually by the Congress, and it and the Bureau of the Budget, when making new appropriations, could redetermine annually the amount of the contracting authority still needed.

For items that do not require a long lead time, as for example most programs of the Veterans' Administration, appropriations, the Commission asserted, should also be placed on an annual accrued-expenditure basis even though little significant change would result. For such agencies this change would be a relatively simple matter.

Other groups have also recommended both to the Bureau of the Budget and to the Department of Defense a system of appropriations on the basis of accrued expenditures.

Obviously, the installation of such a program would produce transitional problems. One necessary prerequisite to its operation would be for Congress to cancel the large balances of unexpended appropriations and to substitute for them annual appropriations to liquidate accrued expenditures and to authorize supplemental contracting authority. Administrative changes in the budget and accounting procedures and reeducation of agency staffs would also be necessary.

Congress has been accused of precluding annual control over expenditures by the way it frequently sets up programs. For example, proponents of such programs as grants-in-aid for old-age assistance say that Congress must appropriate the funds the agency indicates it needs to match State funds. This leaves the appropriations committees of both houses, as well as Congress itself, little discretion in determining the amount of funds to be appropriated in any one year. The Bureau of the Budget asserts that, as a consequence of such situations as this, annual control over the size of the budget is impossible. The bureau estimated that for the fiscal year 1955 more than $15,300,000,000 of the expenditures, or 24 per cent of the total, was relatively uncontrollable.

Probably the bureau actually has more control over these programs than it likes to admit, for it could exercise control by recommending substantive changes in current legislation. The Hoover Commission believes that, where Congress provides for programs not susceptible to the usual annual budgetary control, it should authorize them for only a limited number of years so that they will be subject to frequent review.

ACCOUNTING

As pointed out earlier, in the Federal Government accounting serves as a device for ensuring that expenditures are made only in conformity with law, makes it possible to enforce honesty on the part of public servants, and provides financial data useful to management for determining the efficiency of Government operations.

Accounting in private industry is a major means of management control, but in Government this is only one among several purposes, and probably the most neglected. The Hoover Commission in its report was deeply concerned with better Government accounting as a help to management. The reason for this is that the Budget and Accounting Act of 1921 and the amendments thereto contained in the Budget and Procedures Act of 1950 largely take care of legal control of funds and of their expenditure honestly. The establishment of the comptroller general in 1921 as an arm of Congress to make an independent audit of all expenditures, with authority to disallow any that he may consider to be illegal, effectively implemented many of these objectives.

Through the Budget and Accounting Act of 1950, Congress imposed on the Bureau of the Budget, the Treasury Department, and the comptroller general legal responsibility for the development of accounting methods designed to provide operating information. Up to the present, however, only a few steps have been taken for the implementation of these programs, and these steps have not accomplished much.

The Commission found that "the stimulus of central accounting direction in the executive branch itself is needed if management is to be furnished the financial information which it requires," but that there has been a failure to take this leadership. This means that the Bureau of the Budget, as the management arm of the President, must take the lead in developing such programs. To date the bureau has not equipped itself to meet this responsibility.

The Commission recommends that there be created a Staff Office of Accounting in the Bureau of the Budget, to be headed by an assistant director. Its purpose should be to develop and promulgate an over-all plan for accounting and reporting for the Government consistent with the broad policies delineated by the comptroller general.

To implement such improvements in accounting as the bureau might propose under this recommendation, each department or agency in the executive branch would have a comptroller who should occupy an advisory rather than a determinative role in its management. This official would be able to assist management in reaching sound decisions in the financial field. He should be responsible for the observance of the standards and policies laid down by the proposed assistant director for accounting in the bureau. His would be a full-time job requiring professional competence.

The proposed accounting division of the Bureau of the Budget should also assist in the selection of agency comptrollers.

The several agencies now charged with the basic requirement for keeping accounting records and data have developed cumbersome systems for the allotment of appropriated funds. These are designed to ensure that more money is not spent on an activity than Congress has appropriated for it. In the Department of Defense alone there are thousands of these special funds, resulting in the creation of a multitude of pockets of obligational authority.

The current system of allotments is an attempt to effect management control over operations, but it is defective and self-defeating. In reality it places emphasis on the ability to live within allotments rather than on the usual management criteria of performance in terms of cost. Further, it is self-defeating because it contains an inherent incentive to spend all allotted funds in order to support succeeding allotment requests. The Commission strongly urged that the allotment system be simplified.

Where the Government conducts business enterprises, cost accounting on an accrual basis is especially required. Both the public and the Congress are entitled to know the cost of each Government undertaking, especially in the case of activities which compete with private industry.

Comparisons are frequently made between Government costs and private-industry costs. To be valid these require costs by the Government on an accrued basis because only on that basis are true costs revealed, and it is on that basis that private business keeps its accounts. The costs of Government enterprises should cover such items as depreciation, rent, interest, taxes, and payroll costs, including the pay of military personnel assigned to the operation, all of which would have to be paid by private business. All too often Government accounting fails to include some or all of these items.

The Commission also urged that all accounts be kept on an accrued basis to show current resources and liabilities, thus permitting effective comparisons between Government enterprises and comparable privately owned ones.

The use of revolving funds is a device of recent years used in an attempt to implement management control over Government-operated business activities. These funds are frequently established where Congress appropriates money to a department to be used in financial operations that furnish services or products to other agencies. Among the advantages resulting from the use of such a fund are: (1) it enables an activity to be operated more flexibly under a single source of money; (2) it permits the consolidation of control over materials used in many activities; and (3) it results in better budget estimates. The major disadvantages resulting from such funds are that they minimize congressional control over agency operations and that their widespread use results in pockets of funds. The Commission urged that the creation and operation of revolving funds be reviewed to determine whether they add to efficient management.

The officers in agencies who are accountable for disbursement of funds are personally liable to the Government. This is necessary if Congress is to maintain control over the purse and if the rule of law is to be preserved. Many laws regulate the disbursal of public funds, and any violation of any of them means that the officer personally is financially responsible. As a consequence, many accountable officers are overly cautious. Therefore, where there is any doubt concerning the legality of a transaction, they refer the case to the General Accounting Office for its approval so that they will have an advance determination on the legal question involved. This means an unwarranted expenditure of public funds to handle these submissions to the comptroller general. To remedy this, the Commission recommended that the comptroller general have the authority to relieve accountable officers from financial liability except when losses result from gross negligence or fraud.

GOVERNMENT-WIDE ACCOUNTING

Several agencies have responsibilities in accounting and reporting on a Government-wide basis. One of the most important of these agencies is the Treasury, which maintains many duplicate accounts. The Commission found that this department "at present maintains various accounts . . . which duplicate one another." In addition, it maintains several thousand accounts which largely duplicate similar records maintained in other agencies. Should the accounts of the other agencies ever be so perfected that the Treasury could rely upon them for detail, that department would need to maintain only broad control accounts taking the place of the detailed statements now being kept.

As a consequence, the Commission recommended that the Bureau of the Budget and the General Accounting Office attempt to determine how best to eliminate both the duplicate sets of accounts kept within the Treasury as well as duplication between the Treasury accounts and those of various departments. Although notable progress has been made in the past five years in improving the Treasury's central reporting programs, still further improvements are necessary. The elimination of these duplications would mean large savings.

The Commission found that the Bureau of the Budget, the second agency responsible for central accounting and reporting, fails to perform this task well. "Existing financial reporting fails to provide comprehensive and meaningful information with respect to the operations, and assets and liabilities of the Government as a whole, as well as for major specific component activities," it reported. The Bureau of the Budget should be responsible for the preparation of such comprehensive reports, it said, and Congress should impose upon that Bureau the obligation to perform this function.

Since the Department of Defense is the largest spending unit in the Government, the application of the Commission's recommendations to it deserves special consideration. The significance of this is evident when it is recalled that the agencies in the Department of Defense spend sixty-one cents out of each tax dollar. Further, the complexity of the organization of the department produces difficult and unique problems of financial management that demand solution.

Most of the backlog of unexpended funds is in the Armed Forces Department. Although this department is aware of the need for better financial management, and although it has done much to improve such operations within the past two years, much still needs to be done, according to the Commission. For example, there is still a lack of knowledge as to what the department owns or owes or how it uses its resources.

As a result of the studies and recommendations of the first Commission on Organization of the Executive Branch of the Government, Congress, by Title IV of the National Security Act Amendments of 1949, provided for accounting machinery in the Defense Department and in the armed services; but that department has not so far been able to implement this legislation. Within the Armed Forces control over funds has been hampered by cumbersome allotment structures. The department has attempted to control operations by a system of ceilings on the amount of funds for a given objective, but the Commission found that "the ability to live within such ceilings is no real gauge of performance." "Such a system," it said, "actually puts a premium on the ability to spend all allotments since the allotments for one year are used as one indication of the amounts required for the succeeding year." It would be much more desirable, it found, to make a single allotment of funds to each organization unit rather than to continue the present multiplicity of funds.

The use of revolving funds has improved accounting in certain areas in the defense field, the Commission asserted, but pointed out that "such funds, however, are not a panacea." The objective of accounting is to discover costs. In many instances these revolving funds fail to assist this objective. Another major defect in accounting in these agencies is the large carry-over of unexpended balances of appropriations.

The creation of a comptroller in the Department of Defense was a forward step in promoting sound financial management, but for effective financial control throughout the department the Hoover Commission felt that it is also necessary to have effective comptrollers in each of the three armed services. "Responsibility for fiscal control at the departmental level in each of the three military services should be clear-cut and centralized in the Assistant Secretary for Financial Management," it reported. The Commission recommended that civilians with broad management and accounting experiences should be selected for the positions of comptroller and that these officials should be responsible solely to the secretary of the department. They should, it held, in no way be responsible to their respective chiefs of staff. Freeing them from this responsibility would be a significant step in restoring civilian control over the Armed Forces. If the comptroller answered to the chief of his armed service, he would not constitute a genuine financial control over his respective uniformed service; but if he is freed from such responsibility he could be a real link in the chain of control over the civilian services and in improved management.

The central auditing function throughout the Government is performed by the General Accounting Office, an arm of Congress. Its role has greatly changed in the past five years. Before 1950 it prescribed rigid accounting systems for agencies, maintained duplicate accounts, and performed detailed audits of agency accounts in its own files. The first Commission on Organization recommended that it conduct a modern commercial type of audit at the site of operations. Under the Budget and Accounting Procedures Act of 1950, implementing these recommendations, Congress provided that the comptroller general prescribe the principles and standards for accounting in the agencies, assist them in organizing an accounting system based on those principles, and audit their financial transactions. The second Commission found that:

> The Comptroller General has been, particularly through the General Accounting Office's Accounting Systems Division, an inspiring and constructive influence in developing consciousness of the need for accounting reforms in the executive agencies.

But it went on to say:

> Yet, excellent as this performance has been, it is only a partial substitute for the motivating forces required within the executive agencies themselves.

Recently, the need for internal auditing in the agencies has been recognized as being necessary for determining whether the financial policies of the management have been adhered to. Such internal audits are a supplement to, and not a substitute for, external audits. The Commission urges that the General Accounting Office and the Bureau of the Budget determine the adequacy of internal auditing, as well as means of improving it.

While many of the recommendations made by the Task Force and adopted by the Hoover Commission on Budgeting and Accounting are highly technical and difficult for the layman to comprehend, both the experts of the Task Force and the Commission feel that when adopted they will bring new efficiency into most Federal operations, permit the President closer and better management of the executive agencies, increase Congress's control of the purse, and provide huge savings for the taxpayer.

CHAPTER 4

Legal Services and Procedure

Ten thousand lawyers are directly employed as attorneys by the Federal Government, and the proper organization of the services they render is of transcendent importance to every individual in the United States, for their work involves the protection of our liberties and of our property. In fact, the tasks they perform affect the very basis of the American system of Government.

Our constitutional Republic is founded on the principle that it is a government of law and not of men. It is the rule of impersonal, evenhanded American law that distinguishes our free democracy from dictatorships like Communist Russia and Hitler's Germany. In tyrannies the irresponsible and autocratic bureaucrat reigns supreme only because there is no rule of law applied by independent courts to check him in his dealings with the individual citizen. In the United States it is taken for granted that the rule of law must shape and direct every Government action.

Thus it is that under our American system the individual is supreme before the law, and the Government is his servant; under dictatorships the individual has no rights except as they are conceded by the Government, and the Government is in fact his master.

In some instances, however, legal services are not as well organized in the United States Government as they should be to maintain the rule of law inviolate. It is with these problems that the Hoover Commission's Report on Legal Services and Procedure is concerned.

Before we deal with its recommendations we should clarify the significance of the rule of law.

THE RULE OF LAW

Chief Justice Stone pointed out almost twenty years ago that Government agencies must act only in conformity to the rule of law. "The agencies of government," he said, "are not more free than the private individual to act according to their own arbitrary will or whim, but must conform to legal rules developed and applied by the courts."[1] Arbitrary action by the Government is the complete opposite of the rule of law. Thus Mr. Justice Sutherland emphatically declared:

> Arbitrary power and the rule of the Constitution cannot exist. They are antagonistic and incompatible forces; and one or the other must of necessity perish whenever they are brought into conflict. . . . To escape assumptions of such power on the part of the three primary departments of the government is not enough. Our institutions must be kept free from the appropriation of unauthorized power by lesser agencies as well. And if the various administrative bureaus and commissions, necessarily called and being called into existence by the increasing complexities of our modern business and political affairs, are permitted gradually to extend their powers by encroachments—even petty encroachments—upon the fundamental rights, privileges and immunities of the people, we shall in the end, while avoiding the fatal consequences of a supreme autocracy, become submerged by a multitude of minor invasions of personal rights, less destructive but no less violative of constitutional guaranties.[2]

The assumption in recent years of far-reaching regulatory functions by the Federal Government makes the maintenance of the rule of law more important and more difficult than ever before. Regulatory activities have increased many fold. Examples of regulatory agencies include the Securities and Exchange Commission, the National Labor Relations Board, the Internal Revenue Service, the Federal Communications Commission, and the Interstate Commerce Commission. In such agencies Congress provided for a great diversity and dissimilarity of administrative procedures. In some instances the laws setting them up were hastily drawn to meet emergency situations and failed to include adequate safeguards for the protection of individual rights.

The rise of administrative agencies with regulatory powers was inevitable if the Government is going to supervise our complex economy and intricate communications. In drafting such legislation Congress could not clearly see every eventuality; therefore it had to confer on bureaucrats the authority to issue rules and regulations. Some discretion had to be left to the administrators of the law.

[1] Harlan F. Stone, "The Common Law in the United States," *Harvard Law Review* (1936), Vol. 50, p. 5.

[2] Mr. Justice Sutherland in *Jones* v. *Securities and Exchange Commission,* 298 U.S. 1, 24, 25 (1936).

It is with how these agencies exercise this discretion that the Commission was concerned.

Administrative agencies in performing regulatory activities engage in quasi-legislative, quasi-judicial, and administrative functions. They issue rules and regulations, grant licenses, issue cease-and-desist orders, award damages, and compel individuals or corporations to do many things. They often combine the functions of legislators, prosecutors, judges, juries, and bureaucrats. Too often these agencies have failed to give parties concerned adequate information on regulations. The functions of prosecutor and judge have been exercised by the same bureaucrat. Decisions have not always been based solely on existing law, and in some instances the courts have not been in a position fully to review the decisions.

Despite the fact that the rule of law is basic to our constitutional system, these new regulatory agencies have been in a position to flout it because no check was imposed on their powers.

No real study had been made of the legal services of the Government recently, especially as they relate to the procedures of administrative bodies. A partial study was made in 1945 by the Attorney General's Committee on Administrative Law, and out of this investigation came the Administrative Procedure Act of 1946, which produced some notable improvements. Despite this law much remained to be done to make the rule of law effective over the bureaucracy.

Because the first Commission on Organization of the Executive Branch was clearly limited in its scope, it did not investigate this problem of legal services for fear that to do so was beyond its authority. Because the authority of the second Commission embraced such problems, it decided that it was imperative for it to examine this complicated and important problem. It organized a Task Force composed of fourteen eminent lawyers to assist in gathering the facts and in suggesting recommendations. This group was headed by James M. Douglas, formerly Chief Justice of the Supreme Court of the State of Missouri. Among its members were three deans, or former deans, of law schools, a former deputy attorney general, a former assistant to the attorney general, two Federal judges, two state judges and the president of the American Bar Association. The late Justice Robert Jackson was a consultant to the group, and so was the chief justice of the Supreme Court of New Jersey.

The report of the Commission on Legal Services and Procedure is divided into three sections: legal services, representation before agencies, and legal procedure.

LEGAL SERVICES OF THE GOVERNMENT

The ten thousand attorneys in Government serve in fifty-four agencies. In addition, there are many other lawyers employed by the Government; but the Civil Service Commission, or the Armed Forces, do not consider that they occupy attorney positions, and consequently these are not included in the Task Force study and the Commission's recommendations.

Among the executive agencies are a multiplicity of uncoordinated legal staffs. These staffs vary in size from one lawyer employed by the Coal Mine Safety Board to 1,773 in the Department of Justice. In many instances the agencies have no clear authority in law to employ legal staffs. Although the attorney general is chief legal adviser of the President, he has no authority over the legal staffs of other agencies.

The independence of these legal organizations has been carried to the point where conflicts between agencies have been taken to the courts for settlement. Thus the Government has been suing itself in the Courts to settle disputes that should have been resolved in the executive branch.

The Commission believed "that the efficient performance of legal services within the executive branch demands positive coordination through the Department of Justice." [3] On several occasions, Presidents by executive order have sought to centralize litigation in the department. But by legislation and by administrative action authority over much litigation was again decentralized among the separate agencies. To effectuate such coordination the Commission recommended that responsibility for all litigation throughout all agencies in the Government be centralized in the Department of Justice. It also urged that Congress provide for a procedure that would authorize the attorney general to resolve all legal disputes between agencies, at least in those cases where the agencies involved voluntarily submitted the disputes to him.

The Department of Justice, it felt, should become in fact as well as in name the chief law office of the Government.

[3] Commission on Organization of the Executive Branch of the Government, *Legal Services and Procedure,* A Report to the Congress, March, 1955, p. 6.

Effectively to perform these and other tasks it suggested, the Commission recommended that the Department of Justice be reorganized. Its work in the fields of legal administration and of litigation should be separated, it found, and it urged that an assistant deputy attorney general be placed in charge of each of these major divisions. Such a separation, it said, would permit the litigation staff to perform more efficiently because it would be freed from routine administrative tasks.

LEGAL CAREER SERVICE

For preservation of the rule of law as well as for promotion of efficiency in Government, a trained and experienced legal staff is important. The Commission emphasized that through the centuries, men trained in the law have been its best protectors and interpreters. Lawyers in Government perform their functions well, according to the Commission, only to the degree that they have individual ability and to the extent that their superiors appreciate them when they do their duty. The Commission declares that if Government lawyers are incompetent, or if they disregard the supremacy of the law, the basic rights and liberties of citizens are infringed and justice is impeded.

It is of paramount importance, therefore, the Commission asserts, that our Government employ as attorneys able men who realize that every action of Government must conform with the law. In a Government agency the lawyer is in a position different from that of civil service employees. He must answer "not only to his administrative superior, but to the people of the United States." [4] In addition, the lawyers must answer to the judiciary for their professional conduct.

Thus Government lawyers occupy a unique position that makes necessary unique treatment.

The personnel system applicable to lawyers must take account of their role in applying the law. Under the Constitution, Congress determines and limits the powers which the Government shall exercise. Nevertheless each statute must be interpreted, and as a result a broad area of discretion inevitably is left for the administrators of the law. In the construction and the application of statutes, Government attorneys should be a restraining influence to keep administrative action within both the letter and the spirit of the law.

[4] *Ibid.*, p. 16.

To perform such grave responsibilities properly, the Commission felt that Government attorneys should have independence from administrative control which would enable them to serve as counsels in the Government and not merely as Government employees.

The Commission's proposals concerning lawyers are designed to meet these requirements. It found that morale among Government lawyers is not as high as it should be because many of them do not have a feeling of professional service. All too often they are considered mere "push-button" lawyers, lawyers who are expected to come up with answers designed to please their superiors or to support their policies. Therefore the Commission recommended the creation of a special career service in the Government for lawyers for the purpose of inducing able lawyers to enter and remain permanently in Federal service. The means suggested for accomplishing this is not to put lawyers under civil service, because their special professional position does not permit them to be integrated into the uniform formal pattern of that service, but instead to create a legal career service under an Office of Legal Services and Procedure in the Department of Justice. This office would recruit on the basis of an unassembled examination a register of persons qualified to perform legal work for the Government. The names of persons eligible for such appointments would constitute a central register from which all agencies would make appointments. All legal positions would be classified for the purpose of determining salaries under a special classification system with top pay of $17,500 a year.

Although tenure has not been a significant factor in the retention of lawyers in Federal service, long-term service is necessary for the effective operation of the Government. The probationary period for lawyers, the Commission felt, should be three years instead of three months as is now the case for civil service employees, because of the time it takes to appraise competence. The removal of persons holding appointments in the legal career service, it added, should be only on the basis of the Lloyd-La Follette Act, as amended, which is applicable to all civil service employees. Finally, it recommended that attorneys in Federal service should not be permitted to engage in outside practice or in business activities which interfere with the performance of their legal duties for the Government.

DEPARTMENT OF DEFENSE

Special problems relative to the legal services in the Department of Defense and the armed services were considered separately in the Commission's report. By Reorganization Plan 6 (1953) the President provided that the general counsel of the Department of Defense should be the chief legal officer for the three military departments. The Commission recommended that he should supervise and be responsible for all legal staffs in the department as well as for those of the three armed services. The general counsel of each department, with the rank of assistant secretary, should have final authority over all departmental legal services, including control over the judge advocate general, who in turn controls the staff of uniformed lawyers. The existence of this authority the Commission held vital to the maintenance of civilian control of the Armed Forces and the maintenance of the rule of law.

In each armed service, it declared, there should be a separate judge advocate general's corps.

The existing practice of providing an undergraduate legal education at public expense for commissioned officers in the three services should be terminated because it is wasteful, the Commission reported. Even while such training is now being provided, many uniformed lawyers are not being employed in legal activities. As a result, their training and experience and the money expended for their education are not being used to advantage.

REPRESENTATION BEFORE AGENCIES

Both to expedite public business and to protect litigants, agencies in the executive branch must have the authority to control representatives of litigants who appear before them in administrative proceedings, the Commission felt. Of course, a litigant has the right to represent himself. While individuals are entitled to be represented by others before agencies, persons engaged in such representation, the Commission found, should be qualified by character and training to perform such tasks. Consequently the Commission believed that agencies should impose reasonable safeguards to ensure that representatives who appear before them are reliable and competent.

Each agency itself, the Commission said, should determine who is entitled to act as such representatives. The Commission carefully pointed out that to engage in such representation "is not a right but a privilege." [5] Unless the competence and character of such representatives are adequate, the person represented may suffer, and the administrative agency may be denied the assistance provided by a proper presentation of the case. "The public interest requires that safeguards exist with respect to admission to practice, and administrative agencies are rapidly establishing such safeguards." [6]

The right to represent clients before agencies, the Commission held, cannot be restricted to a single profession—the law. Non-lawyers can and do perform valuable services in this area. The diversity of the activities of administrative agencies makes it advisable to permit persons of diverse talents to represent individuals before them. Among these various talents are accounting, medicine, engineering, and science. Consequently the Commission believed that each agency should regulate by rule the privilege of engaging in such representation and should subject such practitioners to disciplinary control.

Non-lawyers, it recommended, should not be permitted to engage in the practice of the law before administrative agencies. What constitutes the practice of the law, however, is not always easy to determine, and its final determination is a judicial matter. Any lawyer in good standing, the Commission held, should be permitted to represent clients before Federal agencies. For improper conduct in connection with such representation he would be subject to discipline by the United States district court in the district where he principally engages in the practice of law.

No person, it declared, should be allowed to represent a party before an agency, if he in his official capacity had handled the matter or obtained information concerning it.

LEGAL PROCEDURES

The supremacy of the rule of law in Government depends upon adherence by administrative agencies to approved procedural principles. The Commission believed that "sound procedures are indispensable to sound government." [7] For executive-branch functions in the best interests of the Federal Government and of the citizen, the agencies and departments should fulfill their responsibilities in accordance with sound procedural methods and with strict regard for

[5] *Ibid.*, p. 33. [6] *Ibid.*, p. 32. [7] *Ibid.*, p. 45.

due process of law. This is especially true today when these affect almost every individual and every business.

Above everything else simple, inexpensive, direct, and orderly procedures before administrative bodies are of paramount importance to individuals and small businessmen. The large enterprises and wealthy individuals can afford competent lawyers to cope with intricate and badly devised procedures. It is the little man and the small business that are "pushed around" by arbitrary bureaucrats.

Clear legal procedures help to improve the efficiency of Federal agencies and departments. They aid administrators in performing their duties more effectively and more fairly. At the same time they assure relief to the citizen if his rights are hurt by the activities of his Federal Government. Although economy in the operations of the Government is highly desirable, as the Commission has stressed, procedural safeguards cannot be sacrificed merely for the purpose of reducing expenditures.

There is at least one procedural change that is not only desirable but that also will result in economy.

The Commission recommended that the duplication of legal powers between Federal agencies and between Federal and State agencies be terminated. Because the expansion of the administrative functions did not take place in accordance with any plan, each agency has grown without regard for the jurisdiction of other agencies. As a consequence extensive overlaps and conflicts in jurisdiction have developed.

One of the worst examples of such conflicts and duplications is in the field of labor relations, where the National Labor Relations Board and the various state labor relations boards have overlapping jurisdiction over unfair labor practices. The Commission believed that the elimination of jurisdictional conflicts, where practicable, will promote economy for the Government, and will relieve citizens from the burden of complying with the requirements of several different agencies, State or Federal, in any single regulatory area. Such overlaps or conflicts in jurisdiction are confusing and burdensome to the small businessman, who cannot afford to retain lawyers highly trained in such legal intricacies.

DUE PROCESS, EFFICIENCY, AND ECONOMY

Although the Administrative Procedure Act of 1946 has more than demonstrated its utility as the basic charter of Federal administrative law, experience has shown, the Commission holds, that a number of improvements in it are in the public interest. The Commission presented to the Congress a series of recommendations designed to correct shortcomings or inadequacies unearthed by a decade of experience. Only a few of the more significant improvements proposed by the Commission can be mentioned in the limits of this chapter.

One of the recommendations of the Commission is that before issuing rules and regulations, administrative agencies should give the public an opportunity to present its views. This is important because the issuance of rules and regulations by administrative agencies within the last few decades has become an ever larger aspect of the administrative process. This is because Congress in enacting legislation to be applied to diverse and changing fact situations had to leave to the agencies wide authority to issue regulations expanding and applying the law. In their substantive nature such rules resemble legislation but, unlike Acts of Congress, these rules are not adopted after consideration by committees and discussion in open assembly. To provide some equivalent participation in the proceeding by persons affected by the rules is now generally authorized. In a few instances Congress failed to require the agencies to notify interested parties and to give them an opportunity to present their views.

On occasion some agencies have issued regulations without notice or previous publication, and the courts have set them aside. The Commission recommended that in all cases where the Constitution or existing laws do not require a hearing interested parties should have an opportunity to submit their views and arguments in writing, except in cases of emergency or when secrecy is in the public interest.

In all adjudicating proceedings the Commission believed that administrative agencies should afford the parties an opportunity to be heard in a formal judicial hearing. By far the greater part of all administrative actions in the regulatory field involve adjudication, "that is, the formulation of an agency order which finally disposes of any matter other than by rule making." [8] These orders can have far-reaching application and significance both for an individual's liberty and for his property. They may involve the deportation of

[8] *Ibid.*, p. 56.

aliens or the right of a citizen to engage in an ordinary business enterprise.

The Commission found that with few exceptions every agency of the executive branch adjudicates substantive personal and property rights of private parties. Basic to maintenance of the protection of the individual's liberty is the right of persons affected to be heard by the agency prior to the taking of such action. Because of the gravity of the rights involved, the Commission believed that a formal hearing should be afforded in all instances by all agencies.

To protect the rights of litigants the Commission recommended that administrative agencies should in all instances separate investigating, prosecuting, and adjudicatory functions. The Commission placed great stress on this recommendation. One of the characteristics of administrative agencies engaging in regulatory activities has been the merging of these dissimilar functions. All too often the power to initiate an investigation and complaint is united with the power to determine whether the facts found after the hearing warrant the imposition of a penalty or other legal sanction. This concentration of functions tends to depart from the traditional American principle that no one shall be a judge in his own cause. It means that the individual is not afforded a fair trial by an impartial and disinterested judge.

Combining the role of prosecutor and of judge, the Commission held, is autocratic and destructive of individual liberty.

The Commission recommended that long delays in hearing and deciding cases by administrative bodies should end, and that courts should have authority to expedite such cases. Although Congress through the Administrative Procedure Act sought to get rid of long delays in hearing and deciding cases, nevertheless such undesirable delays still persist.

For example, the Task Force found that five cases had been pending before the Indian Claims Commission for at least three years without the Government making any answer to the petitions.

Cases before the Bureau of Motor Carriers of the Interstate Commerce Commission are reported to take, on the average, about twenty-one months before decision. The same Commission's Bureau of Finance reports proceedings lasting an average of one year.

The National Labor Relations Board, on the average, requires one year for the disposition of unfair labor practice cases and six months for representation cases.

The Commission found that proceedings before the Bureau of Old Age and Survivors Insurance of the Department of Health, Education, and Welfare and before the Veterans' Education Appeals Board average four months and one year, respectively.

The Subversive Activities Control Board reported two years as the average time for an adjudicatory proceeding before that agency.

The Commission recommended that all cases decided without hearings should be settled in three months, and that cases where hearings are held should be settled within six months from the final date of hearing.

It further recommended that in proceedings before administrative bodies the hearing officers should have the powers necessary to conduct hearings under established trial procedures and that the use of appeals before the closing of the record should be restricted. The Commission found that it was the intent of Congress, in enacting the Administrative Procedure Act of 1946, that hearing examiners should "perform a real function rather than serve merely as notaries or policemen." [9] The competence and powers of hearing officers lie at the heart of formal administrative adjudication, the Commission said. Unfortunately, by rule and custom in some agencies, the powers of examiners in conducting hearings have become limited, to the detriment of their independence and proper role as administrative trial judges. This has resulted in injury to agency efficiency and also to the rights of private parties.

The Commission recommended that administrative agencies in adjudicating cases should follow the rules of evidence applicable in the United States district courts. The Commission found that a serious deficiency in the administrative adjudicatory processes was the absence of a uniform method of evaluating evidence. The relative informality of some agency proceedings was believed to be an advantage of the administrative method. But experience has demonstrated, the Commission held, that, without sound rules governing the admissibility of evidence, agency proceedings can become involved and cumbersome, with delays in decisions and difficulties in judicial review. The rules of evidence utilized in the courts are designed to protect the accused by requiring adequate proof of all matters that are significant to a decision.

[9] Senate Document 248, 79th Cong., 2d Sess., 269 (1946).

For example, courts generally forbid hearsay evidence because the source of the evidence does not appear in person. Without confrontation the judge cannot evaluate the witness's honesty, and the opponent cannot cross-examine him.

There should be prompt judicial review available, the Commission asserted, for every wrong resulting from agency action or inaction, and the scope of such review should be similar to that provided in the case of trial courts.

The Commission found many situations in which the action or inaction of administrative agencies affecting citizens is subject only to limited judicial review, or in which the administrative activities have been expressly exempted from any judicial review. Although it is the responsibility of the courts to see to it that administrative agencies stay within the limits of the authority granted to them by the Congress, nevertheless the Commission found that there is a broad area in the rule-making and adjudicatory fields where the statutory provisions for judicial control over administrative action should be expanded and strengthened.

The principle of the supremacy of law requires that every administrative official be under the law and have only such authority as the law grants to him. To make this effective every administrative action must be subject to judicial review. The courts, as the guardians of the law, must be in a position to review all administrative action, or the rule of law is destroyed.

Yet the Task Force found that there are at least six statutes which directly preclude judicial review of administrative action.

Many of these statutory exemptions have been based on the premise that where Congress provides for grants or benefits from the Government, the agents of Congress have the power to determine the recipients of the grants or benefits, and that Congress has the right to preclude judicial review of the selection of the objects of its bounty. Nevertheless, the Congress can be assured, the Commission held, that its objectives are fully complied with only if claimants have a day in court to test the exercise of administrative action in the light of the authority conferred by Congress.

Another procedural recommendation of the Commission for maintaining the rule of law was that agencies should impose on individuals or corporations only such sanctions or penalties as are prescribed by Congress. The authority which administrative agencies exercise must be based only upon delegation by the Constitution or by Congress. Action which goes beyond that authority may be invalidated by the courts as *ultra vires.*

It is a fundamental principle of the law that delegated power should be strictly construed. Otherwise, the constitutional authority of the Congress tends to become diluted, since it would be spread throughout various departments and agencies of the executive branch. The imposition of penalties not authorized by law is of the essence of dictatorship. Here again it is obvious that the man of small means and the small businessman need protection against the bureaucrat ever eager to increase his authority.

The Commission proposed that an Office of Legal Services and Procedures be set up in the Department of Justice. Its task would be to study the procedure of administrative agencies engaged in adjudication and rule making and to supervise the career legal service. This office would analyze agency rules and advise agencies of the steps they should take to bring their rules and regulations into more easily understandable form. All rules and regulations, whether procedural or substantive, should be filed promptly by every agency with this proposed office, the Commission held, and every agency should be required to comply with the orders of the office's director for bringing about simplification, clarification, and uniformity of rules.

The Congress, the Commission declared, should be able to learn, without engaging in its own study of all agencies, facts needed for evaluating legal procedures, so that it could determine whether appropriations for regulatory agencies should be reduced or increased, or whether certain functions should be added, modified, or eliminated. At present there is no central place to which Congress may turn for this information. The Commission proposed that the Office of Legal Services and Procedure compile information and statistical data relating to legal services and procedures of all agencies of the executive branch for the use and information of the agencies themselves, for the use of that office, and for the use of the Congress.

HEARING COMMISSIONERS

To hear cases in the first instance that fall within their jurisdiction many administrative agencies use trial examiners. They are an important element in the administrative process because the integrity of the quasi-judicial process depends upon their impartiality and reliability. The record on which a decision is based is made by these examiners. Thus in a real sense, the rights and property of every litigant are in the hands of these petty bureaucrats.

The Commission believed that the titles of these officials should be changed to "hearing commissioners," and that their position and tenure should be improved. These officials should not be subject to influence from any quarter, it felt, and should have the independence of judgment expected of judges. They should not be subject to appointment and personal supervision, it added, by an authority interested in the outcome of the hearings which they conduct. At the same time they should not, it felt, be entirely free from such supervision and control.

To organize this system of hearing commissioners, the Commission recommended that there should be an Office of Chief Hearing Commissioner who should be responsible for the selection and supervision of hearing commissioners employed by all agencies. Because the hearing commissioners should have long tenure and superior status, it felt that it is desirable that they be appointed by the President with Senate confirmation for a term of twelve years.

The chief hearing commissioner should be located in the judicial rather than in the executive branch, the Commission said, and his primary responsibility would be to recruit outstanding men for the positions of hearing commissioners. He should be aided, the Commission recommended, by a presidentially appointed advisory committee of five members. One of the major tasks of this board would be the promulgation of qualifications for the selection of hearing commissioners, and it should advise the chief hearing commissioner concerning the qualifications of nominees to fill vacancies. The chief hearing commissioner should assign and transfer hearing commissioners from agency to agency as requirements dictate.

The Commission proposed that the removal of such officials "should be only for incompetence, neglect of duty, misconduct in office involving moral turpitude, or physical or mental disability, established and determined after opportunity for hearing and upon the record thereof." [10] Removal of hearing commissioners should be only after a hearing conducted by a judge of the Administrative Court, and removal should only be made by that court.

[10] *Legal Services and Procedure,* p. 91.

TRANSFER OF FUNCTIONS TO THE COURTS

Probably the most important recommendation of the Commission on legal services was that some of the more vital judicial functions of administrative agencies be transferred to the courts. This would be important especially to the individual citizen because it would mean that he would be protected by impartial courts instead of being "pushed around" by bureaucrats. There are two ways of doing this: first, the functions can be directly transferred to the regular courts, or second, courts of specialized jurisdiction can be created to handle specific types of cases.

Concerning the first, there are some activities of administrative agencies that are strictly judicial in nature because they provide remedies comparable to those granted by courts. In some situations the private rights involved in administrative proceedings can be protected only if there is separation of the prosecuting function from the function of making decisions. This separation can best be attained in the courts, especially where the remedies are comparable to those provided by the judiciary. Such proceedings are those involving monetary penalties, the award of reparation or damages, and the issuance of cease-and-desist orders.

The Interstate Commerce Commission and the secretary of agriculture, the Commission felt, should be divested of their existing authority to issue orders for reparations or damages. It suggested that further study be made of this problem "with a view to removing typically judicial functions from the agencies in the executive branch." [11]

For functions of administrative agencies that cannot readily be imposed upon existing courts, but which, nevertheless, should be removed from under administrative control, the Commission recommended that they be placed in a court to be known as the Administrative Court of the United States. In at least three administrative areas, it felt, the functions should be transferred from administrative bodies to this court. These are: taxation, trade regulation, and labor relations. It recommended that the Administrative Court be composed of three sections, one vested with authority over each of these three areas.

The present Tax Court of the United States is the only strictly

[11] *Ibid.*, p. 85.

administrative tribunal now in the United States. The Commission recommended that it be removed from the executive branch and be made a legislative court comparable to the Court of Claims. Transforming this court into a regular court would not involve any large change, but it would make it a court of record.

Trade regulation, unfair methods of competition and unfair practices are now being regulated by a number of agencies, including the Federal Trade Commission, the Federal Communications Commission, the Department of Agriculture, and the Food and Drug Administration in the Department of Health, Education, and Welfare. As a result there is confusion as to which agency has jurisdiction. In fact the jurisdiction of these agencies often overlaps. If these functions could be transferred to a single administrative court, enforcement would be improved, and the individuals and business would be greatly benefited.

The third section of the Administrative Court should assume the jurisdiction now exercised by the National Labor Relations Board in unfair-labor-practice cases. This would not include the board's work relative to representative cases. It would mean that litigants would be freed from added heavy costs now imposed upon them because to get a fair judicial trial they must appeal the decisions of the National Labor Relations Board to the courts.

The proposed Administrative Court would not have general jurisdiction over the judicial functions of administrative agencies, but the Commission was of the opinion that the court would be an instrumentality to which additional adjudicatory functions in special areas could be transferred as it proved its effectiveness. The Administrative Court thus would serve as an intermediate stage in the evolution of administrative adjudication.

The primary objective of the Commission's recommendations on legal services and procedure is to reestablish the supremacy of the rule of law throughout the administrative agencies and Government. The growth of the powers of the agencies has been at the expense of the constitutional separation of powers. As a result such agencies are able to transgress in an unconstitutional manner the liberties and rights of American citizens. The enactment of laws to implement the Commission's recommendations would go far toward reestablishing our constitutional rights.

CHAPTER 5

Paperwork and Red Tape

Each year the Federal Government handles more than 25,000,-000,000 pieces of paper. If these papers were laid end to end they would stretch from the earth to the moon thirteen times. Yet this colossal figure does not include pamphlets and books. In producing this mass of paperwork, the Government employs more than 750,000 full-time workers and spends more than $4,000,000,000 yearly. This sum would have paid the entire cost of the Federal Government in 1932.

The filing of correspondence, forms, reports, directives, and other records has resulted in more than 24,000,000 cubic feet of Federal records. This is enough to fill seven buildings the size of the mammoth Pentagon.

The first Commission on Organization of the Executive Branch of the Government made a study of a segment of this problem of paperwork—that was records management. Its recommendations led to the Federal Records Act of 1950 which gave the General Services Administration the task of promoting a program for the improvement of the management of Government records. Three years later the General Services Administration reported that its efforts had resulted in a yearly saving of $34,170,000. Other studies of the first Hoover Commission pointed up additional aspects of the problem. For example, the Task Force report on the Federal Supply System showed that each year the bureaucracy made out 3,000,000 purchase orders to buy supplies and equipment. On the average this paperwork for one such order cost at least $10, although more than 1,500,000 of these orders involved an expenditure of less than $10 each.

Because of the significance of the problem in terms of efficiency and because of the potentialities for savings, a general study of the problem was undertaken by the second Hoover Commission. This investigation sought to measure the costs and dimensions of paperwork activity in general, to identify the areas of potential savings, and to suggest such organizational changes as may be necessary to improve paperwork management and reduce red tape.

It dealt with the problem in two phases. The first covers paperwork management inside the Government itself. The second considers the burden of paperwork that the Government imposes upon private industry and the general public.

GOVERNMENT PAPERWORK

The $4,000,000,000 that paperwork costs the Government each year the Task Force distributed as follows:

Correspondence	$1,000,000,000
Forms	867,000,000
Reports	700,000,000
Directives and Instructions	100,000,000
Record Keeping	650,000,000
Mail Handling	104,000,000
Supervisory and Miscellaneous	579,000,000
	$4,000,000,000 [1]

Each year Government bureaucrats write more than 1,000,000,000 letters, and these cost the taxpayer $1 each. These letters when inserted in envelopes would make a stack 390 miles high. In a little more than forty years the production of letters per Government employee has increased almost tenfold, rising from 55 letters per employee in 1912 to about 522 at present. With the number of employees having increased sevenfold in that time, the total of Government letters has increased seventy times.

A number of agencies have discovered that huge savings result from improved letter writing. Thus, the Baltimore Office of the Internal Revenue Service cut its expenditures for letter writing by more than $157,000 a year through use of standardized texts and wider use of postcards and forms. If these methods were extended throughout the Internal Revenue Service, annual savings of

[1] Commission on Organization of the Executive Branch of the Government, *Paperwork Management*, Part I, "in the U.S. Government," A Report to the Congress, January, 1955 (Washington, D.C., U.S. Government Printing Office, 1955), p. 14.

$5,500,000 might be attained. In a period of less than nine years the Veterans' Administration has made annual savings of $10,860,200 in letter writing. It found that for each $1,000 spent on correspondence management studies, annual savings of $32,000 resulted.

The Government uses more than 18,000,000,000 printed or mimeographed forms each year at a cost of about $867,000,000. The Commission found that great savings can be effected through the reduction and simplification of such forms. The Navy Department has shown the way by cutting the number of its forms in one project from 3,161 to 752. In one year that department eliminated 21,000 forms at a saving of $3,000,000. The Internal Revenue Service and the Social Security Administration have indicated that if two forms could be consolidated, an annual saving to business firms of $22,000,000 would result. This one, however, would require legislation.

More than 25,000 reports are required annually by the Government itself for its own internal use. The Government spends more than $700,000,000 a year on these. In addition, the Government imposes 4,700 different reporting requirements on private industry. The Commission, after studying this problem, found that "many reports do not appear to be well conceived as tools for management control, nor is the data properly integrated and maintained for this purpose." [2] Each adds to the burden of red tape. Many were found to be unnecessary.

The Commodity Stabilization Service of the Department of Agriculture has shown the way by reducing from 1,400 to 600 the number of reports it requires from its field service, and this alone made possible 43 per cent fewer employees engaged in reporting.

This demand for reports also permeates the Armed Forces. An army division, for example, has to prepare 126,000 reports each year. Their preparation takes the full-time services of ninety uniformed personnel. Of course, a man who is busy filling out forms cannot fight, or even prepare himself to fight.

Filing or record keeping costs too much also—about $50,000,000 a year. The Commission found that, "unfortunately, this large item of expense has received little attention from top management. Indeed, no agency of Government appears to have made a thoroughgoing survey of its total filing problem." [3] Out of the 24,000,000 cubic feet of Government records, 16,000,000 occupy 2,000,000 file

[2] *Ibid.*, p. 7.

[3] *Ibid.*, p. 9.

cases and these fill 16,000,000 square feet of valuable office space. Engaged full-time in filing operations are 159,000 employees. Many of these files duplicate one another.

For example, although the headquarters of the air force in 1948 required that all records be kept in the central files, actually only 5 per cent were so transmitted; the balance were kept in the operating offices. As a result the central files were useless. Later, each major segment of the air force was directed to maintain its own files. As a result, the air force could dispense with the services of the twenty-two persons employed in the central files.

The Government produces great numbers of various types of technical manuals. These cover such things as the repair and overhaul of each type and model of aircraft. In most instances these are prepared and printed by the contractors who manufacture the equipment. The Navy Department has estimated that it spends over $20,000,000 a year on such manuals, and it believes that if the requirements for their production were eliminated from all of its contracts an annual saving of from $10,000,000 to $14,000,000 would result.

The Government owns several hundred million dollars of office machines, and the Commission found that the best use was not made of them. The Government maintains no central pool of such equipment, though automobiles are pooled.

Despite the Government's work in pioneering the development of the large-scale, high-speed electronic computers, it is far behind the times in using them for business purposes. Big savings result from the use of such equipment. For instance, a computation that costs $25 to do by hand costs $4 by tabulating equipment, and only $1 if done by an automatic machine. These are costly machines, of course, and for a Government agency to buy one of them under present conditions it would have to pay out a large portion of a single year's appropriation. This is one reason why the Government has been slow in buying and utilizing them. Another reason is that it is costly for an agency to hire the skilled technicians to operate such equipment. Joint action by several agencies or a pooling system could solve the problem.

The Government is also a large owner and buyer of small office machines: typewriters, adding machines, and so on. It owns about $200,000,000 worth of such equipment, and it buys about $20,000,000 additional each year.

The Task Force found that throughout the Government there is great need for skilled workers to supervise and study the management of paperwork operations. Although the Civil Service Commission has spent three years in developing standards to determine the skills and experience necessary for positions in this field, it has failed to arrive at definitions and thus offers no examinations for such positions. This delay has made it difficult to get attention focused in each agency on paperwork management problems and their solution. The Task Force felt it is imperative that the Civil Service Commission develop clear-cut classification standards for such positions.

The Hoover Commission concluded that "agencies too often lack a clear-cut concept of the value and economies possible from careful attention to paperwork management. . . . On the whole, agency heads and their principal subordinates have not given proper attention to potential economies in this $4 billion activity." [4]

The Task Force estimated that approximately $250,000,000 can be saved each year. To facilitate economies in this field, the Commission recommended that the President establish by executive order a government-wide paperwork management program under the supervision of the General Services Administration. In each agency under this program there would be an official to review all forms with a view toward their simplification and toward a reduction in the number of copies of them.

Steps have been taken to improve the Government's paperwork management since the Commission's report was sent to Congress in January 1955. One of the proposals it made was that the agencies reduce the amount of records designated as permanent. During the fiscal year 1955 the proportion of records designated as such was reduced from 26 per cent to 21 per cent. Large segments of Selective Service, Veterans' Administration, and personnel records have been affected. Large savings in the cost of record handling and storage have resulted.

The General Services Administration also decided that one-half instead of one-third of permanent records should be kept in record centers, and transfers to such locations have greatly increased. Again, this means savings.

The Commission recommended that the more uneconomical agency record centers be closed. The Veterans' Administration has been carrying this out, with annual savings of about $1,077,000.

[4] *Ibid.*, pp. 13–14.

Likewise, many record centers of the Selective Service System are being liquidated. Here annual savings might amount to $1,360,000.

Despite this progress, there is still much room for improvement.

PRIVATE INDUSTRY AND GOVERNMENT PAPERWORK

Elimination of many of the 4,700 requirements imposed by the Federal Government on private industry to report statistical data would result in large savings both for industry and for the Government. Already, as a result of preliminary work done as a part of the investigations of the Commission's Task Force on Paperwork Management, savings of $5,000,000 a year have been realized for the Government and $10,000,000 for private industry. The Task Force studies demonstrate that savings of at least $100,000,000 a year to Government and private industry are possible through further cooperation between private industry and Government.

The Task Force on Paperwork Management got committees representing 29 industries to meet with representatives of 33 bureaus or departments to study 328 paperwork items in a move to discover where savings were possible. For each of these 328 items the study groups sought one or more of the following five results:

Eliminating an unnecessary report.
Reducing the frequency of a report.
Reducing the number of copies of a report.
Simplifying or consolidating necessary reports.
Eliminating unnecessary detail, delay, or cost of reporting.[5]

Before it ended its work the Task Force was able to report that 49 of these results had already been accomplished, and that 26 had been partially accomplished. There remained at least 169 that required further follow-through by Government agencies. In connection with these studies the representatives of private industry, according to the Task Force, "could not have been more cooperative," [6] and concerning the Government agencies the group found

[5] Commission on Organization of the Executive Branch of the Government, *Task Force Report on Paperwork Management,* Part II, "The Nation's Paperwork for the Government; An Experiment," June 1955 (Washington, D.C., U.S. Government Printing Office, 1955), p. 5.

[6] *Ibid.,* p. 5.

that "in no single case did we fail to gain some acceptance of industry recommendations." [7]

The Task Force's analysis of reporting requirements imposed on individuals and business was divided into five major parts:

Redtape in Its Purest Form.
The Hoarding Instinct.
Is Everyone a Thief?
Statistics Unbound.
Government's Unpaid Workers.[8]

REDTAPE IN ITS PUREST FORM

Dictionaries define redtape as "necessary official delay"; but the Task Force felt that there is reasonable doubt as to whether most of the delay is "necessary." By the elimination or cutting of redtape, sizable savings for private industry and for Government can be attained. Let's see what this means. A utility company, subject to Federal regulation, desiring to make an addition to an existing plant, must obtain a certificate from the Federal Power Commission. Many of these proposed plant additions are small. In fact, 2½ per cent of all of the additions to plants in terms of dollars accounted for 67 per cent of the total number of the certificates. By setting a minimum value figure for such plant additions requiring certification, a saving of at least $1,750,000 a year can be obtained.

Before the Federal Power Commission licenses a project of a utility company subject to its jurisdiction, it requires proof of the cost of the undertaking. The Federal Power Commission's request for such data covers 82 pages, and the utility's report often runs to 1,000 pages and costs more than $25,000 to prepare. After its receipt, the Power Commission checks it in detail, even using field men who spend long periods surveying the project and checking the accounts. The Task Force suggests that the detail required in the initial application form could be greatly restricted, and that extensive detail should be supplied only after the Federal Power Commission's auditors and the utilities come to an agreement on what is required. The Federal Power Commission has given tentative approval to such a proposal. This would also mean a saving.

Through the elimination of unnecessary forms and reports the Bureau of Customs also can make great savings for industry, accord-

[7] *Ibid.*, pp. 5, 7.

[8] *Ibid.*, p. 7.

ing to the Task Force. In 1954 there were 4,900,025 entries of imported goods into the United States, and industry's paperwork bill for these was about $22,000,000. Thus a 10 per cent saving in costs in this field would amount to $2,200,000. Only five years ago the bureau had some 400 different forms covering procedures for entry into the United States. On its own initiative it reduced the number to 150.

One example of the potential savings involved is in the 960,000 forms prepared annually by airlines authorizing consignees to clear shipments through customs. Through the use of a rubber stamp applied to the airway bills of lading and invoices, the need for this form could be eliminated. This would save $2,000,000 a year to the airlines alone. The Bureau of Customs is willing to make this change.

One of the most startling illustrations of unnecessary Government expense and redtape was a lawsuit brought by the Government to recover a loan of 31 cents plus interest of 28 cents due on it. The original loan of $80 had been made by the Government almost twenty years ago. Probably thousands of dollars of expenditure will be incurred to recover these few cents.

HOARDING

The Task Force found that companies regulated by a Federal commission store twice as many records at twice the cost as do companies not regulated by the Government. Often there is no limit on the time that these companies are required to keep records.

For example, the Federal Deposit Insurance Act set a five-year limitation on the period in which recovery could be made of any assessments due to the Federal Deposit Insurance Corporation from an insured bank. In order to have their records available for auditing by the Federal Deposit Insurance Corporation, many banks have to keep records in costly storage places for as long as six to eight years. But that corporation recently has decided to conduct audits on the basis of a cycle of not more than three years. This reduces by 50 per cent the volume of records that banks must keep available, and cuts costs accordingly.

A division of the Department of Agriculture requires that anyone who acquires, stores, or disposes of raisins must keep records of his activities.

Eighty-five out of one hundred regulations of the Department of Labor requiring the keeping of records fail to state how long such records must be preserved. As a result, theoretically, they must be kept permanently, and that means forever.

Five industries reported that the annual cost of storing old records comes to $26,782,000. The cost to the trucking industry alone is $5,200,000. Savings to that industry as a result of the work of the Task Force on Paperwork Management will be $1,300,000 a year, and in the banking field the savings will be $1,500,000 a year.

Many of the record-keeping demands by Government agencies appear to rest on the assumption that all people are thieves. This is especially true in income-tax matters. The Internal Revenue Service requires anyone who pays money to another person to file with it a notice of such payment. About 60,000,000 of these separate notices are submitted each year. The cost to industry of compiling these reports runs to about $14,500,000 a year. The Task Force reports that "one large well-known company admitted that several years ago it stopped sending in its hundreds of thousands of these reports. So far, nothing has happened. They have not been missed." [9]

GOVERNMENT STATISTICS

The Budget of the United States reports that the Federal Government spends about $43,400,000 on its statistical work a year. No one knows how much it costs American industry to compile the statistics that the Government demands. The chemical industry alone reports that each year it spends $8,850,000 to supply statistical reports demanded by three departments of the Government. The utility industry spends $32,000,000 a year in preparing reports for Government agencies. At one meeting between the Federal Power Commission and representatives of this industry, twenty specific paperwork targets were examined and solutions to sixteen were agreed upon.

All industrial users of peanuts must report their consumption to the Department of Agriculture. Some companies consume such small amounts that their reports are negligible for statistical purposes. Upon the intervention of the Task Force, the Department of Agriculture agreed that henceforth only those that consume more than ten thousand pounds a year need report.

The railroads must report quarterly to the Interstate Commerce Commission the commodities they transport both by type and by amounts. The shippers have to report the same information only once a year. Such reports are not required of highway truckers and

[9] *Ibid.*, p. 30.

this, these carriers assert, results in a saving to them of $685,000 a year. The Task Force recommended that the railroads also only file these reports once a year. This would mean a saving to them of $630,000 a year.

If small alterations are made in two reports, the Task Force says, one industry alone can save $800,000 a year in statistical reporting.

UNPAID WORKERS COLLECTING STATISTICS

Many employees of private industry are occupied with the collection of Government statistics. This is especially burdensome to small businesses. A small hardware store owner in Ohio estimated that 29 per cent of his time is absorbed in filling out such reports.

Not infrequently people dealing with the Government have to keep several sets of books to fit the diverse and dissimilar requirements of Federal agencies. For example, trucking companies have to keep one set of books showing depreciation on one basis so as to conform to requirements of the Internal Revenue Service and another set showing it on a different basis to conform to regulations of the Interstate Commerce Commission. If the requirements of these two agencies could be made identical, the trucking industry reports that its members would save $300,000 a year.

The three military services have at least three separate and distinct procedures which a privately owned company must follow in reporting on Government property in its possession.

> For example, if a contractor had side by side in his plant three identical lathes which he had received respectively from the Air Force, Navy, and Army, he would have to maintain records on three separate forms. For the Air Force lathe, he would use "Industrial Equipment Inventory Record," for the Navy lathe "Property Record Card," and for the Army lathe, "Production Equipment Record." [10]

ROLE OF BUREAU OF THE BUDGET

Since 1942 the Bureau of the Budget and its Advisory Council of Federal Reports supposedly have been charged with the task of reviewing the reports required of private industry by the Government. Although this bureau and its council may have done much to improve governmental statistical reporting, they have not done much to reduce the burden imposed upon private industry by Government

[10] *Ibid.*, p. 51.

reporting requirements. The Commission found that the accomplishments of the bureau do not compare favorably with the achievements of its Task Force, although the latter worked only for four months. So the Commission recommended that the President direct that the Bureau of the Budget, with the help of its Advisory Council on Federal Reports and with the cooperation of the General Services Administration, give increasing emphasis to protecting the public from unnecessary reporting burdens. The Bureau of the Budget should continue, the Commission felt, the methods of cooperation between industry and Government that were developed by the Task Force.

In one industry that annually spends several million dollars compiling statistical reports for the Government, the Task Force found that certain executives had agreed that every year they would omit a different page from this statistical compilation. "They have waited to see what would happen." [11] So far nothing has happened.

In order to claim exemption from a law enacted in 1935, all financial companies are required to make a certain report to the Internal Revenue Service. "In recent years," the Task Force said, "more and more of the hundreds of companies involved simply stopped submitting the report. Today, only nine, the largest, abide by the law. These big companies feel that however small the risk, they must conform to this meaningless requirement to avoid even the shadow of controversy." [12]

Under the so-called Anti-Kickback Law, certified copies of payrolls covering employees of certain Government contractors must be filed with the Government. So many of these reports come in that the agency concerned with the administration of the law does not have time or money to file them. A bureaucrat responsible for administering the law states that "he dumps them in barrels or on the bare floor of empty storage rooms." In the case of one small business the proprietor states that "some time ago she stopped sending copies of the payrolls in the required format to the Government. Although the Government has yet to miss these payrolls and question her, it is a constant source of worriment to the lady." [13] It is futile and highly costly, the Task Force asserts, for the Government to use reporting and record keeping by all people to forestall dishonesty and error on the part of a few people.

The burden of filling out Government reports and forms is espe-

[11] *Ibid.*, p. 41. [12] *Ibid.*, p. 42. [13] *Ibid.*, p. 33.

cially heavy on the small-business man, the Task Force pointed out. He is literally swamped with forms, questionnaires, and reports. Because he is not able to employ high-priced skilled accountants, statisticians, and lawyers this burden falls on him personally. It is estimated that the 4,000,000 small business firms in the country spend at least 5 per cent, and in some instances as high as 29 per cent, of their time on Government paperwork.

Since everyone is eager to help the small-business man, he is caught in a peculiarly difficult situation. He is swamped with the answering of thousands of questions designed to identify him as a small-business man. For instance, to ensure that small business gets its share of Government contracts, prime contractors must report on their contract to small business, but this information is only available through questionnaires sent out to be answered by small-business men themselves.

CONCLUSIONS

Sizable savings to both Government and private industry are not the only worth-while results from improved paperwork management. The Government can save at least $255,000,000 a year from its own expenditures on paperwork. The recommendations of the Task Force concerning the paperwork burden imposed on private industry have produced savings of $10,000,000 for industry and $5,000,000 for the Government. If all of the group's proposals in their area are carried out, savings of $100,000,000 a year are possible.

By freeing private business from the burden of making out unnecessary reports and forms not only will money be saved, but businessmen will be able to devote more of their time and effort to producing more goods and services and more profits to tax. This will be a benefit to the entire nation. The small-business man will be relieved from what are, to him, intolerable burdens. The elimination of excessive Government reports and forms will reduce redtape, speed business, and give millions of Americans a new freedom.

CHAPTER 6

Real Property

The Federal Government owns one-quarter of the land area of the forty-eight States of the Union. Within the continental United States it possesses 472,000,000 acres, and outside the territorial limits of the country it has an additional 366,000,000 acres, making a grand total of 838,000,000 acres. This real property is administered by twenty-seven different agencies.

Every government has to use some real property to carry out many of its activities, and the management of such property is a difficult housekeeping task in the same general category as personnel, budgeting, and legal procedures.

Outside the public domain, the Federal Government has acquired 63,200,000 acres in more than 36,000 locations. For this property it has spent $44,600,000,000. Much of this land was acquired in the last quarter of a century. In addition, it leases 2,449,000 acres in 24,000 locations.

Situated on property owned by the Government are 2,475,000,000 square feet of floor space, the equivalent of 1,250 Empire State buildings. In addition the United States leases 94,500,000 square feet of floor space.

SCOPE AND NATURE OF THE PROBLEM

There exists no adequate inventory of the real property owned by the Federal Government. Nor has there ever been an adequate management study made of how these vast holdings are operated.

Because of the sheer magnitude of the problem and because no study ever had been made of how the Government performs its role as landlord, the Commission on Organization of the Executive Branch of the Government created a Task Force composed of eight experts to study the problem and advise the Commission. This group was headed by John R. Lotz, formerly chairman of the board of

Stone & Webster, a leading engineering firm. The other members of the Task Force were qualified to advise on this problem by experience as business executives, engineers, lawyers, and bankers.

Based on the study of this group, the Commission reached the shocking conclusion that there is "little in the nature of modern real property management in the Government. There is a lack of property records and of financial accounting for property." [1]

Six agencies own 90 per cent of the real property acquired by the Federal Government outside the public domain. The Department of Defense has real property that cost $24,800,000,000; the Atomic Energy Commission, $4,900,000,000; the Department of Interior, $3,500,000,000; the General Services Administration, $1,300,000,000; the Housing and Home Finance Agency and the Veterans' Administration about $1,000,000,000 each. Eleven agencies, each with property costing not less than $100,000,000, account for another 10 per cent of the total. The remaining $200,000,000 of realty belonging to the Government is distributed among ten agencies.

Most of the Government's realty outside the public domain was acquired in recent years, and 79 per cent of the Government's expenditure of $54,200,000,000 for new construction during the entire life of the United States was spent between 1937 and 1953. Present administrative problems are the result of this enormous expansion.

An annual rental of $107,417,000 is paid by the 23 agencies that lease the 2,449,000 acres. About half of this total rent is paid by the General Services Administration, about 22 per cent by the Post Office Department, and 19 per cent by the Department of Defense.

REAL PROPERTY MANAGEMENT

The first effective attempt to introduce order into phases of the Government's management of real property resulted from the recommendations of the first Hoover Commission. In 1949 Congress, in creating the General Services Administration, indicated that that agency should have general charge of the utilization and disposal of all available Government property, including realty. This law

[1] Commission on Organization of the Executive Branch of the Government, *Real Property Management*, A Report to the Congress, June 1955 (Washington, D.C., U.S. Government Printing Office, 1955), p. 2.

gave the President vague and general authority to prescribe policies and directives on property management, but the "Declaration of Policies" that this agency is to carry out is far from clear.

Under an executive order of the President the General Services Administration has received authority to promulgate standards, regulations, manuals, and procedures to guide executive agencies in determining whether their real property operations are efficient and economical. But the General Services Administration has seen fit to exercise this authority only to a limited degree, and all too frequently operating agencies have ignored its directives and advice.

In performing this function the General Services Administration has carried on limited surveys of real property management in a few agencies; but it limited itself to the activities of their central offices, thus failing to survey the field services where most of the problems of property management exist. The regulations relative to real property management that have resulted from such surveys have not been complied with by the owning agencies, possibly because the General Services Administration makes no effort to enforce them.

The Hoover Commission concluded that "the Administrator of General Services appears to have far-reaching responsibilities for real property management, but his authority to accomplish these responsibilities is unclear and diffused." [2]

The Bureau of the Budget also has wide authority to improve the administrative management of the Government, including the administration of real property. It has had this power since its establishment in 1921, and Congress reinforced and strengthened its authority in 1950. And although the President has specifically directed it to review real property management plans of agencies in conjunction with their requests for appropriations, it has done nothing to carry this out.

Despite the fact that present laws relate in a limited way to real property management, Congress has failed to develop a fundamental concept of management. No agency is responsible for developing real property policies and procedures, nor are the operating agencies required to follow existing management policy directives. No single agency, whether in the General Services Administration or in the Bureau of the Budget, is charged with the task of over-all real property management.

[2] *Ibid.*, p. 9.

Many agencies and buildings are specifically exempted even from the limited control of the General Services Administration. All of the public domain, the national forests, and the national parks are entirely outside its jurisdiction. All of the real estate of the Atomic Energy Commission and of the Central Intelligence Agency is wholly exempted. Certain types of property owned by other agencies are also exempt. Residential property owned by the Housing and Home Finance Agency, Department of State properties in foreign countries, the Departmental Reserve of the Department of Defense, and the properties of the Commodity Credit Corporation are all outside its authority. Certain types of buildings are also specifically excluded, such as all post-office buildings used predominantly for the Post Office Department, the main building of the Treasury Department as well as the building of the Bureau of Engraving and Printing, the buildings of the Bureau of Standards and of the Smithsonian Institution, any building in the Department of Defense, unless a permit for its use has been issued to another agency, as well as any building which is predominantly used by one agency.

Under these exclusions and restrictions, it is almost impossible under existing law for the General Services Administration to exercise needed responsibility.

For efficient real property management the Commission believed that there must be accurate records showing the location and title of each piece of property. It suggested an accounting system covering both quantity and dollar value of the properties, including reserves for depreciation. It is also necessary, it felt, to have a constantly corrected national inventory of properties, prompt disposal of surplus, and an agency designated with responsibility for carrying out these functions.

The Commission recommended that Congress enact a definite "Declaration of Policy" stating its intent regarding real property management. The administrator of the General Services Administration, it declared, should establish standards, prescribe regulations, and prepare and issue manuals and procedures to guide agencies in their management of real property. To ascertain that these directives are being complied with, it said, the administrator of this agency should make periodical inspections. Where noncompliance is found, it affirms, he should request the President to direct compliance.

All statutory exemptions from the authority of the General Services Administration over real property management should be terminated, the Commission said. In their place the President should be authorized to make exemptions from the Act when such exemptions are fully justified and in the public interest.

GENERAL SERVICES ADMINISTRATION

Although, as previously stated, Congress in 1949 conferred upon the General Services Administration general responsibilities over real property, in actual practice its activities in this field have been limited to the operation, maintenance, repair, and assigning of space in general-purpose buildings owned or leased by the Government. It has authority to acquire additional buildings by lease or construction. It has authority also to develop methods and standards for the management of real property. These management principles are applied by its regional offices to property under its own jurisdiction and not to property held by other agencies.

Because the General Services Administration is decentralized, its administrator and headquarters office exercise no actual, direct control even over the properties under its own jurisdiction. To each of the ten regional offices the administrator has delegated both authority and responsibility for the management and operation of public buildings under its control, along with the assignment of space in Government buildings, as well as the disposal of surplus real property. In 1953 even the operating records of the General Services Administration were decentralized. The Hoover Commission found that "currently, the central office is policy-making in character, with regional directors virtually autonomous in their areas. The central office does not possess continuing reports on operating conditions and costs within the regions." [3]

The Public Buildings Service of the General Services Administration administers public buildings valued at $2,000,000,000, and has an operating budget of about $160,000,000. The central office has neither the staff nor the funds to check on how thoroughly its own regional offices are complying with its programs and policies. The Commission stated:

> The result has been a delegation of complete authority and responsibility for operations and operating management without maintaining in the

[3] *Ibid.*, p. 18.

central office of the Public Buildings Service the necessary staff authority and responsibility to establish, review, and enforce the standards and policies by which such delegated responsibility is carried out.[4]

The process of decentralization in the administration of the General Services Administration has also led to other difficulties.

For example, if the regional office of an agency housed in a building controlled by the General Services Administration is dissatisfied with its space or how it is being remodeled, it can complain to its own central office; but the central office is simply referred by the central office of the General Services Administration back to its regional administrator for relief.

Although the General Services Administration is responsible for the upkeep and repair of all general-purpose buildings of the Government, Congress frequently gives funds for the alteration of specific buildings to the tenant agencies rather than to the General Services Administration, the landlord. As a result it is not able to administer its property uniformly, and, further, disputes are encouraged and provoked between that agency and incoming tenant agencies.

There are also numerous conflicts between the General Services Administration and the Post Office Department. Buildings in which the post office occupies less than 50 per cent of the space are the responsibility of the General Services Administration for operation and maintenance, but where the post office occupies more than half the space that department is responsible for their operation and maintenance. The Commission found that "such a division has resulted in much confusion, friction, delay, and other inefficiencies." [5]

Thus, although the General Services Administration supervises the repair and improvement of about 4,619 general-purpose buildings, the Post Office is responsible for the operation and maintenance of 3,174 of these buildings. The Post Office Department is supposed to report semiannually to the General Services Administration on the portion of space it uses solely for office purposes, but it does not have to report on space used for other postal purposes. Data supplied to the Task Force by the General Services Administration and by the Post Office Department concerning their respective responsibilities over the same real property did not coincide.

[4] *Ibid.*, p. 19.
[5] *Ibid.*, p. 22.

The Commission recommended that the President authorize the administrator of General Services, after consultation with the Bureau of the Budget and the comptroller general, to prescribe a uniform system of recording and reporting Government-owned real property designed to bring about full disclosure of its operation and management. The administrator, it held, should also prescribe the form and content of real property accounts, and receive, review, and consolidate inventory reports on real property. It further recommended that all executive agencies maintain a perpetual inventory of the real property leased by them and submit a report to the General Services Administration at the end of each fiscal year.

The General Services Administration, the Commission recommended, should be made responsible for real property management for all buildings partially or wholly occupied by the Post Office Department. All funds for the operation, maintenance, repair, and alteration of all general-purpose buildings should, it said, be appropriated directly to the General Services Administration. That agency should, it held, seek to consolidate Government office space in large urban centers into a small number of large buildings and should gradually seek to improve the quality of such office space while promoting its relocation out of high-cost areas.

DEPARTMENT OF DEFENSE

The $24,800,000,000 in real property held by the Department of Defense, which amounts to 61 per cent of all the real property held by the Federal Government outside the public domain, costs about $1,500,000,000 a year for maintenance and operation. Here the Commission felt that "modernization of management methods will result in substantial savings to the taxpayer." [6]

Although the secretary of defense is responsible for the administration of the real property of the three services, he has delegated to the assistant secretary of defense for properties and installations the task of developing standards and procedures. But to the secretaries of the three departments he has delegated all necessary authority to perform management functions for their respective real property. In addition, under existing law the heads of these three services have authority to acquire property.

[6] *Ibid.*, p. 27.

These three service secretaries in turn have delegated certain aspects of property management to their assistant secretaries; but both the extent and the nature of such delegation is not uniform in the three services.

The real property used for defense purposes falls largely into two major categories: command establishments and industrial facilities.

Command establishments valued at $13,800,000,000 are the larger group. These are used for the administration, training, and other activities of the three armed services.

Approximately $8,660,000,000 of the department's real property consists of 288 plants in the Departmental Industrial Reserve and the National Industrial Reserve. Their operation involves grave issues of public policy. These plants fall into two major categories.

1. The Departmental Industrial Reserve created in 1947 includes arsenals, shipyards, other industrial facilities, and many war plants not considered excess after the end of World War II. There are 249 facilities that cost $8,330,000,000.

2. The National Industrial Reserve established in 1948 includes such excess or salable plants as have been earmarked by the military departments for production during another emergency. This group consists of 39 facilities that cost $330,000,000. Should any plants in this reserve be sold or leased, the law requires that there be a recapture clause in the agreement. This requirement has inhibited the sale of most of these plants.

At least a hundred of the 288 plants in the two categories are either inactive or in poor physical condition. The Commission believed that in all possible cases it is desirable to return these facilities to private industry where they will contribute to the national production. Should this be done, Government expenditures would be reduced and the tax receipts of the Federal, State, and local governments would be augmented.

For instance, six plants in the National Industrial Reserve that originally cost $132,000,000 were sold for $42,000,000. But since being turned over to private industry they have produced more than $100,000,000 in taxes for Federal, State and local governments. Thus through their sale they have brought in $10,000,000 more than their original cost, while at the same time the Government has been freed from maintenance costs. The Commission stated:

The management of the real property of the defense establishment is complex and is made more complicated by the restrictions of legislative procedures and regulatory controls that have accumulated, and by the continual change in total holdings, either through emergency increases or more gradual decreases.[7]

The 249 plants in the Departmental Industrial Reserve are under the jurisdiction of the military departments, while the 39 plants in the National Industrial Reserve are under the jurisdiction of the General Services Administration. Such a division of responsibility makes impossible effective management either by the Department of Defense or by the General Services Administration.

The Commission recommended that authority over properties in the National Industrial Reserve be transferred from the General Services Administration to the Department of Defense. Control over property in the Departmental Industrial Reserve and in the National Industrial Reserve should, it asserts, be unified and vested in the Secretary of Defense. Finally, the Office of the Director of Defense Mobilization should be directed by legislation, it declared, to establish the general policies governing the retention and disposition of all industrial property acquired by the Government for defense purposes.

FEDERAL RURAL LANDS MANAGEMENT

Thus far only urban realty property and property used for an industrial purpose have been discussed; but in addition the Federal Government owns vast quantities of rural lands. These include the public domain, the national forests, the national parks, Indian reservations, as well as other lands owned by the Department of Agriculture, the Department of Defense, and the Tennessee Valley Authority.

These rural lands present difficult administrative problems, and their use raises fundamental problems of national concern. Serious problems of land management result, for example, from the geographic intermingling of lands administered by the Bureau of Land Management and the Forest Service. The Forest Service of the Department of Agriculture is responsible for administering 189,400,000 acres of forest land. This agency won commendation from the Task

[7] *Ibid.*

Force both because of its organization and because of the way that it manages public land. The Bureau of Land Management in the Department of Interior is responsible for the administration of about 180,000,000 acres of public land in the United States and for vast areas in Alaska.

The difficult interrelations between these two agencies have to do both with forest lands and with grazing lands. Some of these problems are caused by the lack of uniformity in the policies of the two agencies. For instance, the administration of Forest Service grazing lands is left largely to the discretion of that service, while numerous acts of Congress regulate the administration of grazing lands under the Bureau of Land Management.

The Commission found that "as an over-all management operation, there are gaps and duplications in both responsibilities and practices." [8] As a consequence, the Commission recommended that the President appoint a committee to study the problems of Federal rural lands and to make recommendations for their improved management. This special study committee, it believes, should include representatives from Federal and State governments, as well as members representing forestry, agriculture, conservation, and mining interests.

FOREIGN REAL PROPERTY

In foreign countries the United States Government owns property that cost $2,700,000,000. These properties are at 4,260 locations. These foreign holdings range from embassies and consular establishments to air bases, military posts, hospitals, warehouses, and fueling stations. Most of the foreign properties are owned by the Departments of Defense and State, the Panama Canal Company, the Canal Zone Government, and the Foreign Operations Administration.

"There is no centralized responsibility in the executive branch," the Commission found, "for the management of real property owned and leased by the Government in foreign countries. There is no consolidated inventory of this property, and no steps are being taken to make one." [9]

[8] *Real Property Management,* p. 39.
[9] *Ibid.*, pp. 41–42.

The existing policies and procedures for such real property are inconsistent and uncoordinated.

Because the Office of Foreign Buildings Operations in the State Department apparently efficiently administers the property under its jurisdiction, the Commission recommended that the President be authorized to direct that the secretary of state be responsible for operating and maintaining all general-purpose buildings owned or leased by the Federal Government in foreign countries.

The secretary of state should also be directed, it held, to get from other operating agencies financial operating reports covering all real property owned by the United States in foreign countries. It was also recommended that he should submit to the General Services Administration annually a consolidated financial statement concerning such properties.

Finally, the Commission urged that Congress appropriate directly to the State Department all funds required for the operation, maintenance, repair, and alteration of general-purpose buildings owned or leased by the Government in foreign countries.

CONCLUSIONS

What important questions are raised by this study of the Government's real property? Among them are:

First, does the Federal Government need all the real property it now holds?

The answer is no. One-quarter of the acreage of the entire country, plus improvements which bring the acquisition cost to almost $41,000,000,000 (exclusive of the public domain), is a tremendous amount of land and buildings for the exercise of the essential functions of the Federal Government.

However, a realistic evaluation of the situation is impossible pending adequate inventories or other management records.

Second, does the Federal Government make good use of its holdings?

Again, the answer is no. The Commission points to the possibility of finding improved office space at less cost. There appears to be an excess of storage space. The worst type of problem is exemplified by the fact that two agencies (General Services Administration and the Post Office Department) do not agree with respect to the property for which they have joint responsibility.

Third, how does all this affect each of us, the national economy as a whole, as well as our basic principles of government?

The Federal Government's holding of unnecessary property is reflected in our tax bills in several ways. It raises Federal taxes because the Government must pay for the property and its maintenance. It raises state and local taxes because these Government units cannot tax Federal property and, therefore, raise the rates on remaining taxable property. Despite higher rates, local and State units find themselves short of funds for carrying on functions which traditionally, and appropriately, are sponsored by them. It then becomes easier to convince them of the need for various forms of Federal aid.

Financial aid, however, is accompanied by control. Thus, practices which increase Federal taxes, and simultaneously reduce the income of local units of government, pave the way for increased Federal control over State and local governments. This poses an ever greater threat to our constitutional liberties.

Further, through the sale of unnecessary industrial plants Government competition with private industry will be reduced, and as a result the capacity of industry to pay taxes to support the Government will be augmented.

If the recommendations of the Commission were carried out completely, annual savings of $185,000,000, it is estimated, will result to the taxpayers. In addition, $1,250,000,000 of capital funds could be returned to the Federal Treasury through the sale of properties that would become surplus under the Commission's proposals.

3.

Big Government

CHAPTER 7

Water Resources and Power

The Hoover Commission examined many phases of Government activities that have far-reaching implications to the people because of the nature of the activities and because of the size of the operations involved.

For example, practically every person realizes the importance of water for drinking, for the disposal of waste, for navigation, for industrial purposes, and for the generation of electric power. Again, credit activities of the Government have a significance for anyone desiring to buy a home or a farm, or to enter into business, or who has money in an insured bank. Medical services are provided by the Government for a large segment of the population either in whole or in part. Finally, although it is widely recognized that the most significant factor making possible the high level of prosperity of our nation is the free private enterprise system, this Government nevertheless operates a multitude of business enterprises that compete unfairly with private business.

In this and the three following chapters the Government's activities in the fields of water resources, lending, medical services, and business enterprises will be reviewed, and the Commission's recommendations relative to each of these problems will be summarized.

THE DEMAND FOR WATER

The nation's demands for water exceed available supplies. During 1950 roughly 180,000,000,000 gallons of water were being withdrawn every day from the ground, lakes, and rivers of this country for use on farms, in municipalities, and in industrial enterprises. This was enough to take care of the needs of 180 New York Cities. By 1975 it is estimated that the demand for water will increase by an additional 138,000,000,000 gallons. This increase would be equal to the flow of eleven Colorado Rivers and would supply the needs of 145 New York Cities.

In some parts of the country ground water is being used at ten to fifteen times its normal replacement rate. Where the nation will find the water to fill its expected future needs is not apparent.

Thus the intelligent use of water is now, and will continue to be, a problem of grave public concern and will require the development of a sound national policy.

The role of water in our national life has changed dramatically during our history. In our early years water was primarily used for transportation, and in the period fom 1789 to 1910 the Federal Government spent $693,400,000 on water projects, mainly in the form of aid to navigation. Since the early part of this century the increase in population has resulted in pressures on our water supply from many quarters, and now transportation is only one of several competing functions demanding Federal outlays for water projects.

There has been a vast expansion in Federal regulatory and promotional activities in such fields as flood control, irrigation, power production, and pollution control. As a result, today one of the primary problems before us as a people is the equitable distribution of water between various users. There has been competition for the use of water between Federal, State, and local interests. Because water is a primary necessity for all life, it is imperative that our national policies permit the greatest possible use of water resources for all of our people for those purposes which are the most important.

THE NATURE OF THE PROBLEM

From its beginning to the present the Federal Government has spent more than $14,300,000,000 on water-resources projects. Additional projects authorized by Congress but not yet completed will cost $18,494,000,000 more. Thus the grand total will come to $32,-800,000,000. The cost of projects proposed but not as yet authorized by Congress would bring this total to more than $84,000,000,000.

In many areas there is keen competition for the use of available water supplies. In some localities the use of water for irrigation has lowered the downstream level of water for navigation. In the Central Valley of California there is competition for water to be used for irrigation, power, navigation, reclamation, and the maintenance of the balance between salt and fresh water at the mouth of the Sacramento River. Further, there is competition between northern and southern California for the use of hydroelectric power generated on streams in the Central Valley.

Another clash of interests is between those who would erect reservoirs to promote the beneficial use of water and those who would preserve scenic values. Bitter controversies are raging on the damming of streams in the Dinosaur National Monument and in the Glacier National Park for reservoirs where such construction would interfere with the recreational use of national parks.

The Hoover Commission found that "the most difficult problem of water resources development is the balancing of the interests, demands, and responsibilities of individuals, local groups, States, and the Federal Government."[1] One phase of this clash of interests is illustrated by the problem of the management of big reservoirs built for several purposes. If a reservoir designed to control floods, among other purposes, is to result in the maximum amount of flood control, water in it must be drawn down as soon as one flood has occurred so that storage space will be available for the next flood; but if the dam and powerhouse are to produce the maximum amount of electric power the water must be drawn down evenly throughout the year. When reservoirs on the same stream are controlled by different agencies with different responsibilities, inevitably there will be conflict. Further, there are extensive overlaps and conflicts between Federal agencies, among the several States and between the National Government and the States on the use of water.

The multiplicity of Federal agencies concerned with different phases of water development is of itself confusing. For example, twelve agencies deal with flood-damage abatement, nine with irrigation, eight with drainage, seven with improvements to navigation, nine with pollution control, ten with watershed treatment, fifteen with power generation, nine with power transmission and distribution, ten with recreation, fish and wildlife conservation, and thirteen with water supply. And, to climax it all, there exists no machinery to coordinate these agencies.

Moreover, the Federal Government and the States are not in agreement on who has the right to water in streams. In the West people consider they have a vested right to the use of the water. This means that the first users have a superior right. The States in

[1] Commission on Organization of the Executive Branch of the Government, *Water Resources and Power*, A Report to the Congress, June 1955, I, 11.

this region are insistent on protecting the rights of existing users under this doctrine of prior usage. This vested right is valued at between $15,000,000,000 and $20,000,000,000. On the other hand, under Federal law water rights are based upon riparian rights.

Many conflicts involved between these two principles have gone to the courts; but in recent years there has been some progress in settling these controversies through interstate contracts.

NEEDED IMPROVEMENTS

Fundamental defects exist in present Federal policies and structure relative to water projects. These can be corrected only by formulation of new basic policy and development of new Government machinery.

For instance, it is common practice in submitting water-resource projects to Congress for the Federal agencies to develop statements of benefits to justify authorization of the projects and of the appropriation of funds. Should the cost of the project be underestimated, or the projected benefits overestimated, the ratio between benefits and cost would be misleading. Yet the use of misleading estimates has been frequent.

Another reason that the Federal machinery for handling water projects needs improvement is that cost estimates for the construction of many water projects are far below actual costs. The Task Force found that the original cost of 90 reclamation projects was estimated at $1,580,000,000, but in 1952 the figure for the same projects had been raised to $3,317,000,000. In 1944 the reclamation phases of the Missouri River Basin project were estimated to cost $840,000,000; but by 1953 the estimate had been increased to $3,717,000,000, or an increase of about 343 per cent. Again, for 182 Corps of Engineers projects, it was found that cost estimates had increased $3,274,000,000 over the original submission, or an increase of 124 per cent, with only 57 per cent of this rise attributed to increased costs.

If the cost of these projects had been accurately estimated at the start, many of them probably would never have been authorized by Congress.

All too often there have also been gross overestimates of the benefits that would result from projects. For example, the average estimated benefit from reclaiming an acre of land has been $509, but actually the land, when reclaimed, had a market value of only $150 per acre. This means that for a 160-acre irrigated farm the Federal subsidy would exceed $56,000. It is doubtful if Congress would ever have permitted the construction of such costly projects had it been properly informed.

In evaluating flood-control projects, the estimates of benefits are often without foundation and on occasion almost fantastic. The Corps of Engineers estimated the damage resulting from a specific flood at $7,010, while the Soil Conservation Service of the Department of Agriculture estimated the damages from the same flood on the same stream at $47,004. The next year the two agencies got together and estimated the damage at $9,016.

The Commission did not cite these examples for the purpose of casting doubt upon the competence of the Federal agencies. In fact, the Commission hastened to state that "they have been signally free of the taint of dishonesty in administering construction programs. Most of the blame must be placed on the lack of consistent national policies, and the absence of adequate provisions for review, inspection, and coordination of projects at Washington and basin levels." [2]

BASIC POLICY

Although the burden of developing a sound water policy rests on Congress, that branch of the Government has failed to perform this task. The Commission emphasized:

> Policy statements of the Congress deal largely with separate water uses, separately conceived and separately enacted. Other laws enacted from time to time establish individual projects and define areas of authority and in this way to some extent fix the intent of the Congress. But overlaps and gaps occur, and an overall policy for water utilization and the Federal interest therein does not exist.[3]

Congress's failure to formulate a clear and simple water policy is a major defect in the development of the nation's water resources. Concerning the need for such policy the Commission states that

> it must be evident that there is imperative need for a clear definition of the role and policies of the Federal Government in the framework of a consistent national water policy and the coordination of Federal and

[2] *Ibid.*, I, 25.

[3] *Ibid.*, I, 35–36.

State agencies which will progressively promote conservation and development of this vital natural resource for the Nation as a whole, as well as for States and local communities.[4]

For its first and most fundamental recommendation on water resources the Commission outlined the elements for a national policy to be adopted by the Congress. This recommendation is so clearly stated and so important that it should be quoted textually. It reads:

Recommendation No. 1

That the Congress adopt a national water policy on the following nine points:

(*a*) That water resources should be developed to assure their optimum use and their maximum contribution to the national economic growth, strength, and general welfare.

(*b*) That water resources development should be generally undertaken by drainage areas—locally and regionally.

(*c*) That the Federal Government should assume responsibility when participation or initiative is necessary to further or safeguard the national interest or to accomplish broad national objectives, where projects, because of size or complexity or potential multiple purposes or benefits, are beyond the means or the needs of local or private enterprise. Under other circumstances the responsibility for development should be discharged by State or local governments, or by local organizations, or by private enterprise.

(*d*) That in participating in water resources and power development, the Federal Government without waiving its constitutional rights should take account of the rights and laws of the separate States concerning appropriation, use, control, and development of waters within their boundaries.

(*e*) That the Federal Government should provide advisory assistance to those local and State agencies that are undertaking water resource and power development projects.

(*f*) That before Congress authorizes or appropriates funds for Federal participation in any water resource project, it should have substantial evidence that the project is economically justified and financially feasible, and that such project is essential to national interest.

(*g*) That one Federal agency should be made responsible for collecting and reviewing the adequacy of hydrologic data.

[4] *Ibid.*, I, 35.

(*h*) That all Federal agencies administering revenue-producing water resource and power projects should pay all cash revenues to the Treasury as miscellaneous receipts, and receive an annual appropriation for cash operating expenditures.

(*i*) That regulation of rates for sale of electrical energy by all Federal agencies be vested in the Federal Power Commission.[5]

EXECUTIVE REVIEW

With the multiplicity of Federal agencies engaged in water-resources development there is a need, the Commission felt, for coordinating their activities at the highest executive level. In recent years several attempts to develop machinery for such executive coordination have been made, but no significant results have come of these efforts. Consequently, the Hoover Commission proposed the creation of a Water Resources Board in the Executive Office of the President. This board should consist of those Cabinet members primarily concerned with water resources together with five public members, presided over by a non-Government chairman. The primary purpose of this board would be to determine broad water-resources policies that might be transmitted by the President to Congress for its consideration. Another task would be to coordinate the plans and activities of the multiplicity of Federal agencies in this field.

The Bureau of the Budget now has the responsibility of passing on the merits of water-development projects, especially in connection with its recommendations concerning authorizing and appropriating legislation. Because the bureau is not adequately staffed to perform this task, the Commission urged that the bureau's professional staff in this field be increased so that it may properly evaluate the merits of water-development projects.

RIVER-BASIN COMMISSIONS

With but few exceptions, the river basin is the critical area where water-resource development projects must be coordinated. The four big Federal water-development agencies—the Bureau of Reclamation, the Corps of Engineers, the Soil Conservation Service, and the Federal Power Commission—as well as privately owned enterprises, deal with the development of the same river basins. In addition, the

[5] *Ibid.*, I, 36.

States in each basin are interested in the plans of the Federal agencies. As early as 1926, the then Secretary of Commerce Herbert Hoover proposed that each important river basin should have a commission on which the States as well as the major Federal agencies concerned would be represented along with representatives of private development organizations. The objective was to coordinate development activities.

The Hoover Commission recommended that the proposed Federal Water Resources Board should set up river-basin boards to represent Federal, State, and private interests for the sole purpose of planning and coordinating projects in each major basin. These bodies, it held, should not be set up rigidly on the basis of a drainage basin; instead some flexibility should be permitted. It believed such basin boards would do much to develop maximum participation by local governmental and private agencies.

RECLAMATION AND IRRIGATION

Of the 25,800,000 acres of irrigated land in the United States in 1950, approximately 7,147,000 acres were in Federal projects. This means that at least 73 per cent of the irrigated land was in non-Federal projects. The Commission as a justification for a Federal interest in irrigation found that

> irrigation is not solely to provide land for farmers or to increase food supply. These new farm areas inevitably create villages and towns whose populations thrive from furnishing supplies to the farmer, marketing his crops, and from the industries which grow around these areas.[6]

The financial record of Federal irrigation projects indicates that often costs were grossly underestimated, that the period of repayment was much longer than originally expected, and that in some cases there have been financial failures. As part of its investigation of the Federal irrigation program which is under the Bureau of Reclamation in the Department of the Interior, the Commission studied 110 projects that furnish primary water to 5,216,000 acres as well as supplementary water to 5,644,000 acres. These facilities provide some or all of the water for a total of 10,861,000 acres. The original estimate of the cost of these projects was $1,580,000,000, but

[6] *Ibid.*, I, 44.

on June 30, 1952, it was estimated that these projects would cost $3,317,720,000, or an increase of more than 110 per cent. Part of this increase was due to expansion of some projects and part was a result of higher prices. The Commission believed that there can be no doubt that serious underestimation of costs constituted a large part of this 110 per cent increase, and that a number of these projects would not have been authorized if the Congress had been better advised concerning their cost.

On ninety of these projects $1,040,500,000 of the cost was allocated to be repaid by water users, but up to June 30, 1952, these beneficiaries had paid only $95,300,000. On two projects 90 per cent of the costs had been repaid, and on five, less than 15 per cent had been repaid. The repayment of the costs of some projects has been slow. For example, the Milk River Project has repaid only 10 per cent of its costs in forty-one years. At this rate it will take 410 years for it to repay all of its costs that are to be recovered from irrigators. In the twenty-seven years since the Riverton Project has been completed it has repaid only 6.3 per cent of its costs, and at this rate will take 430 years to repay all of the money expected from water users.

The period of construction for many of these undertakings has also been long, and too often it has been much longer than originally estimated. Twenty-one projects were under construction for more than twenty-two years, and seven for more than forty years.

SUBSIDIES

The Federal Government has paid subsidies to irrigation projects, but despite these the load of charges on water users in many instances is still too high for them to bear. This burden of costs still exists, although the Federal Government charges no interest on the unrepaid balance due on reclamation projects. In a project, the cost of which is to be repaid in fifty years, this interest subsidy can account for more than 50 per cent of the costs of the undertaking at the present rate of interest being paid on the public debt. As previously indicated, the farmers have repaid so far only $95,300,000 out of the $1,040,000,000 allocated for repayment.

Many devices have been used to obscure the size of the subsidies. Obviously there is objection to practices which manipulate the returns from a project to provide low-cost power and a subsidy to irrigation. Methods of cost allocation which relieve power revenues of their share of the burden of the payment of project cost, particularly where there are features whose cost is nonreimbursable, is a significant instance of such practice. Another such practice is the recapture of the interest component where the return of interest on power investment is used to pay irrigation costs. This results in a subsidy by the taxpayer to irrigation because the money required to pay interest on the power investment cannot at the same time repay the capital costs charged to reclamation.

APPROPRIATE POLICY

In the field of reclamation the Commission believed that Federal policy should strive to attain the following objectives: (1) to relieve the farmer of the excessive amount which he is called upon to pay for water; (2) to simplify the calculations of direct and indirect benefits resulting from reclamation; (3) to state clearly the amount of subsidy expected from the Federal Government; and (4) to protect the Government from the underestimations of cost and the overestimations of benefits.

In determining the Federal contribution it is desirable that water users who are to benefit should pay a sum approximating the difference between the market value of irrigated and nonirrigated land in the immediate area. For instance, if irrigated land is selling at $200 an acre, and nearby unirrigated land at $50 an acre, a farmer should pay irrigation costs approximating $150 an acre. If Congress believes that costs exceeding this amount will benefit the country as a whole, the Commission felt, it should contribute the additional amount needed as a direct subsidy. Finally, if the costs of constructing a project should be underestimated or the benefits overestimated, some portion of the resulting losses to the Government should be borne, it adds, by the irrigation district.

Generally, the Federal Government has limited the acreage belonging to a water user who could receive water from a Federal irrigation project. In most instances this limit has been set at 160 acres. Although some limitation of acreage may be justified, the Commission asserted that the criteria for determining the appropriate size of the family-type farm should not be based on rigid limitations on acreage but should vary to meet local conditions. Consequently, the Commission recommended that Congress should amend the present laws limiting acreage in irrigation projects to provide flexibility.

These recommendations of the Commission, if adopted, could result in large savings to the taxpayer because the construction of costly, uneconomic reclamation projects would be avoided.

FLOOD CONTROL

For more than a century the Federal Government has been engaged in flood-control activities. Before 1917 its role was relatively minor, involving a total expenditure of about $85,000,000. Since then responsibilities imposed on it have increased rapidly, and the same has been true of its outlays.

Floods are of two sorts. First, there are those that result from the increase in stream flow due to seasonal rains and melting snow, and second, there are those which occur at relatively rare intervals. Although the latter type cannot be wholly controlled they can at least be restricted and the damage reduced.

There are at least five major Federal agencies engaged in flood-control activities—the Army Corps of Engineers, the Bureau of Reclamation of the Department of the Interior, the Soil Conservation Service of the Department of Agriculture, the Tennessee Valley Authority, and the International Boundary and Water Commission of the United States and Mexico.

The Corps of Engineers has primary Federal responsibility for flood control. Under its jurisdiction it has 1,033 past and present authorized projects which will cost $11,100,000,000. Of these, 349 have been completed at a cost of $1,500,000,000. It now has under construction 84 projects which will ultimately cost $4,200,000,000. It has also a backlog of authorized projects that will cost $5,400,-000,000. In addition, the Corps envisages the construction of additional projects that will cost $15,200,000,000. The cost of operation and maintenance of these projects would come to $46,900,000 a year.

The Soil Conservation Service of the Department of Agriculture was authorized by the Flood Control Act of 1936 to attempt to control floods through the construction of minor dams on the headwaters of streams. According to the Task Force, the program of the Soil Conservation Service would cost at least $25,000,000,000 to complete.

Thus the total flood-control program as mapped out by the major agencies of the Government with responsibilities in this field would cost at least $41,000,000,000.

The Army Engineer Corps has been in water-development activities since 1824. It has all too frequently underestimated costs and overestimated benefits. The Task Group on flood control cited the following as an illustration of its practice of overestimating benefits:

> The Corps of Engineers estimated the value of "business income losses" (exclusive of other flood losses) in Kansas City during the 1951 flood to be $154,146,000. It also estimated the value of property in the flooded area at $1,115 million. If it be assumed that the business income losses resulted from a shutdown lasting 1 month, the claimed loss of over $154 million would mean that the annual net return on the investment in the flood plain is about 166 percent. Even assuming a 2-month shutdown, the annual net return would have to be about 83 percent if the claimed losses were correct. This is, of course, a very rough check but it serves to show that the business income losses must have been grossly overestimated.[7]

This Task Group found many defects in the programs of the Corps, but concluded:

> That much of the blame for these program defects must be assessed against the lack of wise and unified Federal policies, and the absence of adequate provisions for review, surveillance and coordination in the executive branch. For these inadequacies the Congress must bear a considerable measure of responsibility.[8]

Nevertheless, the Commission and the Task Force both point out that

> the Corps of Engineers has an enviable record for safe and adequate engineering design, that it has demonstrated its ability to carry out very large engineering projects, and that it has been signally free of any taint of fraud or dishonesty in the administration of the vast construction program with which it has been entrusted.[9]

The Soil Conservation Service in the Department of Agriculture has not done so good a job in controlling floods. So far it has spent

[7] Commission on Organization of the Executive Branch of the Government, *Task Force Report on Water Resources and Power* (Washington, D.C., U.S. Government Printing Office, June 1955), II, 808.

[8] *Ibid.*, II, 821.

[9] *Water Resources and Power*, A Report to the Congress, I, 67.

more than $42,000,000 on 212 headwater control projects. It has generally built earth embankment dams, often on private property and thus belonging to the owner of the land. It frequently has "underestimated the cost of providing storage capacity in headwater reservoirs." [10] Its estimates of flood damages are, in general, much larger than those of the Corps of Engineers. The Commission in fact found that the "Soil Conservation Service estimates of damage per acre are nearly four times those of the Corps of Engineers." [11]

Largely because the Corps of Engineers has high engineering competence, because its staff is operating on all streams of the country, and because another large engineering organization is undesirable in the Federal Government, the Hoover Commission recommended that the program of the Soil Conservation Service for the construction of headwater dams be transferred to the Corps of Engineers.

There has been a general failure to coordinate the Government's flood-control activities. The Task Group on Flood Control wrote:

> On a broader front there is little or no real coordination between flood control, irrigation, navigation, power, and other major elements of river basin programs. . . . The task group also considers past efforts to coordinate at the Washington level as falling far short of success. As indicated previously, the review process sponsored by the Federal Inter-Agency River Basin Committee (now the Inter-Agency Water Resources Committee) has brought about very little real coordination. The Bureau of the Budget, has upon occasion, succeeded in eliminating the more obvious conflicts in plans. But on the whole, existing machinery is, in the opinion of the task group, wholly incapable of providing the degree of coordination needed to protect the public interest.[12]

NATIONAL POLICIES

For more than a hundred years the Federal Government followed the practice of requiring contributions from local sources for flood-control projects. Since 1928 relaxations and confusions have taken place in Federal policy that resulted in an abrogation of that practice. For stream-control projects the local authorities must provide land, easements, rights of way, and the protection of the Federal

[10] *Ibid.*, I, 71. [11] *Ibid.*
[12] *Task Force Report on Water Resources and Power*, II, 800.

Government from damages. For reservoir construction no local participation is required.

The Commission was of the opinion that many flood-control projects now in use or under consideration are of local interest only. The present policy has led to the authorization of many projects "of questionable economic merit which in all probability would not have been adopted had local promoters been required to back their claims with cash." [13]

Although there are definite Federal responsibilities in the field of flood control, the Commission felt that non-Federal agencies, communities, and private businesses that benefit directly from projects "also have a basic obligation to share in financial responsibility in proportion to the benefits they receive." [14] The basic policies outlined earlier that should be used in the evaluation of water projects, it declares, would greatly limit the number of flood-control projects undertaken by the Federal Government, and thus reduce expenditures.

NAVIGATION

The improvement of navigation has always been a function of the Federal Government; but up to 1910 expenditures for this purpose totaled only about $500,000,000. During the next forty-four years Federal appropriations for the improvement of navigation amounted to $4,500,000,000. Thirty-eight per cent of that outlay has been for seacoast harbors, 11 per cent for Great Lakes harbors and channels, and 51 per cent for inland navigation.

The character of traffic on the waterways of the country has changed greatly through the years. With the increased size of ocean-going ships, constant and costly improvements in our harbors have been required. On the inland waterways the traffic was originally carried in shallow-draft vessels transporting both passengers and light freight, but now traffic is carried in large, deep-draft barges and consists primarily of bulk goods.

There is no over-all plan for the development of water-transportation facilities in this country. Although the Corps of Engineers has had primary responsibility in this field since 1824, it has not devel-

[13] *Water Resources and Power,* A Report to the Congress, II, 74.
[14] *Ibid.*

oped any consistent pattern. The Great Lakes offer close to 2,000 miles of deep-water navigation. In the Mississippi River Basin there is a system of river channels running close to 1,500 miles from north to south and a like distance from east to west. Finally, there is a system of inland coastal canals along the Atlantic and Gulf coasts. Concerning the failure of the Corps to develop an over-all program the Commission found that:

> The questions of justification of new projects and justification of maintenance of old projects lie mostly in the rivers tributary to these systems. There are pressures constantly brought to bear on the Corps of Engineers in respect to such projects. Some of these projects already in operation have by shifts in transportation become obsolete or fail to attract enough traffic to warrant their improvement or maintenance.[15]

Many projects authorized in earlier years are not now worth while and should be abandoned. There are projects totaling $3,600,-000,000 now authorized that the Corps considers as constituting an additional fifteen-year program, and there are further "inactive and deferred" projects that would take six years more to complete. Many of these projects were authorized so many years ago that their worth, if finally constructed, is doubtful. The Corps itself has suggested the reduction of the existing backlog by $976,600,000.

The Commission recommended that all projects declared obsolete or unsound by the Chief of Engineers should be removed from congressional authorizations.

The Commission found defective the standards for determining the benefits to result from new projects. In estimating the cost of water transportation the task group found:

> The rates assumed for the prospective water carriers are built up from estimated barge line service costs under the assumed operating conditions. They do not cover charges for the waterway itself, since water carriers do not have to pay for providing, maintaining or operating the waterway.[16]

In estimating the tonnage to be carried the methods were also found defective:

[15] *Water Resources and Power,* A Report to the Congress, II, 82.
[16] *Task Force Report on Water Resources and Power,* II, 875.

Tonnage figures are customarily obtained by field canvasses of potential shippers and receivers of freight. These are sometimes supplemented by analysis of sample waybill records conducted by the Interstate Commerce Commission or other interested agency such as the now defunct Board of Investigation and Research. Here again estimates are prone to be exaggerated because rate differentials counted upon to divert traffic to the waterway are almost certain to be reduced, if not wiped out, by competitive rate cutting.[17]

Because of these defective principles many uneconomic projects are approved and constructed.

USER CHARGE ON INLAND WATERWAYS

The Federal Government makes no charges on those who use and benefit from inland waters, even though tolls have been charged on the Panama Canal since it was opened forty years ago. Presidents Franklin D. Roosevelt and Harry S. Truman urged that tolls be imposed on inland waterways, and the principle has been recognized again in legislation authorizing the St. Lawrence Seaway. The Commission pointed out:

> There is no distinguishing fact, theory, or principle to support user charges for the Panama Canal and on the St. Lawrence Seaway, which does not equally support user charges for inland waterways.[18]

The Government spends for the maintenance of facilities developed for intracoastal and river navigation about $0.74 per 1,000 ton-miles of traffic carried, and on the entire system, including the Great Lakes, the cost is about $0.29. On the other hand, rail transportation of bulk freight such as coal costs in the northeastern part of the country about $17.50 per 1,000 ton-miles. Therefore the Commission recommended that Congress authorize a user charge on inland waterways to cover the cost of maintenance and operation.

POWER

In 1933 the Federal Government owned only seven-tenths of 1 per cent of all electric generating capacity in the United States, but by

[17] *Ibid.*
[18] *Water Resources and Power,* A Report to the Congress, I, 84.

1953 the percentage had increased to 12.4. When presently authorized Federal power projects are complete it will own 17 per cent. The Federal investment in such facilities is $2,311,000,000, and when projects now under construction, or already authorized, are completed the investment will rise to $9,662,000,000.

On the other hand, privately owned utility companies and industrial producers since 1940 spent more than $13,000,000,000 on the expansion of such facilities. During the year 1953 they spent more than $2,600,000,000, and propose to spend more than $35,000,000,000 on electric-power plants in the next twenty years.

DEVELOPMENT OF FEDERAL POLICY

Congress through the Reclamation Act of 1902 authorized the Federal Government to build works for the irrigation of arid lands in the West. Not until 1906 did it authorize the sale of electric power generated as a by-product of such irrigation projects. In 1928, by the Boulder Canyon Project Act, Congress authorized the first large multipurpose dam—the Hoover Dam. This law provided that the project was not to be built until the Government had made contracts for the sale of power to be generated by the project that would yield revenue sufficient to pay 4 per cent interest on the investment (later changed to 3 per cent), amortize the cost of the project in fifty years, and return additional income to the State of Nevada and Arizona in lieu of taxes.

In 1933 Congress created the Tennessee Valley Authority to generate power as a by-product of flood control and navigation works. The TVA proved to be one of the major Federal experiments in power generation and transmission. Also during the depression the Government initiated the Bonneville Power project, Parker and Davis dams on the Colorado River, and the Central Valley project in California. The Southwestern Power Administration and the Southeastern Power Administration were created in the 1940's by the secretary of the interior to market power produced at dams built by the Corps of Engineers in those two areas. These separate laws and the administrative practices developed under them have produced a multiplicity of conflicts and divergences in Federal policies relative to power. Among these are:

1. Significant differences exist in the criteria used for the estimation of benefits to be derived from different projects.

2. Differences exist in interest rates charged on different projects.

3. Differences exist in the methods of determining the rates to be charged for the sale of power from different projects.

4. Interest on capital employed during construction is included in the cost of some projects and not in that of others.

5. Administrative expenditures incurred during construction are included in the cost of some projects and not in that of others.

6. Differences exist in the method of allocating the portion of the cost to be charged to power.

FINANCIAL OPERATION

The Task Force estimated that on seven large project systems the Federal Government in 1953 lost $75,000,000 because of failure to recover from purchasers the true cost of power generated. During the entire life of these projects up to that date the Government, the Task Force estimated, had lost $331,500,000. What this means is that the people who bought this power received a subsidy of that size from the American taxpayers.

In making these estimates of the cost of power produced, the Task Force assumed that the Federal Government should receive 3 per cent interest on its investment. This is the rate charged under the reclamation law and under the Boulder Canyon Act as amended. It was further assumed that the cost of the projects should be amortized within fifty years for hydroelectric facilities and within thirty-five years for steam plants. All expenditures for the acquisition of land, preliminary investigations and design, and so on, should be included in the cost. An allowance was made for the replacement of parts during the period of amortization. Finally, it was assumed that the power phases of these projects should be charged with State and local taxes equal to those paid by public utilities, as well as an allowance representing the taxes paid to the Federal Government by such enterprises.

For the Tennessee Valley Authority the loss was $99,574,000 from 1933 to the end of the fiscal year 1953, and in that year alone the loss was $29,979,000. For the Hoover Dam the total loss was $101,-186,000, whereas the loss in 1953 was $7,941,000. The losses from the latter were a result of the revision by Congress in 1940 of the original contracts made under the 1928 Act.

The only major project where costs through 1953 did not exceed the income was the Central Valley project, which had a net return of $8,596,000.

SUBSIDIES

Thus it is clear that the Federal taxpayer is subsidizing the purchasers of power generated by these large projects. The burden of these subsidies is unequally distributed throughout the country because this power is sold only in a few areas to a small portion of the population. Thus, the States of New York, New Jersey, and Pennsylvania have 20 per cent of the total population, pay 29 per cent of the taxes collected by the Federal Government, and use 19 per cent of all electricity sold in the country, but in these States there are no Federal hydroelectric projects in operation nor are there any under construction or authorized. Actually only 10 per cent of the population is receiving the greater part or all of the Federal power produced. This means that 90 per cent of the population pays a subsidy to 10 per cent.

There is no uniform method for determining the rate to be charged by Federal agencies for power. In only a few cases does the Federal Power Commission determine the charges. There is no independent regulatory agency that fixes the charges imposed by the Bureau of Reclamation or by the Tennessee Valley Authority. The Hoover Commission believed that wherever the Federal Government engages in business activities normally conducted by private individuals "it should charge rates which recover at least the actual costs of conducting them." [19] Therefore, it recommended that Congress empower the Federal Power Commission to fix the sales price for all power sold by Federal projects so that the charges will reflect the true cost of such power, including amortization, interest, payments in lieu of taxes to State and local governments, and the equivalent of the taxes imposed by the Federal Government on comparable privately owned industry.

The proportion of the population receiving subsidies from low-cost Federal power is greatly restricted by the so-called preference laws which Congress enacted, largely since 1933. Under these laws the Federal Government in selling its power must give preference to nonprofit public agencies, mostly to municipalities and cooperatives. These so-called nonprofit agencies pay no Federal and little State

[19] *Ibid.*, I, 110.

and local taxes. Of course, the Federal generating agencies likewise pay little or no State, local, or Federal taxes. It has been estimated that because of these exemptions from taxes and because of other uneconomic rate-making practices, electricity produced by the Federal Government is disposed of at about 40 per cent below its true value.

Under the preference clauses these selected customers are receiving a constantly increasing proportion of the power produced by the Federal Government. In 1942 only 5.9 per cent of the power sold by Columbia River Basin projects went to such customers, whereas by 1953 the proportion had increased to 33.3 per cent. In five years the proportion of power sold by the Southwestern Power Administration to preference customers increased from 1 per cent to 42.4 per cent. In 1938 the Tennessee Valley Authority sold only 18 per cent of its power to preference customers, but by 1953 it was selling 68 per cent. The Commission has found that in 1938, 38.3 per cent of Federal power went to preference users, while in 1953 they got 52.2 per cent.

The Commission said:

> The preference clause has resulted in serious inequities and discrimination between the citizens of the various States. Thus, as of 1953, Washington, in which State there are numerous preference customers, received almost 85 percent of the Federal power produced by the Columbia River projects, and Oregon, where private power enterprise in power distribution is more prevalent, received less than 15 percent.[20]

The Task Force Report points out that whatever the original reason for such preference clauses, they no longer are in the public interest:

> The general Federal policy of preference to public bodies on water-power uses, including hydroelectric generation, developed at a time when utility rate regulation did not exist or was in its infancy, and at a time when the element of taxes for the support of Government was a minor element of cost of production. Both of these circumstances have changed, not only from the time the policy was first inserted in the statutes, but even from the time in the 1930's when it was applied to the first of the Government's large-scale multiple-purpose projects.[21]

[20] *Ibid.*, I, 112–113.
[21] *Task Force Report on Water Resources and Power,* II, 376.

Because preference clauses have outlived their usefulness, the Commission recommended that privately owned utilities should be permitted to purchase power generated at Federal projects.

All too often, to provide power for preference customers or for other reasons, the Federal Government has constructed transmission lines that duplicate and compete with those of private industry. To correct this practice, which hurts both the taxpayer and private industry, the Commission recommended that the Federal Government cease to build transmission lines where such service can be provided by non-Federal agencies.

COMPETITION WITH PRIVATE INDUSTRY

The Federal Government's activities in the production and transmission of electrical energy constitute, the Commission said, the clearest case of unnecessary and undesirable Government competition with private enterprise that has been found. The Commission concluded: "Such competition by the Government with private enterprise in the power field is more extensive than in any other single governmental field and has taken on many aspects which are the negation of our fundamental economic system." [22] And it went on to say that "where private enterprise is driven from the field in large areas, the Federal Government creates an element of monopoly in and must assume for all time the responsibility to furnish power to those areas." [23]

But in attempting to find a solution for this undesirable competition it should be remembered, it adds, that as a consequence of the construction of necessary and desirable multipurpose dams the Federal Government is in the business of producing electrical energy. As a result, the Commission does "not entertain the idea of the sale of dams and their powerhouses." [24] These structures perform important services for irrigation, navigation, and flood control, and the Federal Government has maintained control over them to discharge its responsibilities. The Commission found that "the problems involved cannot be solved by simple recommendations that such activities should cease and these projects be sold." [25]

In determining how the Government can discharge its responsi-

[22] *Water Resources and Power*, A Report to the Congress, I, 115.
[23] *Ibid.*, I, 115–116. [24] *Ibid.*, I, 116.
[25] *Ibid.*, I, 116.

bilities in connection with the necessary features of multiple-purpose projects, while at the same time minimizing its competition with private enterprise, one of the major issues to be resolved is whether the portion of the cost of new multiple-purpose projects allotted to power might be provided by private enterprise or by non-Federal power organizations. Experience has demonstrated that private enterprise and non-Federal bodies are in a position to provide the funds necessary for the construction of these facilities. For example, during the past thirteen years private investment in power facilities has been over $13,000,000,000, while the total expenditure of the Government on power from the very beginning through 1953 amounts to only $2,300,000,000. Thus, the Commission concluded that "financially there is no present or prospective need for Federal financing of power activities." [26]

At one time it might have been argued, the Commission said, that Government production of power was needed because privately owned electric utilities were not being regulated in the public interest. At present, it added, there is no basis for such a belief, because both Federal and State bodies are effectively regulating such enterprises as to rates, service, and sale of securities. Therefore, the Commission recommended two approaches to the problem of Federal power facilities, one to be applied to areas where the Government already has constructed large undertakings and another in areas where the Government has not previously been engaged in this function.

In the first situation the Commission recognized that it will be impossible for the Government to get out of power operations. Consequently, it recommended that the Government's power operations in the Missouri River Basin, the Southwestern Power Administration, the Southeastern Power Administration, the Columbia River Basin, the Central Valley in California, and the Hoover-Parker-Davis dams on the Colorado River should each be incorporated and made subject to the Government Corporation Control Act. This would put them on a sound basis so far as budgeting and accounting are concerned, and would make available to Congress reports by the comptroller general on the efficiency and the desirability of the business policies of these enterprises. This proposal would increase congressional control over the purse.

[26] *Ibid.*, I, 120.

The Commission went on to recommend that these six systems, as well as the Tennessee Valley Authority, should be required, as authorized by Congress, to obtain their future capital requirements through the sale of their own securities to the public. Such securities would only be a lien upon the earnings from the new structures to be built with the capital thus raised. They would not constitute a general lien on the income or assets of these corporations. There should be no subordination, it held, of the existing Federal investment to the interest of such security holders. Finally, the Commission proposed that representatives of the States concerned should be placed upon the governing boards of these corporations. This would keep the corporations close to the people and would stimulate local interest.

In the second situation, relative to the provision of the power components of new multiple-purpose projects, the Commission recommended that private enterprise be offered the opportunity to provide the necessary capital for the electrical facilities, but that the structures when built should be under the control of the Federal Government. If such capital is not available, the power, prior to construction, should be offered to private utilities, States, and municipalities on such terms as will recover the cost of the Federal investment, with interest as well as operating and maintenance expenses. In all probability, if power cannot be disposed of in advance by either of these two methods, the project is not economically sound and should not be undertaken.

CONCLUSIONS

The Hoover Commission made the most extensive and the most penetrating study ever made of the nation's water resources. It poses a number of fundamental issues:

Who is responsible for failures in the national water policy?

The Commission states that the Federal agencies concerned with water development are highly competent. Their record for safe engineering design is "enviable," as is their success in carrying out large engineering projects. Personnel weaknesses are not involved because these agencies are "signally free of the taint of dishonesty." Therefore "most of the blame must be placed on the lack of consistent national policies, and the absence of adequate provisions for review, inspection, and coordination of projects at Washington and basin levels."

Who is to determine the priorities to be given to the major uses of water?

As water shortages make the problem increasingly acute, there must be some machinery for an intelligent decision. A national policy is necessary, but it cannot be a rigid policy dictated from Washington. The major uses of water vary from region to region, as does the competition among users or beneficiaries. Therefore, a policy must be established which recognizes broad, general national needs and which, at the same time, permits problems to be resolved on the basis of local and regional needs.

Development of sound Federal policy for water resources is of fundamental importance to the national economy. The imperative need for such policy will become more obvious during the next decade. The Commission's objective in this field was to delineate the elements that should be made a part of such a sound policy. The first recommendation, discussed early in this chapter, is the most important step in the formulation of such a policy.

The recommendations of the Commission are designed largely to reduce the impact of the Federal Government on private enterprise, that is, to lessen competition. The recommendations relative to the construction of steam plants and transmission lines, the sale of power to preference customers, and the fixing of rates to be charged on Federal projects are all designed to meet this objective.

Another objective of the Commission is to reestablish congressional control over the purse. The recommendation that revenues from Federal water projects should be paid directly into the Treasury and not be spent by the projects without congressional approval promotes this objective. The recommendation for the development of improved methods of calculating benefits from proposed projects and of estimating the cost of such projects will also help to reestablish congressional control over the purse. Only when Congress knows what a project is likely to do for the Nation and how much it is likely to cost can it intelligently appropriate money for its construction.

The proposals of the Commission to accomplish these objectives are similar in all important respects to the water-resources and power policy developed by President Eisenhower and the leaders of his Administration.

CHAPTER 8

Lending, Guaranteeing, and Insurance Programs

The Federal Government had $244,000,000,000 of loans, guarantees, insurance, and contingent liabilities outstanding on June 30, 1954. Thus without doubt it is by far the biggest moneylender in the country, if not in the world. Its lending activities are carried on by 104 different entities, some incorporated, others not. Through these agencies it exercises a powerful influence over the privately owned credit and lending facilities of the Nation.

The Government's direct obligations under these programs, however, are much less than the $244,000,000,000 mentioned above.

For instance, the Government's involvement in the insurance of bank deposits is nominally limited to the authority of the Secretary of the Treasury to lend to the Federal Deposit Insurance Corporation not more than $3,000,000,000. In the insurance of building and loan associations and savings bank deposits the Government has contributed $66,779,000 of capital to the Federal Savings and Loan Insurance Corporation, and the Secretary of the Treasury is merely authorized to lend the Corporation up to $750,000,000. However, since both the Federal Deposit Insurance Corporation and the Federal Savings and Loan Insurance Corporation are Government instrumentalities created by Congress to provide insurance for the deposits of private citizens, the Government has a moral liability to aid these programs in the event the reserves of these two corporations are inadequate to cover losses.

Accordingly, it is appropriate to regard the total amount of deposits thus insured, $106,509,000,000 for the Federal Deposit Insurance Corporation and $22,602,000,000 for the Federal Savings and Loan Insurance Corporation in 1954, as contingent liabilities of the Government. But the first source of funds for making good such an obligation would be the assets of the insured banks. Presumably, the Government would become the owner of these assets if it should be called upon to make good the insurance and guarantees, and their liquidation would reduce the amount of Treasury funds required.

NATURE OF THE PROBLEM

The Hoover Commission was most commendatory of the administration of most of these lending agencies.

"With relatively few exceptions these agencies have developed methods of organization which assure integrity, efficiency, and great public service," it said. "They have made great contributions to national security, to the strengthening of our economy, and to the standards of living of the American people."[1]

The Commission made the fundamental policy decision that lending money or guaranteeing loans are functions which the Government should undertake only when private enterprise cannot or will not perform them, and then the Government should do this only in furtherance of a justifiable national purpose.

The objectives of the Commission's study of lending functions were to promote economy, to eliminate waste, to restore congressional control over the purse, and to eliminate unnecessary Government enterprises that are competitive with private enterprise. The Commission did not seek to eradicate Government lending activities, but rather to preserve and to continue their desirable aspects on a sound business basis with efficient administration. Every effort was made to indicate the methods of organization and operation that have proved successful. Existing weaknesses were pointed out only because this was a necessary prerequisite for making recommendations for their elimination. A major objective was either to eliminate completely or to publicize all subsidies to special interests, especially when hidden. Only if such special favors are known is it possible for the public to make an informed decision on their desirability.

APPROPRIATE FORMS OF ORGANIZATION

The multitude of lending agencies created in the past forty-two years have a diversity of forms. Some have a single head; others are

[1] Commission on Organization of the Executive Branch of the Government, *Lending Agencies,* A Report to the Congress, March 1955 (Washington, D.C., U.S. Government Printing Office, 1955), pp. 1–2.

run by a board. Twenty-three of them are parts of regular departments; the remaining ones are independent or parts of other independent agencies. Many have been incorporated, but most of those in departments are not.

To determine the best form of organization for lending agencies, it is necessary to appraise their existing weaknesses. Among their more obvious defects are:

1. These agencies tend to expand their functions beyond Congress's original purpose, and thus to go in for empire building.

2. When the function for which they were established has been completed, there is an inner impulse to continue even though they should be liquidated.

3. The Government tends to create activities which could be undertaken more appropriately by private agencies.

4. In some agencies there are concealed subsidies.

5. Congress permits agencies to make loans or guarantees to individuals or concerns without adequate equities.

6. Loans or guarantees are made without adequate premiums or fees, or there is a failure to charge borrowers interest rates sufficient to cover the cost of money, to pay administrative expenses, and to build reserves against losses.

7. Departmental lending or guaranteeing programs have a political attraction. Pressure groups, whether composed of businessmen, labor unions, farmers, or veterans, often force the abandonment of standards of prudence in the operation of these agencies.

8. Where easy money is obtainable from the Government, financial integrity tends to deteriorate, and windfalls and corruption may flourish.

A study of the lending agencies that have operated most effectively indicates two fundamental steps that have contributed to their success. First, the operations of many have been made subject to the Government Corporation Control Act. Second, Congress has provided for the mutualization of the organization and finances of a number of them. These two measures are not applicable to all agencies nor can they be considered cure-alls, but the Commission believed that their application to many lending programs would be in the public interest.

GOVERNMENT CORPORATION CONTROL ACT

Among the major requirements of the Government Corporation Control Act of 1945 are:

1. The corporation or agency must adopt budgeting, accounting, and management methods similar to those of private business instead of the cumbersome forms applicable to Government departments.

2. The General Accounting Office is required to audit their accounts annually in accordance with the customary auditing practices applicable to privately owned commercial corporations. The comptroller general is directed to report on the expenses of each agency, the origin of its funds, and its financial status, together with comments on irregularities.

3. Each corporation must annually present a business-type budget to the Bureau of the Budget, to the President, and to the Congress. Congress annually approves of their expenditures for operating purposes; but outlays for loans when made in conformity with existing laws need no annual appropriation from Congress.

4. All banking and checking accounts of more than $50,000 must be kept with the Treasury.

5. Purchases or sales of United States obligations in amounts exceeding $100,000 by Federal corporations are prohibited unless approved by the Secretary of the Treasury.

The net effect of bringing an agency under the Government Corporation Control Act is greatly to simplify budgeting, accounting, personnel management, and the use of revolving funds. Moreover, the use of the corporate form generally brings about a much more flexible organization, provides more checks and balances upon management, and ensures an effective audit by the comptroller general.

It is for these reasons that the Hoover Commission proposed that several additional lending agencies should be brought under this law.

MUTUALIZATION

Mutualization is the second important step that Congress has taken to improve the organization of many of these enterprises.

What mutualization meant to the Commission can be indicated best by its own words:

"Mutualization" has been attained by requiring the beneficiaries of loans, guarantees, or insurance to make proportionate payments to retire capital stock owned by the Government. Thus, in several instances, great numbers of individuals and firms interested in these problems become the stockholders and the management in practice passes into their hands subject to Federal regulation. In those instances, inclusion of this private ownership has proved to be a valuable check on management much needed by Government agencies. Mutualized agencies pay their own administrative expenses and set up their own reserves against losses, subject to Government control.[2]

Thus, this device combines the advantageous incentives of private ownership and management with the desirable fiduciary restraints resulting from Government supervision.

The following agencies have been mutualized in whole or in part:

The Federal Reserve banks
The Federal land banks
The home-loan banks
The banks for cooperatives (partly)
The Federal Deposit Insurance Corporation
The Federal Savings and Loan Insurance Corporation (partly)

In many ways these corporations resemble privately owned mutual savings banks and mutual life insurance companies, but they are still subject to Government supervision. The Commission proposed that a number of lending agencies should be mutualized, but because these serve a variety of functions it was not feasible to develop a uniform pattern for doing so.

HOUSING

Depression pressures, the need for providing housing at defense establishments in World War II, the desire to aid veterans, and the demands for better housing for the general public combined to create a demand for Federal lending programs in the housing field. The diverse methods used by the various resulting agencies comprise loans, mortgages, guarantees, and insurance of mortgages and loans, grants-in-aid, and the purchase of mortgages.

[2] *Ibid.*, pp. 11–12.

To encourage the construction of housing and home ownership several Federal agencies are engaged in lending or the insurance of loans. Most of these are under the Housing and Home Finance Agency. They include the Federal home-loan banks and the Federal Savings and Loan Insurance Corporation under the Home Loan Bank Board, the Federal Housing Administration, the Public Housing Administration, and the Federal National Mortgage Association. The Veterans' Administration gives similar aid for veterans.

Housing loans, commitments, insurance, and guarantees outstanding on June 30, 1954, totaled $55,800,000,000, and there was further authority to lend or insure $3,100,000,000 more. The Federal Government held $88,779,000 of capital stock in these agencies. It had lent them $3,994,000,000, and the Treasury was authorized to lend them an additional $3,554,301,000.

HOME LOAN BANK SYSTEM

The Home Loan Bank System in the opinion of the Commission is a good example of a mutualized lending program. The Home Loan Bank Board and the Federal home-loan banks were established in 1932 under President Hoover to encourage home ownership and home building by making advances on the security of mortgage loans held by building and loan associations, savings banks, and insurance companies.

The capital of the eleven federally incorporated home-loan banks was supplied initially by the Government. With its repayment, the banks have been mutualized so that all of the stock is owned by the members and the management is now in their hands, subject to regulation by the Home Loan Bank Board.

From their creation to June 30, 1954, the banks advanced more than $5,500,000,000 to borrowing institutions. During this period they have, in addition to the repayment of the Federal capital, declared dividends totaling $63,152,000, and have also built up an earned surplus of $39,362,000. Member institutions have paid in $420,533,000 on capital stock subscriptions to the different banks. To encourage their development the Treasury has been authorized to lend them up to $1,000,000,000.

The Federal Savings and Loan Insurance Corporation, governed by the Home Loan Bank Board, was established in 1934 to insure the deposits of cooperative savings banks and building and loan associations. The Government subscribed to its capital stock to the amount of $100,000,000, and the Secretary of the Treasury is authorized to lend it up to $750,000,000. About $33,200,000 of this stock had been repaid to the Treasury as of June 30, 1954, but existing law precludes the corporation from using more than half of its net income for retiring Federal stock.

Despite this, the corporation has large holdings of Government bonds. The significance of this is that money received from the Government through the subscription to stock is invested in the Government's own bonds, and the interest paid on these bonds is an indirect subsidy to the corporation. The Commission recommended that Government bonds equal to the value of the Government-owned stock be surrendered in return for a cancellation of the stock or that bonds to the value of the stock be surrendered to the Treasury in return for non-interest-bearing certificates of indebtedness. Either method would end the subsidy.

The Commission felt that it is not desirable to have both the Federal Savings and Loan Insurance Corporation and the Federal Home Loan Bank System controlled by the Home Loan Bank Board, as their interests in some instances are dissimilar. For example, the banks might desire to expand credit while the Loan Insurance Corporation, because of its fiduciary role relative to depositors, might believe that a contrary policy is required. Therefore the Commission recommended that no person should be permitted to serve on both boards at the same time. It also urged the cancellation of the Treasury's authority to lend $1,000,000,000 to the Home Loan Bank System and $750,000,000 to the Federal Savings and Loan Insurance Corporation.

FEDERAL HOUSING ADMINISTRATION

The Federal Housing Administration, through nine programs, is insuring mortgages on housing in return for premiums paid by borrowers. Under existing law these mortgages can extend for as much as thirty years and cover from 80 to 95 per cent of appraised value. Up to June 1954 it had insured $26,489,000,000 of mortgages and $7,956,000,000 of home-improvement loans. Its losses through all forms of insurance totaled $86,555,000. No Federal funds are invested in the agency, but in paying off holders of defaulted mortgages it can issue to them debentures guaranteed by the Government.

The Federal Housing Administration has made a valuable contribution to home financing and has, in large part, been responsible for the sustained high level of construction activity since World War II; but serious doubts have been raised concerning the adequacy of its reserves to support its huge insurance programs. On June 30, 1954, it had $17,921,000,000 insurance outstanding, and to meet its potential obligations it had reserves and surplus of $338,826,000. These reserves amounted only to 2 per cent of commitments, whereas savings banks reserves are about 6 per cent. The Commission recommended that an independent study be made of the adequacy of these reserves, and such a study is now being made.

The Commission also proposed that the President should receive authority to increase the equities required in housing for such insured mortgages. As of August 1, 1955, the required equities were increased and the repayment period of the loans reduced. Finally, the Commission recommended that the Federal Housing Administration be mutualized like the home-loan banks and the Federal Savings and Loan Insurance Corporation so that it will provide its own funds and will not have to call on the Treasury for additional money.

The Hoover Commission felt that a number of activities of the Housing and Home Finance Agency should be terminated. As of June 30, 1954, the Public Housing Administration owned 84,441 permanent dwelling units and about the same number of temporary units with a book value of $698,456,000. As a carry-over from the liquidation of the New Deal Greenbelt Towns programs it had $11,251,000 in mortgages. From the programs to aid prefabricated housing the agency held assets of $6,847,000, and its outstanding loans on Alaskan housing totaled $9,272,000. The Commission urged that these assets be liquidated with dispatch.

In addition, the agency has authority to lend $300,000,000 for college housing. It may lend $50,000,000 to States and public bodies for the construction of public works, and it also has authority to make loans and grants to cities for urban planning and for the advanced planning of public works. The Commission recommended that all of these programs be ended.

VETERANS' ADMINISTRATION

The Veterans' Administration guarantees loans to veterans without the payment of a fee; thus any loss resulting from defaulted mortgages is a direct charge on the Treasury. The guarantees outstanding on June 30, 1954, were $9,618,000,000. The total cost of grants, losses, and administrative costs of housing for veterans has amounted to $500,000,000. Only about 4,000,000 of the more than 21,000,000 living veterans have benefited from these programs. Veterans of wars before World War II are not entitled to these loans.

"The establishment of these special aids to veterans," the Commission said, "was no doubt justified by the special emergency which veterans faced upon demobilization. In keeping with the emergency nature of these programs and with the original congressional intent, they are scheduled to be terminated on dates fixed by the Congress." [3] These guarantee provisions end in 1957 for veterans of World War II and for those of the Korean War in 1965. These dates the Commission declared should not be extended when they expire.

AGRICULTURE

Federal agricultural agencies had lent or had made commitments to lend more than $8,200,000,000 at the end of the fiscal year 1954. The Government had $371,000,000 of capital stocks of these agencies, had lent them $8,443,000,000, and was authorized by law to lend $2,912,727,000 more.

Financial aid to farmers dates from the establishment of the Federal land banks in 1916, the Federal intermediate credit banks in 1923, the Federal Farm Board in 1929, and the authority of the Reconstruction Finance Corporation to extend financial aid to farm organizations in 1932. A multitude of institutions and programs followed.

FARM CREDIT ADMINISTRATION

Congress undertook a constructive step recently to improve the organization of some of the Farm lending agencies.

By a law effective December 4, 1953, the Farm Credit Adminis-

[3] *Ibid.*, p. 31.

tration, which supervises about fifty corporations giving financial assistance to farmers, was removed from the Department of Agriculture and set up as an independent agency reporting to the President. Twelve of these corporations (land banks) have been fully mutualized.

The Commission recommended that the banks for cooperatives should also be mutualized and their hidden subsidies ended. When these banks were created in 1923, the Government subscribed $178,500,000 to their capital stock. The member borrowers in more than thirty years have retired only $28,500,000, leaving $150,000,000 outstanding. Meanwhile these banks have $52,078,000 invested in United States bonds. "Since the Government has not been paid any return on its $150,000,000 investment," it reported, "a part of which has been used to buy Government bonds, the payment of interest on these bonds is simply a hidden subsidy from the taxpayers at large to a small group of beneficiaries." [4]

The Commission recommended that the borrowers accelerate acquisition of the stock in the banks and that the banks' holdings of Government bonds be surrendered to the Treasury in return for non-interest-bearing credits.

Comparable recommendations were made by the Commission for several other agricultural lending agencies.

The entire capital stock of the Federal intermediate credit banks, amounting to $62,800,000, is owned by the Government, while the banks hold $50,209,000 of United States bonds. Their mutualization should be speeded up, the Commission said, and their holdings of Government bonds should be treated like those of the banks for cooperatives.

In the production credit corporations the Government has $90,000,000 invested while these corporations hold $41,809,000 of Government bonds. The production credit corporations, the Commission felt, have ceased to have any important function which could not be performed by the Federal intermediate credit banks. Liquidation of these corporations would save the cost of management, would reduce the public debt by about $45,000,000, and save the interest paid on the Government securities held by them. The corporations should be liquidated, it declared, and, pending that, their Government bonds should be handled like those of the banks for cooperatives.

[4] *Ibid.*, p. 52.

FARMERS HOME ADMINISTRATION

All of the four lending agencies remaining in the Department of Agriculture need to be put on a sound business basis, according to the Commission. These include the Farmers Home Administration, the Commodity Credit Corporation, the Federal Crop Insurance Corporation, and the Rural Electrification Administration.

Even though the price of farms is inflated, the Farmers Home Administration makes loans for the purchase of small farms by farmers who could not get loans otherwise and who in many cases are unable to make any down payment. This agency is the present version of the Resettlement Administration founded in 1935, and it and its predecessors have lent or insured loans totaling $3,235,-104,000. Of these, $161,530,000 have been written off as complete losses. On June 30, 1954, out of a total of $813,158,000 in loans outstanding, about $115,000,000 were delinquent. "A reserve of $105,431,000 is carried against further losses. This would indicate a possible ultimate loss of principal of more than $260 million." [5]

From 1935 to 1954 the Farmers Home Administration and its predecessor agencies realized from interest and other sources a total income of approximately $447,500,000. During this period the cost of administering the program, together with all grants made, approximated $839,000,000. Therefore, the taxpayers at large have paid approximately $391,500,000 for these programs; but this amount does not include any losses of principal resulting from defaults on loans. It can be estimated roughly that the total cost of these programs to the present is close to two-thirds of a billion dollars.[6]

The net effect of the Farmers Home Administration operations is that the taxpayers are subsidizing the agency and its borrowers (*a*) to the amount of its administrative expenses, (*b*) to the amount of its losses on loans, and (*c*) to the amount of the interest paid by the Federal Government on $750,000,000 of United States securities issued to provide its capital.

As a matter of national policy the Hoover Commission, except in disaster and emergency loans, was opposed to "subsidies being given indirectly to a fraction of the people by the taxpayers at large without their knowledge and approval. Incidentally, these taxpayers include also over 90 percent of the farmers who do not benefit from the Farmers Home Administration themselves." [7]

[5] *Ibid.*, p. 60. [6] *Ibid.* [7] *Lending Agencies*, p. 64.

The Commission urged that this administration be required to tighten its lending programs to minimize the cost to the taxpayer. It also recommended that the administration charge interest and fees sufficient to cover administrative expenses, as well as the cost of money to the Treasury, and that it should require adequate equities under its mortgages.

THE COMMODITY CREDIT CORPORATION

The Commodity Credit Corporation, wholly owned by the Government and founded in 1934, is not primarily a lending institution, but an instrumentality to maintain farm-crop prices. In the main, the commodity price levels to be maintained are stipulated by the Congress based upon a computed "parity." The corporation uses several different methods in its price supports: outright purchases, conditional purchases, loans without recourse to the borrower, purchase agreements, and guarantees to private lenders. The corporation has a capital of $100,000,000 subscribed by the Federal Government, and it can borrow up to $10,000,000,000 from the Treasury or from private sources.

Borrowings from the Treasury are made on notes at interest rates set by the secretary of the treasury, recently increased from 1 to 1⅜ per cent (as of February 1955). The dividend paid on capital stock in the fiscal year 1955 was at the rate of 1 per cent. Funds from private sources have been obtained at rates ranging from 2⅛ to 3 per cent.

The corporation's total loans on commodities (which can be canceled by surrender of the commodities), were, on June 30, 1954, $2,337,289,000. There was a loss reserve of $96,252,000 against these loans. Of the commodity loans, $2,002,184,000 was held by lending agencies, mostly commercial banks. For the most part these loans are paid off by the Commodity Credit Corporation, which takes ownership of the farm products held as collateral. Loans for storage facilities and equipment were $30,585,000. The purchase of commodities represented $3,727,751,000, against which there were carried loss reserves of $926,193,100.

The price-support activities of the Commodity Credit Corporation could be greatly simplified, the Commission found, a considerable amount of administrative expenditures saved, and the use of Treasury loans diminished by a change in the method of handling price-support operations.

The Commission recommended:

To achieve these ends, instead of the Department's making loans to the farmers based on price support levels pending his decision as to when he wishes to sell the commodity, the Commodity Credit Corporation should enter into contracts to purchase the commodities from the farmer at the support level and leave to him, as before, the determination of when he sells them. This would result in no change in the farmer's situation; but for the Commodity Credit Corporation it would reduce the enormous detail of managing the multitude of loans and it would enable the farmer to borrow from private banks any advances he wishes to secure within the limits of the level of the price-support program.[8]

RURAL ELECTRIFICATION ADMINISTRATION

The Commission found that the Rural Electrification Administration, another highly subsidized agency, also needs to be put on a sound financial basis. Its principal purpose is to supply financing for electrical and telephone services for rural areas. It operates by making direct loans to local cooperatives composed of farmers, to some public agencies, and to a few private companies. In 1954 it had approved electrification loans of $2,885,000,000, about 95 per cent to cooperatives. More than $500,000,000 of this total was for generating and transmission facilities. Its loans can have terms as long as thirty-five years.

Interest charged to the Rural Electrification Administration by the Treasury may not by law exceed 2 per cent, although the actual rate of interest now being paid by the Treasury itself on comparable long-term loans is about 3 per cent. The Rural Electrification Administration in turn charges cooperatives and other borrowers only 2 per cent interest, and payments due during the first five years are deferred.

The administrative expenses of the Rural Electrification Administration are met from congressional appropriations, and to June 1954 they totaled more than $85,000,000. In the fiscal year 1954 the agency received income, mainly from interest on loans, of $41,885,000. Administrative expenses of $7,284,000 plus interest on funds borrowed from the Treasury resulted in a net loss of $5,480,000 for that year. The total subsidies received from the Treasury since 1935 have amounted to about $72,000,000.

Thus, the Government has subsidized the sale of electric power to

[8] *Ibid.*, p. 69.

the members of cooperatives at considerably less than its economic cost. These subsidies result from:

1. The charging of interest at 2 per cent per annum which is about 1 per cent less than the interest which the Treasury must pay on long-term issues to provide the money.
2. Deferring to later years the interest due during the first five years, which results in an effective rate of return of even less than 2 per cent.
3. Granting of exemption from all Federal taxes (in some States these bodies are exempt from all or some local taxes).
4. Providing administrative expenses at the expense of the taxpayers. In the past five years these have averaged $7,750,000 annually.

By June 30, 1954, at least 92.3 per cent of all farms in the nation had been electrified; 54 per cent of these get their energy from systems financed by the Rural Electrification Administration, while 46 per cent get it from privately owned utility companies. On the basis of this analysis the Commission concluded:

> In view of the great advance made in farm electrification, it is our belief that the time has arrived for the reorganization of the Rural Electrification Administration into a self-supporting institution securing its own finance from private sources in a manner similar to that of the other agencies discussed previously. Moreover, the operations of Rural Electrification should be made subject to the Government Corporation Control Act in order to secure the advantages of more efficient organization under that act.[9]

This would remove the Government from another form of unfair competition with private enterprise and reduce Government expenditures.

LOANS TO BUSINESS

Loans made to business by the United States Government totaled $2,335,394,000 on June 30, 1954. In addition, the Government had insured or guaranteed loans to the amount of $540,316,000. In the agencies engaged in these operations the Government held $1,100,000,000 of capital stock; it had lent them $1,408,764,000; and the

[9] *Ibid.*, pp. 75–76.

Treasury by law could advance them $2,153,000,000 more. At least eight agencies made such loans, one of which, the Reconstruction Finance Corporation, has since been liquidated. Our attention will be directed only to the Federal Deposit Insurance Corporation, the Export-Import Bank, and the Small Business Administration.

FEDERAL DEPOSIT INSURANCE CORPORATION

The Federal Deposit Insurance Corporation was established by congressional act in 1933 to insure deposits in banks which are members of the Federal Reserve System and in other banks which wish to participate. Deposits are now insured up to $10,000 for each depositor.

It was founded with paid-in capital stock of $289,000,000, of which the Federal Reserve banks subscribed $139,000,000, and the Treasury $150,000,000. The Secretary of the Treasury is authorized to lend the corporation up to $3,000,000,000, which the Hoover Commission believed should be carried on the Government's financial records as a contingent liability. The insured banks pay an assessment to the corporation of one-twelfth of 1 per cent of their deposits, and out of this assessment all of the capital stock has been retired, administrative expenses have been met, and strong reserves built up. After paying the expenses of the Federal Deposit Insurance Corporation, 40 per cent of the remaining income is used to build up further reserves and 60 per cent is credited pro rata to the insured banks to be used by them against future assessments. The effect of this has been to reduce the assessments to approximately one twenty-fourth of 1 per cent. It is thus evident that the corporation considers its present reserves adequate.

The corporation is mutualized to the extent that its capital has been retired, but the insured banks do not participate directly in its management. Its net income for calendar year 1953 was $86,640,000 after paying total expenses and losses of $7,584,000. From the inception of the program until December 31, 1953, losses have been $28,200,000. This figure represents only the amount of losses charged against the corporation's funds. From the beginning, disbursements of about $280,000,000 have been made to protect the depositors of 422 banks, but liquidation of assets recovered 89 per cent of disbursements.

EXPORT-IMPORT BANK

The Export-Import Bank was established in 1934, during the depression, as an emergency agency. It has since been federally incorporated as an independent establishment with a capital of $1,000,000,000, reporting to the President. The bank is managed by a board of five directors with a managing director and an advisory committee of nine members appointed by the directors.

In addition to the original capital, it has authority to borrow from the Treasury up to $4,000,000,000. Since March 15, 1953, it pays the Treasury 2⅜ per cent for long-term borrowings and 1 per cent for short-term borrowings. It charges higher rates for its loans to business and thus earns profits.

On June 30, 1954, the bank had loans outstanding of $2,699,004,000, against which there were reserves of $216,000 for losses on loans already in default and $330,509,000 as a reserve against possible losses on other loans. It had contingent liabilities of about $532,000,000, mainly for undisbursed commitments. In the year ending June 30, 1954, it paid the Treasury dividends of $22,500,000, and its retained earnings were $34,888,000.

The bank's total outstanding loans to finance export and import trade on June 30, 1954, were $1,428,192,000. During the fiscal year 1954 total private American imports and exports were $23,057,000,000 and loans from the Export-Import Bank were $250,400,000, or only about 1 per cent of the total of such trade. The other 99 per cent were handled by private enterprise.

When the bank was established in 1934 it was designed to act only through the emergency, and to supplement and not to compete with private capital. The Commission felt it should be reorganized because (*a*) the need for Government finance of normal, short-term commercial export and import loans is no longer urgent, (*b*) the bank has been partially transformed into an agency making export loans for longer periods than are normal in commercial practice, and (*c*) its loans for the development of foreign resources to foreign governments have been greatly expanded.

The Commission recommended that the bank cease to make normal short-term commercial loans, that it be the only Federal agency making foreign development loans or loans to foreign countries, and that Congress appropriate annually the funds needed for these purposes. This proposal for annual appropriations would assist Congress in reestablishing control over the Federal purse.

SMALL BUSINESS ADMINISTRATION

The Small Business Administration was created by Congress in 1953 to take over from the Reconstruction Finance Corporation the task of lending to small business. This is an independent agency responsible to the President. Its management is vested in an administrator and three deputy administrators. Loans are made directly to small business concerns as well as in participation with banks or private agencies. They may not be made if financial assistance can be obtained otherwise on reasonable terms. No concern may borrow more than $150,000.

Certain types of small business are excluded from such loans. These include newspapers, radio and television operators, alcoholic-beverage concerns, and institutions engaged in lending or investment. The law contains certain requirements designed to prevent monopoly and to ensure that loans are used only to promote business and not for the relief of creditors or the owners.

The agency's revolving fund authorized by the Congress totals $275,000,000. The whole amount had not yet been appropriated in 1954. Up to January 31, 1955, 391 direct loans had been approved for a total of $17,768,000 and 775 participation loans had been approved of which the agency's portion was $43,948,000. One thousand and forty disaster loans, partly to homeowners, had been approved amounting to $6,082,331.

The type of credit advanced by the Small Business Administration is illustrated by its loan, approved in March 1954, for $120,000 for seventy-three months at 6 per cent to facilitate the expansion of a partnership in California engaged in the manufacture of machine parts and special tools. This business began in 1946 with $6,000 in capital and reported a net worth of $62,000. Of the proceeds of the loan $61,000 was used to repay a loan from the Reconstruction Finance Corporation, $18,000 to pay existing indebtedness on machinery, and $41,000 for working capital. According to the files on this case, the borrower previously had difficulty in meeting the monthly payments on the RFC loan, which were less than those required under the new SBA loan. Other indebtedness was overdue at the time of the application, and competition was forcing the company to lower its prices and its expectations of profits.

Despite numerous unsound loans of this type, the Commission believed "that there are areas of business activity where the Small Business Administration can legitimately provide services helpful to small business." [10] As a result it recommended that the Small Business Administration be made subject to the Government Corporation Control Act, that it charge interest and fees sufficient to make it self-supporting, and that Congress continue it for two years. Congress has since extended its life for that time.

SUMMARY AND GENERAL RECOMMENDATIONS

To facilitate their reorganization on a sound, businesslike basis the Hoover Commission recommended that a number of lending agencies be made subject to the Government Corporation Control Act, and that some be mutualized. The Small Business Administration, Rural Electrification Administration, Housing and Home Finance Agency, and the Veterans' Life Insurance Program, it felt, ought to be made subject to the Government Corporation Control Act. The Rural Electrification Administration and the Federal Housing Administration it felt should be mutualized. The process of mutualization, it urged, should be speeded up for the banks for cooperatives, Federal intermediate credit banks and the Federal National Mortgage Association. This is most desirable "to make them self-supporting, to relieve the Federal Government of expenses and liabilities, to assure better management, and to merge them into the private enterprise system." [11]

Numerous forms of subsidy have become an integral part of many Government lending programs. Several of the agencies making loans pay a lower rate of interest to the Treasury than that Department must pay to the public for loans with comparable maturities. The Farmers Home Administration, the Rural Electrification Administration, and the Commodity Credit Corporation are examples. When the Treasury allows an agency to borrow at such interest rates it is granting a hidden subsidy. The beneficiaries of such agencies are but a fraction of the people, and the burden of paying the subsidy to them must be borne by all taxpayers. Therefore, the Commission recommended that the Treasury charge lending agencies a rate of

[10] *Ibid.*, p. 91.

[11] *Ibid.*, p. 108.

interest on loans or advances equal to the going rate paid by that department on loans of comparable maturities.

The administrative expense of at least seven lending agencies is paid out of direct appropriations made by Congress. These come to about $95,000,000 annually and are another subsidy from the taxpayer. The Commission proposed that all lending agencies charge fees sufficient to cover their administrative expenses.

Sizable amounts of Government bonds are owned by lending agencies in which the Federal Government has invested large amounts of capital, and all too often on these capital advances little or no return is received by the Treasury. This means that the Government has provided such agencies with excess capital which they are able to invest in Government bonds, and the interest on these constitutes a hidden subsidy to the beneficiaries of the loan programs. The Commission found that at least $210,875,000 was so invested in 1954, and the annual interest paid on it is about $5,000,000. These corporations, it declared, should surrender Government bonds held by them to the value of the Government's invested capital and receive in their place non-interest-bearing evidences of indebtedness.

Wherever it should be necessary to continue subsidies in the lending field, the Commission was eager that they be made public. Therefore, it recommended that each nonmutualized lending, guaranteeing, and insurance agency should report to Congress annually the amount that its earned income failed to cover of the total of the following: operating expenses, interest on money borrowed from or advanced by the Treasury, losses on loans and reserves against future losses, and the amount of interest received on Government bonds where inadequate or no return was paid on the Government's investment.

There is no mechanism whereby the financial policies of the lending, guaranteeing, and insurance agencies are coordinated with the credit policies of the Treasury. Thus, the lending practices of individual agencies may conflict with the credit policies of the Treasury. On the boards or commissions of all agencies that are able to affect the fiscal policy of the United States, the Hoover Commission urged that there be an ex officio representative of the secretary of the Treasury. His major task in this capacity would be to inform the agencies of the Government's credit policies.

CONCLUSIONS

These proposals of the Hoover Commission in the lending field would mean sizable financial relief for the American taxpayers. The annual savings resulting from implementing all items in the program could total $200,000,000. In addition, there would ultimately be returned to the Treasury $4,933,000,000 of capital funds now invested in agencies to be mutualized or liquidated. This total could be realized only over a period of years. Finally, Congress could cancel $1,114,249,000 of unused authority to borrow from the Treasury.

In addition to promoting economy, the Commission's proposals would assist Congress in regaining control over the purse through the canceling of improper or unnecessary authority of the Treasury to make loans to a number of agencies. Undesirable competition with private enterprise would be mitigated through the mutualization of some of these agencies and by the termination of subsidies.

This discussion presents the reader with three crucial questions that are of fundamental importance:

First, does the American public want the United States to compete with private enterprise in the lending field?

Because Government lending is not limited to essential projects which private enterprise is unable to finance, the United States Treasury in many instances is in the position of competing with private credit agencies.

Since Government loans and guarantees are sometimes available where private enterprise considers the risks unattractive, the Government's financial aid to such enterprises or groups introduces a factor which works against the normal operation of a free market. In this way marginal entrepreneurs, who could not continue to operate if subjected to the same economic standards as are applicable to their competitors, continue to function and are helped by the Government to compete with their more economically efficient rivals. This is contrary to the basic principles of the free private enterprise system.

Second, do the American people want special segments of the community to be subsidized by public funds?

In some instances, as for example the Rural Electrification Administration, or the loan and guarantee programs for veterans, members of the very groups that are presumed to be helped are being taxed to permit a part of the group to receive extra benefits not received even by all members of the select class.

Although in a number of cases the original special need for the help no longer exists (electrifying farms), the program is nevertheless continued to provide other services which cannot be justified on the same or comparable grounds. Thus, some Rural Electrification Administration funds are now used for the generation and transmission of power, rather than for its distribution to farmers.

Third, if subsidies are considered necessary, should they not be clearly labeled as such, instead of being hidden?

Throughout the Government taxpayers are indirectly extending credit to activities which they would not necessarily help to underwrite voluntarily. Most people are aware of their tax bills, and a good many know that some of their savings are invested directly or indirectly in Government securities. They do not realize, however, that this means that both their taxes and their savings are being used to underwrite certain programs. The recipients of subsidies almost universally are anxious that existence and size of the subsidy be concealed. They fear publicity, realizing that secrecy is their best ally. In most instances when the public appreciates the nature and size of the special gift at their expense, the people demand that it be terminated.

Whether or not the Hoover Commission's proposals in this area are implemented, the discussion of these three basic questions raised by the Commission will result in a better informed American public.

CHAPTER 9

Business Enterprises

After two years of study the Commission on Organization of the Executive Branch of the Government was unable to discover the full extent of the business enterprises owned and operated by the Government. No one knows how much goods and services are produced by them or how much profit or loss they make in any year. Nevertheless, it is obvious that the Government is in business in a big way and that it competes unfairly with privately owned business.

Such competition threatens the efficient operation, if not the very foundation, of the free private enterprise system.

The Hoover Commission considered recommendations for the elimination of unnecessary Government business enterprises one of its major tasks. The Congress, in creating the Commission, clearly indicated this. Public Law 108 of the 83rd Congress provided in its first section: "It is hereby declared to be the policy of Congress to promote economy, efficiency, and improved service in the transaction of the public business . . . by– (5) eliminating nonessential services, functions, and activities which are competitive with private enterprise." [1]

THE NATURE OF THE PROBLEM

On several previous occasions Congress had committees study Government competition with private business. A special Committee of the House of Representatives found in 1933 that 232 Government-owned business enterprises started during World War I were still existing fourteen years later. This group reported:

> The evidence in general indicates that the operations of the Federal Government in the field of private enterprise have reached a magnitude

[1] Commission on Organization of the Executive Branch of the Government, *Business Enterprises*, A Report to the Congress, May 1955 (Washington, D.C., U.S. Government Printing Office, 1955), p. xiv.

and diversity which threaten to reduce the private initiative, curtail the opportunities, and infringe upon the earning powers of tax-paying undertakings while steadily increasing the levies upon them.[2]

Twenty-one years later the House Committee on Government Operations concluded after a year of investigation and study:

Though economy in Government operation may be proved in a given case or the necessity for the Government to operate a service may be proved at one time—it is essential to develop competitive industries as soon as possible and the Government should step out of the picture at the earliest date. Government's continued monopoly in a field may prevent free industry from entering.

From 1929 to 1948 public wealth has grown 278.5 percent while private wealth has increased only 78.7 percent. . . . In 1929 the public wealth represented only 15 percent of total national wealth, in 1948 the public wealth amounted to 27.3 percent of the total (appendix 4). The trend continued. Is this "creeping socialism"? [3]

The Government has found three major pretexts for creating its own businesses that invade the field of private enterprise: (1) the existence of economic emergencies; (2) emergencies caused by war; and (3) the need for development of projects which are not adaptable to private industry because of their nature or magnitude. A large proportion of the business enterprises presently conducted by the Government originated during World War I, or the depression or World War II. Once started, they have an impressive capacity for perpetuating themselves after their original purpose has ended. A major reason for this is that their employees and the population of communities where they function resist termination. For example, the Inland Waterways Corporation, created in World War I to meet a wartime need, survived for thirty-five years despite the fact that it lost money practically every year.

Primarily, the American economy is based on free private enterprise, regulated in some instances to prevent monopoly and to maintain freedom of competition. The genius of this system is that it generates initiative, ingenuity, inventiveness, and thereby a high level of productivity. On the other hand, because of rigidities that are inherent in Government operations, especially where the rule of

[2] H.R. 1985, 72nd Cong., 2d Sess., p. 13.
[3] H.R. 1197, 83d Cong., 2d Sess., p. 4.

law exists, the same forces that produce excellent results in private industry fail to have the beneficial consequences in Government-owned enterprises.

Private enterprise has proved its ability to produce for the national defense in preparing this country to meet the needs of war. It manifested an inventiveness and productivity which, second only to the valor of our troops, made possible victory in both World War I and World War II. In another such emergency it would again provide the sinews of victory.

Government competition is almost always unfair competition. The Hoover Commission found that Government businesses, except in rare instances, pay no taxes and pay little or no interest on the capital invested in them by the Government. They seldom include depreciation in their costs, and frequently all of their personnel costs are not charged to their operations. Similarly, payments to provide fringe benefits for their employees generally are not included. Finally, the existence of such enterprises deprives the Government of the taxes which it otherwise would collect from private enterprise.

As a consequence, the Commission concluded that "therefore, their claims of financial success are often wholly invalid." [4]

As a fundamental principle in approaching the problem of Government business activities, the Commission declared that "the continuance of such activities by the Government must be made subject to rigid justification; occasionally this can be done, but the burden of proof in all instances must be on the Government. Unjustified continuance is a definite injury to the vitality of the whole private enterprise system." [5]

It was on this basis that the Commission approached the multitude of business activities of the Government.

Not all of the Government's business enterprises are surveyed in this chapter. Chapter 7, which examined the Government's policies relative to water resources and power, showed how the United States generates and transmits electric power in competition with private industry. In Chapter 8 the Government's lending activities were analyzed; these compete with privately owned banks and lending institutions. The Government's medical activities, considered in Chapter 10, are in competition with private practitioners of medicine and privately owned hospitals.

[4] *Business Enterprises*, p. xii. [5] *Ibid.*, pp. xii–xiii.

The business enterprises operated by the Department of Defense, because of their magnitude and variety, will be treated in a separate section of this chapter. Later, similar activities of the other departments and agencies will be considered.

ENTERPRISES IN THE DEPARTMENT OF DEFENSE

There are no fewer than 2,500 separate industrial- or commercial-type facilities owned by the armed services, according to the Commission, and the Government's investment in them is in excess of $15,000,000,000. Among them are at least 47 different types of enterprises. These are:

Aluminum sweating
Scrap metal preparation
Clothing factories
Coffee roasting plants
Motion picture studios
Paint factories
Ropewalk
Sawmills
Bakeries
Clothing reclamation shops
Furniture repair shops
Ice cream manufacturing plants
Laundries and/or dry-cleaning plants
Chain manufacturing
Acetylene manufacturing
Automotive repair shops
Caustic soda manufacturing
Cement mixing plants
Chlorine manufacturing
Surgical and medical instruments and supplies
Photographic equipment and supplies
Watch, clock, and jewelry repair shops
Plastic laminating operations
Cobbler shops
Ice plants
Office equipment repair shops
Oxygen and nitrogen manufacturing
Powerplants
Tire retreading
Tree and garden nurseries
Wood preservation
Dental manufacturing
Orthopedic manufacturing
Medical and dental repair shops
Post exchanges
Commissaries
Cafeterias (civilian type)
Meat cutting plants
Marking devices
Ophthalmic goods manufacturing
Watches, clocks, and parts
Air transportation
Sea transportation
Panama Canal Company
Panama Railroad
Industrial reserve plants
Warehouses and depots [6]

Not all of these activities are competitive with private enterprise.

[6] *Ibid.*, pp. 1–2.

Moreover, some are essential parts of the military service. But many of them could be performed better by private enterprise.

The armed services attempt to justify these productive activities on several grounds. These include (*a*) inability of private enterprise to provide the service; (*b*) maintenance of a mobilization base; (*c*) geographic isolation of the military installations; (*d*) classified nature of military requirements; (*e*) hazardous nature of certain manufacturing operations; (*f*) training of personnel; (*g*) maintenance of morale; (*h*) the provision of fringe benefits for personnel; (*i*) need for research facilities; and (*j*) the need for the determination of standards and the development of specifications.

Too often these supposed justifications are pretexts. In each instance the Commission and its staff examined the justifications advanced for these activities in an effort to determine the major services which not only are competitive with private enterprise but which could be partially or wholly dispensed with. The objective was to discover those functions where large capital investment could be recovered and where unnecessary expenditures and losses could be eliminated. Some of the activities listed on page 157 are reviewed elsewhere in this work. For example, the transportation activities, including Military Air Transport Service, Military Sea Transport Service, and the Panama Steamship Line, will be considered later in the chapter dealing with transportation. The industrial reserve facilities have already been mentioned in Chapter 6, "Real Property."

COMMISSARY STORES AND POST EXCHANGES

The armed services operated 438 commissary stores that sold $306,000,000 of groceries in 1954. This is one of the largest chain-store operations. Of these commissaries, 199 are in the United States and 239 are abroad, but the major part of the sales occurred in this country. They had 12,861 employees of whom 5,851 were in the armed services. This means that the equivalent of close to two army regiments were employed in selling goods. While thus occupied they can neither train to fight nor defend the country.

The prices charged for goods sold in these stores do not cover the full cost of operation because such items of expense as the pay and subsistence of military personnel, depreciation, interest, and other operating charges are not included. Clearly a privately owned grocery would have to meet these costs. In determining retail prices the commissaries use a markup of from 3½ to 5 per cent on the original cost of goods. According to information supplied by the comptroller general, an additional charge of from 10 to 14 per cent would be required to make their operation self-supporting, and even then there would be no allowance for taxes paid by comparable privately owned enterprises.

The armed services in 1954 also operated 450 post exchanges in this country, and these sold about $470,000,000 worth of merchandise. They employed 19,780 civilian employees with an annual payroll in excess of $48,000,000. Outside this country there are an additional 2,700 post exchanges (including branches) that did a business of $540,000,000 in 1954. These employed more than 49,900 civilians, mostly foreigners, with a payroll of about $39,000,000.

The Government largely subsidizes these post exchanges, since the prices charged for merchandise do not reflect the true cost of doing business. For example, the salary and allowances of 1,300 military personnel are not included in the selling prices of merchandise. Further, the operations of post exchanges are mostly tax exempt.

Congress by various means has attempted to restrict post exchanges and commissaries to isolated locations and has sought to require them to charge prices to cover the costs of doing business. But the military services have disregarded the intent of Congress. When anyone raises the issue of the need for these stores, the Armed Forces assert that they are required to maintain morale of uniformed personnel who have come to look upon their low prices as a part of their compensation.

The Hoover Commission recommended that post exchanges and commissaries be restricted to localities where adequate, convenient service is not otherwise available, in conformity with the declared intent of Congress. Moreover, it held that the use of these facilities should be confined to military personnel. The Commission also urged that the prices charged should cover the cost of doing business. It suggested that consideration be given to contracting out to private industry for the operation of commissaries and post exchanges where such facilities are necessary.

Finally, the Commission proposed that Congress request the comptroller general to determine the real cost of these operations.

On the basis of such a study, Congress and the public could determine the extent of the fringe benefits provided for the armed services, and what the true costs of these operations are to the public. Then the American people can decide whether the fringe benefits are worth the price.

BAKERIES

The armed services operate 46 large commercial-type bakeries in the United States. These are in addition to baking facilities maintained as parts of general messes, galleys, or kitchens. They employ 730 military personnel and 123 civilians with an annual payroll of $2,000,000. They compete with the 6,800 commercial bakeries which have large excess capacity; only a small part of the facilities of the commercial bakeries would be needed to supply all of the needs of the Armed Forces in the United States. The Commission believes that "if all expenditures for military personnel and other overhead, such as depreciation, interest on the investment, etc., were taken into account, bread could probably be obtained from commercial bakeries at the same or less cost." [7]

MEAT CUTTING

The armed services have 71 meat-cutting plants in the United States employing 1,150 military personnel and more than 100 civilians, with an annual payroll of nearly $3,000,000. In these plants meat is cut up, boned, trimmed, and processed for preparation in military kitchens. Throughout the country, there are 4,000 privately owned wholesale meat-packing plants that perform comparable operations. Since the meat handled by these military meat-cutting plants in 1954 was less than 2 per cent of that processed in all privately owned, federally inspected plants, it is obvious that private industry could take care of these needs. Further, these plants are not required for the training of meat cutters for deployment overseas since all meat shipped out of the country is already boneless and prepared for kitchen use.

LAUNDRIES AND DRY-CLEANING FACILITIES

Government departments operate 360 laundries with a staff of 12,000 employees and an annual payroll in excess of $28,000,000.

[7] *Ibid.*, p. 28.

Of these, the armed services are responsible for 125, with a staff of 7,500 and a payroll of $16,000,000.

In practically every instance, these facilities function at less than their optimum capacity, and in most cases they are in areas where there are numerous privately owned commercial laundries that are capable of performing the service, and willing to do so. For example, in the vicinity of Norfolk, Virginia, the navy has three commercial-type laundries which are used at an average of less than 38 per cent of capacity. At San Diego the Marines have two laundries which operate at only 50 per cent of capacity. In both areas privately owned laundries have idle capacity.

Despite the excess capacity in the laundries of the armed services, in 1954 more than $1,000,000 was spent on new equipment for them.

The prices charged by these Government laundries are not adequate to cover their costs of operation. Not included in their charges are interest on the investment, the rent of buildings, utilities, trucking costs, and depreciation. Yet privately owned laundries are generally willing to provide the same service at identical or lower prices.

The armed services operate 38 commercial-type dry-cleaning plants in the United States, employing 550 civilian employees and at least 50 uniformed military personnel. These plants operate at only a small part of their capacity. For example, the average for all dry-cleaning plants of the Marines is 24 per cent and for the air force 28 per cent. In almost every section of the country the privately owned dry-cleaning plants have excess capacity and could supply service at comparable costs. Actually, the army and the air force now have at least 311 contracts with private industry for laundry and dry-cleaning services, and it is agreed that private industry is performing satisfactorily under these arrangements.

The Commission recommended that bakeries, meat-cutting plants, laundries, dry-cleaning plants, and clothing manufacturing establishments operated by the armed services should be closed except where they are in isolated or overseas areas.

PROGRESS IN REDUCING FACILITIES

Athough numerous orders have been issued by the secretary of defense for the elimination of commercial- and industrial-type facilities, often they have not been obeyed. Secretaries of defense issued directives in November 1952 and again in 1953, and a new one was issued by Secretary of Defense Wilson on February 8, 1955. Recently the department has taken additional steps to carry out this program, and orders were issued in 1955 for the elimination of 97 facilities in 20 categories.

The Commission considered that this "action of the Department of Defense is most constructive," [8] but it believed that probably a thousand of these 2,500 different facilities could be eliminated without injury to the national defense.

BUSINESS ENTERPRISES IN THE CIVILIAN AGENCIES OF THE GOVERNMENT

No one knows the total number of business enterprises operated by civilian agencies of the Government. Similarly, the total amount of capital invested in them is unknown, as is the number of their employees, the value of goods and services produced, or the profit or loss resulting to the Government from their operations. Many of these publicly owned businesses compete with private enterprise, while a few of them even enjoy a monopoly position since private enterprise has been excluded from their special field. Here again the Government has made progress in the past few years in the reduction of unnecessary activities.

DEPARTMENT OF JUSTICE

The Department of Justice conducts two kinds of business enterprises, neither of which can be eliminated.

The Office of Alien Property, created in 1942 to administer the property of enemy aliens seized during World War II, owns a diversity of enterprises. Although many of these businesses compete with privately owned firms, it is impossible at the present time to rid the Government of them.

During World War II the Government took over all, or substantial parts, of 434 business enterprises owned by enemy aliens. Approximately 333 of these already have been placed in liquidation, and of this group 70 still were in the process of being closed down in the summer of 1954. Approximately 100 domestic business enterprises were conducted as active concerns. Since 85 of these have been disposed of, 15 remain as active enterprises. The total assets of

[8] *Ibid.*, p. xiii.

these 15 are valued at $170,644,000; the Government has a vested interest of $103,098,000 in these businesses. The General Aniline and Film Corporation accounts for $94,000,000 of this, while the remaining businesses are relatively small.

Existing laws make it impossible for the Government to dispose of most of these concerns. A statute which permits non-enemy claimants to bring actions against such property held by the United States prevents the return of many of them. Of the 15 properties now being operated, 7 are involved in such litigation. The United States' interest in the eight properties that could be disposed of amounts only to $1,007,000.

Although their operation by the Department of Justice has been efficient and financially sound within the restrictive limits of Government administration, actually the Government, in managing them, has been inefficient and lacked financial ability when judged in terms of private enterprise. This was the conclusion of a subcommittee of the Senate Judiciary Committee in 1954, and the Hoover Commission indicated its agreement with this finding. The Commission commended the energetic efforts of the Department of Justice to dispose of the remaining enterprises.

The other business activity of the Department of Justice is Federal Prison Industries, Inc., and here again its nature makes continued operations by the Government necessary. This enterprise was incorporated by Congress in 1934 to take over existing prison industries. The corporation carries on thirty different types of industrial activity in nineteen Federal prisons. Out of a total prison population of 20,000, about 3,525 do work for the corporation. All goods and services produced are sold to Federal Government agencies. In 1954, $20,000,000 worth of products were sold, three-quarters of which went to the armed services.

In pricing articles manufactured the corporation charges the agencies the same prices they would have to pay had the merchandise been bought from private industry. Although these activities to some extent compete with private industry, "The Commission believes that the social importance of occupation, discipline, vocational training, and rehabilitation outweigh any question of minor competition with private industry." [9]

[9] *Ibid.*, p. 49.

POST OFFICE DEPARTMENT

Three phases of the work of the Post Office involve competition with private industry: the postal savings system, parcel post, and the manufacture of mailbags and locks.

The Postal Savings System, created by Congress in 1910, offers competition with privately owned banks. It was designed to provide a safe repository for the funds of small savers before the insurance of bank deposits. During the first eighteen years of its life total deposits averaged about $135,000,000; but with the depression they increased to $1,268,000,000 by 1937. During the next decade, because of the unsettled conditions arising out of World War II, they further increased to $3,393,000,000 in 1947. Since then they have declined, and in 1954 were $2,251,000,000.

One of the original purposes of postal savings was to provide savings facilities in towns without banks. This objective has not been attained.

Actually, there are fewer than 1,200 postal savings offices in bankless towns, but there are 12,000 post offices in bankless towns, all of which sell government savings bonds. Although there are 7,872 postal savings depositories, 80 per cent of these are in first- and second-class post offices, which are situated in larger communities, by far the greater number of which have banks. More than 98 per cent of all deposits have been made in this group of depositories.

The Postal Savings System, then, operates mostly in large cities where there are ample private institutions to take deposits and to insure them. Further, the system is not conducted primarily for the benefit of small savers, since the average deposit is in excess of $750.

Repeatedly, the termination of this service has been recommended. The General Accounting Office and the secretary of the treasury, as well as the postmaster general, have indicated that there is no need for its continuation. Finally, the Commission on Organization of the Executive Branch recommended that the Postal Savings System be terminated. The public should be informed, it held, that after some reasonable period, for instance one year, no further deposits will be accepted, and that depositors will be allowed a certain period, not to exceed five years, to close their accounts.

The parcel-post system in recent years has offered subsidized competition to the Railway Express Agency and to other carriers of freight and packages. From its inception in 1912, Congress made it clear that this service was not to compete unfairly with private enterprise. In at least two ways such detrimental competition was to be minimized. Congress provided, first, that the size and weight of packages to be carried was to be limited, and second, that the charges for the service should be enough to cover all costs.

Although for a time large packages were carried, Congress has recently restricted their size.

It was always intended that the charges for parcel post should cover the cost of the service. Rates are fixed by the Interstate Commerce Commission on the request of the postmaster general. Despite this objective, the parcel post has mostly operated at a deficit, and this deficit has tended to increase. The cost of the service exceeded revenues by about 9 per cent in 1930; this rose to 16 per cent in 1946, and finally to more than 20 per cent in 1953. Since 1950 Congress has required that if revenues are not sufficient the postmaster general each year must submit to the Interstate Commerce Commission proposals for increased rates that will yield the needed income.

But under existing law, sizable items of costs are not included in making these determinations. Among these are the Government's contributions to the employees' retirement fund, compensation for employees' injuries, custodial costs, and depreciation. For the entire Post Office system, these total about $151,000,000 a year, but no official estimate has been made of what portion of these additional costs should be allocated to parcel post.

A few years ago the Senate Committee on Interstate and Foreign Commerce observed: "In the opinion of the subcommittee there is no justification for the action of the Government in subsidizing its own parcel post service in competition with private railway express service. A subsidized Government transportation service in competition with a nonsubsidized private service cannot be squared with the declared national transportation policy." [10]

The Commission came to the conclusion that "this failure of parcel post rates to cover the full cost of service constitutes a subsidy to the users of parcel post." [11] Therefore it recommended that the postmaster general be required to seek further increases in parcel-post

[10] *Ibid.*, p. 60.
[11] *Ibid.*

rates to cover all costs of the service, including those items not now included.

The Post Office Department has been manufacturing and repairing mailbags and locks for more than eighty years. It contends that by making mailbags it gets them at a price at least 4 per cent less than it could buy them from private industry. But actually this saving was estimated on a false basis because it rested upon the premise that the bags used would have to be delivered to Washington, and therefore transportation from the place of production was added to bids. Actually, most bags are not used at the Capital. If prices had been computed on an f.o.b. basis, as is the case generally, this alleged saving would disappear.

Federal Prison Industries, Inc., now manufactures the canvas out of which mailbags are made. The production of these bags and locks is similar in many ways to the industries carried on in the Federal prisons. Their transfer to Federal Prison Industries, Inc., would involve only slight competition with private industry and would furnish needed employment for convicts. The Commission recommended such a transfer.

DEPARTMENT OF THE INTERIOR

In the last few years the Department of the Interior has been striving to reduce its business activities. One of its most costly ventures has been the Alaska Railroad, a standard-gauge rail line 512 miles long, running from Anchorage to Fairbanks, that cost more than $160,000,000. As part of this transportation service the department has operated a steamship service on the Yukon River, several hotels, restaurants and commissaries. The river-boat service on the Yukon has lost money steadily—in 1954 it was $184,000. Within the past year, the department has arranged for its operation by private enterprise on a contract basis.

From its inception in 1914 through 1947, the Alaska Railroad incurred deficits totaling $14,281,000 and in computing this loss no allowance was made for depreciation. In 1954 the railroad reported a profit of $742,123, but in arriving at this figure it failed to include interest on Federal funds invested in it. Moreover, the rates charged have not been revised since 1937 despite increases in wages and in prices. On several occasions the General Accounting Office and congressional committees have urged that rates be increased.

In 1953 a study made for the Interior Department indicated that, with certain improvements and higher efficiency, the line might ultimately be able to earn a profit of $2,000,000 annually.

Under present conditions it would be difficult to dispose of the railroad to private enterprise. As a result the Hoover Commission concluded: "We can only express the hope that an increase in rates and the continued vigorous efforts of the Department of the Interior since 1953 will improve its earnings," [12] and went on to recommend that the rail rates be raised to a more adequate level, that the line be incorporated, and that it be made subject to the Government Corporation Control Act.

Although the major function of the Bureau of Mines is mining research, it has engaged in the production of helium, titanium, zirconium, and shale oil. Most of these activities, the Commission felt, should be terminated or curtailed.

Ever since 1918 the bureau has produced helium, and since 1938 it has monopolized the field. About 85 per cent of the gas produced is used by the Government. The plant utilized cost about $17,000,000. A survey in 1954 by a committee appointed by the Office of the Secretary of the Interior urged that the helium facilities be sold to private industry if a buyer can be found. The Commission joined in this recommendation.

Titanium, a metal used especially in paints and as a hardening alloy, was produced by the Bureau of Mines from 1944 to 1954. The bureau pioneered the development of its production. Because of its efforts, private industry is now producing this metal, and the bureau has retired from the field.

The production of zirconium, a rare metal, also was pioneered by the Bureau of Mines. Here again, a number of private concerns have undertaken its production, and the bureau is now leaving the field to them.

During the past ten years the production of oil from shale rock has been one of the bureau's major activities. More than $20,000,000 has been spent on plant and equipment for this purpose. Despite this investment the Commission found that "the present cost of extraction, however, results in a product which cannot compete with the prices of petroleum products." [13] The Commission recommended

[12] *Business Enterprises,* p. 67.
[13] *Ibid.,* p. 71.

that the bureau continue to produce oil from shale only until adequate cost data are available. When this information has been developed, a decision should be made on whether to continue the work or to dispose of the facilities.

Although most hotel, restaurant, and recreation facilities in the national parks are privately owned and operated, a few are operated by the National Park Service through the National Parks Concessions, Inc. Efforts are now being made to terminate at least some phases of this business. National Parks Concessions, Inc., is a Delaware membership corporation created in 1941 under the authorization of Secretary of the Interior Ickes. A majority of its directors are employees or former employees of the Park Service. Congress never authorized the company nor has it given the enterprise any funds. The General Accounting Office does not authorize the business accounts, and Congress has no control over it.

The corporation operates concessions in the Mammoth Cave Park in Kentucky, on the Blue Ridge Parkway in Virginia and North Carolina, in the Olympic National Park in Washington, and in a number of other parks and national historical sites. It got its original funds through an unusual transaction when the Federal Government acquired the Mammoth Cave National Park from the State of Kentucky. With the income resulting from the facilities in this park, the company expanded its activities into other parks. Its total assets in 1954 were about $339,000. Its gross revenues in that year were $1,070,606, and it claimed a profit, after depreciation and other charges, of $18,745. On the Mammoth Cave concessions it made a profit of more than $53,000, but on practically all other operations it lost money.

Some steps have been taken by the department to reduce the corporation's activities. The Commission recommended that the corporation be dissolved, that its assets be transferred to the National Park Service, and that the service lease or sell these facilities to private persons to be operated as are the other concessions in the national parks. If these activities cannot be operated at a profit, it asserted, there is a lack of public interest in them and they should be terminated.

The Virgin Islands Corporation is another business enterprise of the Department of the Interior that probably cannot be completely terminated. Since the United States acquired these islands in 1917 it has spent more than $75,000,000 on them, or about $3,000 per inhabitant. Despite this the islands are still impoverished. In order to develop their industries, the Government in 1934 created the Virgin Islands Corporation, which owns and operates a sugar plantation and mill, an electric power system on St. Croix and St. Thomas, and a distillery which it leases to a private company. It formerly owned a hotel, which it sold in a profitable transaction a year ago.

Generally the corporation has lost money, and this is due to the operation of its sugar plantation and mill. It harvests cane grown on 4,000 acres of its own land and it buys cane grown on 2,000 acres of privately held land. Sugar production on St. Croix can never compete effectively with that of the other West Indian islands because of inadequate rainfall. In addition, the corporation is hampered by a labor force which is 50 per cent less efficient than that on the other islands, as well as by the local minimum-wage law which provides for higher wages.

The Department of Agriculture reported that "existing wage rates are not justified by the present level of labor productivity—present rates have been induced by minimum-wage legislation of the municipal council." [14] Similarly, the General Accounting Office found in 1953 that "most of the native Virgin Islanders are reluctant to work in the fields and perform such work only because of necessity. Consequently, their productivity has always been far below other comparable areas." [15]

Although the corporation has lost money almost every year, it is difficult to see how its activities can be dissolved. The Commission concluded its appraisal by pointing out:

> The dilemma is that the production in St. Croix and St. Thomas are dependent upon the sugar plantations, the refineries, and the distilleries. They will close unless supported by the United States. The only bright spots in the economy are that the electric plants are likely to become self-supporting, the growth of tourist traffic from about $1,000,000 in 1950 to $5,000,000 in 1953, and the successful disposal of the hotel.[16]

The Island Trading Company of Micronesia is the one business enterprise of the department that has been completely liquidated.

[14] *Ibid.*, p. 75.
[15] *Ibid.*, p. 76.
[16] *Ibid.*, p. 77.

This was incorporated in Guam in 1947 by the navy for trading purposes in the Trust Territory of the Pacific. Its major function was to buy copra from the natives and to sell it in the world market. It was subsidized by a navy advance of $1,800,000 on which no interest was paid. Because the corporation violated the Government Corporation Control Act of 1945, Congress decreed that it had to be liquidated by the end of the calendar year 1954. This has been done, and the subsidy received from the Navy Department has been repaid to the Treasury. The Commission commended "the liquidation of the Island Trading Company as a desirable step in getting the Government out of business enterprises." [17]

GENERAL SERVICES ADMINISTRATION

The General Services Administration, created in 1949, operates Government buildings and procures supplies and equipment for civilian departments and agencies of the Government. In connection with these functions it provides a multitude of service activities. Some of these are obtained through contracts with private enterprises; others it supplies directly through its own operations.

The policy of the present administrator is to let contracts to private industry for all possible service activities. Thus, by retiring from competitive business enterprises, he sets an example to other Government agencies. There are about seventy-five different types of service by the administration that are subject to procurement under contract with private industry, and for fifty-eight of these 2,622 contracts were in force at the end of 1954. Often these provide service to the Government more economically than direct Government production did.

For example, in Washington the General Services Administration had been charging other Government agencies $1.25 to wash an automobile. This is now being done under contract with private industry for $0.90. The GSA has been delivering warehouse stocks to agencies in Washington at a cost of $6.65 a ton. This is now being done by private contractors at $4.95 a ton. This means an annual saving of over $28,560. Twenty-four contracts have been made with private concerns for washing the windows in sixty-six Government buildings in Washington. When the Government did this directly, the cost was $102,000 yearly; now it is being done for $74,000. The

[17] *Ibid.*, p. 78.

General Accounting Office Building is now being cleaned by a private contractor at a cost of $22,978 a month as compared with $26,506 when the Government did this itself.

The General Services Administration also produces abacá and nickel that go primarily into the Government's strategic stockpile. It loses money on both operations. Abacá is produced for the Government by the United Fruit Company on a contract basis. This rope fiber is now grown on 15,000 acres of land owned by the fruit company while the Government has an investment in the program of more than $13,600,000. The Government's stockpile of abacá has reached its desired level, and the fiber is being sold on the commercial market, although it is not moving rapidly. Losses on the operation have occurred in most years, ranging from $2,500,000 in 1951 to an estimated $3,500,000 in 1955. The losses from the program are actually larger than indicated because of the Government's policy of selling abacá only at a price comparable to that of similar grades of Philippine fiber. Because the trade does not regard this abacá as the equal of that grown in the Philippines, it is difficult to move it at that price except to the stockpile. As a consequence, late in 1954 the Government held in storage outside the stockpile about 16,000,000,000 pounds of fiber, or six months' production. The Commission believes that "when the abacá in the stockpile and this supply in storage are sold in the open market a large loss is likely." [18]

The production of nickel by the Government, begun during World War II, is being continued at a loss. This is carried on by the Cuban Nickel Company, which the Government owns. Ultimately the Government's investment in the program will be about $90,000,000. These facilities are operated for the Government by the Nickel Processing Corporation on a cost-plus-fixed-fee basis. The General Services Administration acquires the entire output of nickel and sells it either in the open market or to the stockpile. The price charged for nickel moving into the stockpile is set to cover operating costs. In 1953 this project lost $249,000 without allowing for interest on the Government investment. The Commission believes that the continued operation of this Government enterprise is justified because there are no known significant nickel deposits in the United States and because the major nickel production of the world is controlled by foreign corporations. The Commission believes that "the

[18] *Ibid.*, p. 85.

maintenance of this reserve abacá and nickel production serves to diminish the need for stockpiling these products." [19]

PRINTING

Although no precise estimate is available of the money that the Government is spending for printing, it is believed its bill is in the neighborhood of $370,000,000 a year. About $55,000,000 of the work is done in the Government Printing Office; another $30,000,000 is done under contract with privately owned commercial plants; while approximately $285,000,000 is done by the executive departments and agencies in their own plants. In addition to the Government Printing Office and its branch plants, there are in the executive departments and agencies 327 printing and duplicating plants, of which 196 are operated by the armed services.

The Congressional Joint Committee on Printing has authority over the Government Printing Office and also exercises control over printing plants in the executive agencies. Because of the important role that Congress has given to this committee, there is no focal point in the executive branch where attention is given to the need for or usefulness of these plants. Nor has any study been made concerning the economies that might result from the use of private printing facilities.

The Commission recommended that the Bureau of the Budget study the feasibility of central control over Government printing plants and that it make suggestions concerning the amount of printing that executive agencies can appropriately place with private printers or with the Federal Prison Industries, Inc.

FERTILIZER PROGRAM OF THE TENNESSEE VALLEY AUTHORITY

The Tennessee Valley Authority has been in the business of manufacturing fertilizer since its creation in 1933, and its annual production now amounts to about $19,800,000. This fertilizer is sold in competition with the products of private industry. The TVA produces primarily phosphate and nitrate fertilizers and the 360,000 tons manufactured by it account for about 4 per cent of the national production. There is no clear evidence as to whether or not the authority in selling this fertilizer is competing unfairly with private industry. Inasmuch as the authority is tax exempt, its prices do not

[19] *Ibid.*, p. 87.

have to include the taxes paid by private industry nor do they cover other costs of production.

The Commission recommended that Congress instruct the comptroller general to determine what the real cost of the Tennessee Valley Authority fertilizer production is, and that its prices should reflect its total cost. The Commission further recommended that TVA's fertilizer research activities should be transferred to the Department of Agriculture.

CONCLUSION

It is a tremendous task to implement these recommendations for the elimination of unnecessary or undesirable Government business activities. Some progress has been made in the last two years to rid the Government of some of them. The Inland Waterways Corporation was sold in the summer of 1953. The plants for the production of synthetic rubber were profitably disposed of in 1955. The Virgin Islands Company got rid of its hotel and distillery. The Department of the Interior liquidated the Island Trading Company of Micronesia, and the Bureau of Mines has ceased to produce titanium and zirconium. Some of the activities of the National Parks Concessions, Inc., have been eliminated. The General Services Administration is making increased use of private industry to supply service activities such as cleaning of public buildings, washing of windows, and the trucking of supplies and equipment. The armed services have taken steps to rid themselves of unnecessary productive activities. The Bureau of the Budget has enunciated a public policy calling for the elimination of many of these activities throughout the Government. Despite these valiant efforts, much remains to be done.

Senator John L. McClellan, Chairman of the Senate Committee on Government Operations and a member of both Hoover Commissions, introduced in Congress in 1955 a bill designed to restrict Government competition with private industry. This proposed legislation (S. 1003) declares that as a general policy the Federal Government should cease to engage in business-type operations which compete with private industry. It would direct the secretary of commerce to receive and examine reports from private industry concerning such competition, and he should then attempt to limit or terminate the Government activities involved.

The bill also provided that, except for activities specifically authorized by law, no agency could undertake any new business-type activity in competition with private industry or request funds for such a purpose unless a report on it had been submitted in advance to the director of the Bureau of the Budget, who would report to the President on such requests. The bill directs the President to inform Congress each year of what action he had taken on such requests.

The Hoover Commission was of the opinion that the enactment of this bill would be highly desirable.

It is not possible to estimate the dollar savings which could result from implementing these recommendations of the Commission. Far more important than any monetary savings, however, are the benefits that will result to our economy from the elimination of Government competition. The Commission pointed out that "the private enterprise system is the basis of the military strength of this Nation and of its unparalleled standard of living. Further strengthening of the private enterprise system is the best way to further these objectives." [20]

This problem of Government business activities poses a number of fundamental questions that every American citizen must answer. Among these are:

1. Is the continuance of Government-owned business activities consistent with the American philosophy of Government?

According to the basic principles of our Constitution, the Federal Government is designed primarily to perform regulatory and protective functions. It was not created to produce goods and services. The few instances where normal private business cannot produce goods and services should be recognized as exceptions to the general rule. This is a different philosophy from the one that prevailed for many years that the increase of Government productive facilities was a good thing for its own sake.

2. Does the Government really compete with private industry?

Yes, it does, although not in the sense in which we normally use the term "unfair competition." Normally, costs are considered to be a factor in determining the ability to compete. The more efficient producers have the lower costs. On the other hand, Government business enterprises usually do not have to carry many important

[20] *Ibid.*, p. 103.

charges which private industry must include: taxes, interest, depreciation, the full costs of payrolls and of fringe benefits for personnel. For all practical purposes, the exclusion of these items of cost constitutes a hidden subsidy to Government-owned producers. Therefore, when they compete with private producers the latter are at a disadvantage because their prices must be high enough to cover all costs. It is then easy for the proponents of Government ownership to allege that these Government businesses can produce more economically. The fact is that the taxpayers pay the difference in higher taxes or by an increased national debt.

3. Does the existence of these Government business enterprises affect the level of taxes?

Because these Government businesses, except in a few cases, pay no taxes, the United States Treasury is unable to collect the revenue that it would derive from the same activities if carried on by private business. Thus, if we maintain Government-subsidized bakeries to provide the Armed Forces with "cheaper" bread, we are also losing the taxes that commercial bakeries would have to pay on such business. Thus, the American taxpayer must pay sufficient taxes (*a*) to provide the capital for the Government-owned businesses, (*b*) to subsidize them through the payment of hidden costs, and (*c*) to make up the loss of revenue that is a consequence of the lower volume of private business.

It is no wonder that a congressional investigating committee, after it had conducted a long inquiry into this problem, asked, "Is this creeping socialism?"

CHAPTER 10

Medical Services

The Federal Government has assumed responsibility for all or a part of the medical care of about 30,000,000 Americans. In addition, it has taken on a large measure of responsibility for the protection of the health of the Nation's entire population of more than 165,000,000.

Close to 4,000,000 persons, mostly in the Armed Forces, are entitled to complete medical care from the Government, and about 3,500,000 veterans can claim care for service-connected disabilities. About 20,000,000 people are eligible for hospital, surgical, and medical care from the Government where services are available. Of these about 17,500,000 are veterans with no service-connected disabilities.

Through a multitude of agencies the Federal Government spends $4,270,000,000 a year on medical services. Almost two-thirds of it is spent by the Veterans' Administration and a quarter of it by the Defense Department. There are twenty-six Federal departments or agencies engaged in health activities, and within them there are sixty-six administrative units in this field. More than 10 per cent of the Nation's active medical practitioners are employed by the Government, as are also 6 per cent of the nurses and 9 per cent of the dentists. Out of 1,573,000 beds in all types of hospitals, 200,535 are in hospitals under the Federal Government, or 13 per cent of the total. In 1953 there were about 19,900,000 admissions to all hospitals, and of these 1,461,000 were to Federal institutions.

NATURE OF THE PROBLEM

These Federal medical services came into being at different times during the past 150 years, and each has its own history and traditions. Each had different objectives. The major purposes of many are dissimilar. They care for disability resulting from war; they cure and return soldiers to combat; some agencies protect civilians from epidemics, while others care for the mentally ill. In addition, they do much to advance research in the medical sciences.

Nothing has been done to integrate this diversity of agencies so that they serve common goals without duplication. With sixty-six administrative units spending billions of dollars yearly on medicine and operating under a multiplicity of unrelated laws, huge savings probably can be attained through improved policies and increased efficiency.

In 1949 the first Hoover Commission stated:

> The enormous and expanding Federal medical activities are devoid of any central plan. Four large, and many smaller Government agencies, obtain funds and build hospitals with little knowledge of, and no regard for, the needs of the others. They compete with each other for scarce personnel. No one has responsibility for an over-all plan. There is not even a clear definition of the classes of beneficiaries for whom care is to be planned. The Government is moving into uncalculated obligations without an understanding of their ultimate costs, of the lack of professional manpower available to discharge them, or of the adverse effect upon the hospital system of the country.[1]

Sad to say, this conclusion is just as true today as it was then. Many of the difficulties the first Commission indicated resulted from the enormous expansion of Federal medical services, the obscure and conflicting laws which accompanied this growth, and the complexities produced by Congress's effort to eliminate waste and duplication by unifying the military services.

Throughout its analysis of this most vital problem, the Hoover Commission was eager to reduce unnecessary expenditures and to lessen Government competition with the private practice of medicine. It should be stressed here that the great advances in medicine in recent years were achieved by private practitioners and not by Federal bureaucrats.

There is another more fundamental problem that must be faced in appraising the Government's medical services. The vast majority of the American people do not want socialized medicine, but

[1] The Commission on Organization of the Executive Branch of the Government, *Medical Activities,* A Report to the Congress, March 1949 (Washington, D.C., U.S. Government Printing Office, 1949), p. 7.

already the Government has assumed a large responsibility for the medical care of huge segments of the population, and it has seized control over a sizable portion of the medical and health resources of the Nation. Some of these responsibilities and functions of the National Government are appropriate and necessary. The basic problem is how the necessary medical services of the Government should be organized so that they will not result in socialized medicine.

In this chapter the lack of coordination in the various Federal programs will be considered in some detail. This will be followed by a discussion of proposals for improving the medical services of the Armed Forces, of the Veterans' Administration, and of the Department of Health, Education, and Welfare. Then specialized problems such as medical supplies and the use of health insurance for Federal employees and their families will be considered, and finally, the Hoover Commission's general recommendations will be presented.

LACK OF COORDINATION

The excess of hospital services provided by Federal agencies in certain metropolitan areas shows lack of coordination and wasteful duplication.

In and around San Francisco the Government owns sixteen hospitals operated by four agencies. These have 11,565 beds, but 5,233 were unoccupied in March 1954, when the Commission's staff made its survey. Actually, 45 per cent of the beds in Government facilities in this area were unoccupied. In the hospitals of the navy and of the air force only 38 per cent were occupied, and in army hospitals 48 per cent were in use, whereas in the Veterans' Administration the figure was 81 per cent. Both the Task Force on Federal Medical Services and the Hoover Commission believed that at least six of these sixteen installations could be closed to advantage, thus reducing the number of hospital beds by 1,454. This would allow the 233 physicians, dentists, and nurses working in them to move to posts where their services could be used more effectively.

The maximum use of such skilled personnel is imperative because of perennial shortages of medical manpower.

In the New York area, where there are twelve hospitals with 12,841 beds, 3,010 were unoccupied at the time of the study. Thus almost 25 per cent of the available beds were not being used. The portion in use ranged from a low of 43 per cent in the army hospitals to a high of 86 per cent in the hospitals of the Veterans' Administration. At least five of the hospitals in this area could be eliminated through a more efficient use of facilities.

In the Norfolk area where there were eleven hospitals with 3,971 beds, the unoccupied beds totaled 1,659. Thus only 58 per cent of the available beds were being used. In both the army and the air force hospitals 80 per cent of the available beds were not occupied, whereas in those of the Veterans' Administration 86 per cent were utilized. At least one of the hospitals in this area could be closed, releasing 277 trained personnel.

The three armed services do little cross-servicing of their respective hospital needs. When the Commission's task force made its study it found that out of a total of 102,280 constructed beds in all the facilities, only 2,255 of them were being used to cross-service the needs of the other services. This meant that only 72 navy personnel were receiving service in army hospitals and that only 297 army personnel were receiving medical attention in navy hospitals. This is surprising because at this time no use was being made of 52,760 beds, or 51 per cent of the total of 102,280 then available. On a theoretical basis at least, the unused facilities of either the army or the navy at that time could have accommodated all of the air force patients.

Waste is also evident in the large Federal expenditures for providing new hospital beds at the very time the number of unused beds was increasing. For example, the armed services in 1952 had 48,889 unused beds, or 46 per cent of all constructed beds. In that year $11,822,000 was spent for constructing new hospitals for these services. In 1955 the number of unused beds had increased to 58,899, or 63 per cent of the total available; nevertheless $62,227,000 was spent on new hospital construction in that year. Actually, a total of more than $128,000,000 was spent for army hospitals for the four years from 1952 through 1955.

In the Veterans' Administration there were 115,945 constructed beds in 1951; of these, 11,554 were unoccupied. During this period when its unoccupied beds increased from 10 to 14 per cent of the total, the Federal Government spent more than $375,000,000 for constructing added hospital facilities for the Veterans' Administration.

During the fiscal year 1953 more than 31 per cent of the beds in all Government hospitals were unoccupied; nevertheless the Government spent more than $40,000,000 in 1954 and $79,000,000 in 1955 for the construction of new hospitals.

Another cause of waste is the overly long stay of patients in Federally operated hospitals as compared to that in voluntary hospitals. For example, for the removal of an appendix the average stay in a voluntary hospital is only 7.8 days, but in the Public Health Service hospitals it is 11.9 days and in the navy 20.3 days. For removing tonsils the average stay in the voluntary hospitals is 1.4 days, while in the Veterans' Administration it is 8 days and in the army it is 16.1 days. The Task Force on Medical Services reported:

> Military personnel on active duty receive relatively large amounts of hospital service, an average of 8 days a year (exclusive of battle casualties), as compared to 1 day a year in general hospitals for the United States population. . . . In general, the amount of hospitalization given to military personnel seems excessive in terms of good medical care. The stay of many cases is too long and is influenced strongly by administrative considerations. Convalescent facilities, which require less staffing and less expensive operation than hospitals, should be used much more widely in the military than they are at present.[2]

The General Accounting Office found that these longer periods of hospitalization were due in part to "factors, such as absence of cost to the patients and probably some tendency in hospitals with light patient loads to continue care beyond necessary limits." [3]

FEDERAL ADVISORY COUNCIL OF HEALTH

Despite the multiplicity of agencies and the diversity of their statutory authority, there is no one point in the Federal Government where its medical activities can be reviewed in order to develop over-all policies, to facilitate coordination, and to eliminate duplication. The Commission believed most strongly that "there should be an agency within the Executive Office of the President charged with these responsibilities." [4] To fill this need the Commission pro-

[2] Commission on Organization of the Executive Branch of the Government, *Federal Medical Services,* A Report to the Congress, February 1955 (Washington, D.C., U.S. Government Printing Office, 1955), p. 19.

[3] *Ibid.,* p. 19.

[4] *Ibid.,* p. 21.

posed that there should be created a Federal Advisory Council of Health. This council it felt, should comprise members of the medical profession as well as lay members with distinguished records in other fields. The members, it added, should serve at the will of the President, and it should have a small staff.

The major functions of this council would include:

1. Making continuous evaluations concerning Federal policies and programs relating to medical care and national health, and presenting to the President recommendations based on its analyses.
2. Advising on measures designed to ensure adequate hospital facilities and manpower for the Nation's health needs.
3. Reviewing all hospital construction programs involving the expenditure of Federal funds.
4. Advising upon regional coordination of hospital services of all Federal agencies.
5. Making proposals for systematic cross-servicing between medical agencies.
6. Advising Federal departments on all medical policies and programs.
7. Reviewing and appraising Federal grants-in-aid for health research.

The Commission believed that "such a Council would be the beginning of the end of the present chaos." [5] Both the Task Force and the Commission considered that the establishment of this council would be the most important step that the Government could take in the field of medical and health services.

DEPARTMENT OF DEFENSE

As already indicated, the Hoover Commission found duplication and waste in the medical services of the armed services. The excessive hospitalization given to military personnel has resulted in unnecessary capital expenditures for hospitals as well as in the inefficient use of existing facilities and manpower.

The rapid growth in the number of dependents of military personnel receiving care at military hospitals has been another cause for the high costs. For example, in 1948, 42,000 babies were born in military hospitals in the United States, and by 1953 the number had

[5] *Ibid.*, p. 22.

increased to 145,000. On an average day in 1953 there were 6,300 dependents of military personnel in military hospitals in the United States and 23,000 received outpatient care.

When unification of the armed services was proposed and finally legalized in 1947, one of the major arguments for it was it would facilitate the unification of their medical services, but this has not been realized because of the unrelenting opposition of the armed services. Actually there is duplication and even competition between the army, navy, and air force in providing medical services. The first Hoover Commission found:

> There is duplication and even competition in the provision of services by the Army, Navy, and Air Force. There are too many small hospitals and infirmaries within easy reach of large facilities which have empty beds and not overburdened staffs. Medical specialists are too scattered—many of them are in hospitals which cannot make full use of their valuable training or skills.[6]

The situation has not improved in the ensuing years. Since unification of medical services has not been and probably cannot be attained, the Commission felt that under the circumstances regionalization of the military medical services is the best practical solution of the problem. Already in certain overseas areas regionalization of responsibility has proved to be advantageous. As thus developed, one service receives responsibility for the care of patients of the other services in a certain area. A similar plan might be advantageous in the United States.

Under this proposal responsibility for medical care for the three services in a locality would be assigned to the service having the predominant interest in the area. This could be done so as not to alter materially the nation-wide proportion of total responsibility for medical care now assumed by each of the three departments. This would permit the services to dispose of many small facilities. The situation revealed in Norfolk, New York, and San Francisco gives some indication of the size of the savings possible.

The secretary of defense, the Commission urged, should exercise strong control over the medical policy of the services, and already some steps have been taken to make his existing authority effective. The establishment in 1953 of the position of assistant secretary of

[6] *Ibid.*, p. 25.

defense (health and medical) was an advantageous move. But despite the creation of this new post, there are still weaknesses in the organizational pattern. The authority and responsibilities of the surgeons general of the three services are not identical. If each received a comparable responsibility, the Commission believed that coordination by the assistant secretary of defense (health and medical) could be attained more readily.

VETERANS' ADMINISTRATION

In the next few years the medical responsibilities of the Veterans' Administration are likely to increase substantially under existing law. In 1955 the Veterans' Administration spent more than $3,800,000,000 on all of its activities, and at least $2,700,000,000 of this went for medical services, including compensation to living veterans. The veteran population of the United States now numbers more than 21,000,000 and has been growing at the rate of 1,000,000 a year since 1949. It will probably continue to grow at this rate for several years more, and by 1958 the number of veterans eligible for hospitalization from non-service-connected disabilities will reach 24,000,000.

The Hoover Commission found that at present "there are more Veterans' hospitals than are necessary. Many are uneconomic to operate; some because of size, location, or inadequate number of patients." [7] Therefore it recommended that the Veterans' Administration immediately close all hospitals determined to be surplus, and that all present outstanding authorizations and appropriations for new hospital construction should be rescinded, except where work is already under way.

Non-service-connected cases are the major problem in medical care for veterans. The primary administrative concern is not with the 3,500,000 veterans who have service-connected disabilities, but with the 21,000,000 who under existing law can receive hospitalization as a result of illnesses not connected with their military service provided that they claim inability to pay.

Originally, Veterans' Administration hospitals were only for the care of veterans with service-connected disabilities, but when the demand for beds for such cases began to decline after World War I,

[7] *Ibid.*, p. 33.

Congress in 1923 authorized the use of such facilities for veterans of certain specified wars with non-service-connected disabilities. Ten years later their use was authorized for all veterans with any non-service-connected disability provided that they were unable to pay for treatment. The law required merely that the veteran swear he was not able to pay the cost. The Veterans' Administration was forbidden to challenge his declaration of financial incapacity.

It was believed originally that such service would involve no additional cost to the Federal Government, but this has proved wrong. Actually, the construction of new hospital beds for the care of such cases has cost at least $1,000,000,000. In addition, the taxpayer has been burdened with the expense involved in providing medical care and subsistence. The 40,000 beds in Veterans' Administration hospitals in 1933 would have proved adequate to care for all service-connected patients up to the present, but the number of beds in veterans' hospitals has been increased to 128,000. In 1954 an average of 65,000 out of a total of 110,497 occupied beds were taken up by cases with non-service-connected disabilities.

At present their medical and hospital care costs the taxpayer about $500,000,000 annually.

The Veterans' Administration needs a firm legal basis for determining the eligibility for medical care of veterans with no service-connected disability, according to the Commission. Its greatest difficulty is its inability to challenge the veteran's statement that he is unable to pay. "It is difficult to believe," the Commission report says, "that all of the approximately 369,000 such veterans given care last year were actually unable to pay for at least part of their hospital and inpatient medical care." [8] In 1952 the General Accounting Office found that out of a sample of 336 cases of veterans with annual incomes of more than $4,000 and receiving hospitalization, one had an annual income of $50,000, at least four had assets of between $100,000 and $500,000, and twenty-five had assets of more than $20,000.

The Commission recommended that the veteran's declaration of inability to pay should be subject to verification. It also proposed that a veteran should assume the liability to pay for care received if he should become able to do so within a reasonable time.

The Veterans' Administration has found it difficult even to collect

[8] *Ibid.*, p. 36.

on the health-insurance policies of veterans treated for non-service-connected disabilities. Frequently these contracts provide that the insurance company need make no payment for treatment received in veterans' hospitals. As a result these companies refuse to reimburse the Veterans' Administration on the ground that the veteran has had no personal loss. In such circumstances the Veterans' Administration does not even bill the company. In 1954 the administration billed insurance companies for $15,000,000, but collected only $3,300,000.

Outpatient service for non-service-connected disability cases would in some cases considerably lessen the hospital load and the cost to the Government. Therefore the Commission recommended that outpatient service should be available to veterans for non-service-connected disabilities (other than neuropsychiatric cases) where they are unable to pay.

In granting pension compensation to disabled veterans the Commission found that the standards used for determining disability were lax, and that sizable savings would result from putting them on a sound basis. Where compensation is claimed for partial disability resulting from service-connected injuries, the existence of the disability and its extent are determined by rating boards. These boards tend to assume that a disability is continuing and progressive, thereby avoiding the need for reexamination.

Where a pension is granted for a low percentage of disability (30 per cent or less), there is a failure realistically to relate the disability to the loss of earning power, the Commission discovered. For example, a 30 per cent disability is granted to a veteran for amputation of a great toe. For this he gets a pension of $50 a month regardless of his other income or of his actual earning capacity.

Some veterans are also eligible for total-disability benefits as a result of non-service-connected disabilities. These payments are only made where the recipient has an annual income of less than $1,400, or less than $2,700 if married. Actually, these limitations are not rigidly applied because their application depends upon the veteran's own estimate of anticipated income at the beginning of the year, and this declaration is rarely compared with his actual earnings at the end of the year.

Sizable savings could be attained through improving the disability rating system, the Commission found. Of the 1,998,000 veterans receiving compensation in 1953, 1,465,863 were rated as being 30 per cent disabled or less. They received an average monthly payment of $28, or a total of $487,000,000 for that year. Those rated 100 per cent disabled totaled 123,290; they received an average monthly payment of about $209, or a total of $309,000,000 for the year. A general tightening up of the rating philosophy and a reexamination of the whole program, the Commission declares, would probably save the Government as much as $180,000,000 a year.

In addition to such steps the Commission recommended a codification of all the laws and regulations relative to veterans' benefits and medical service.

DEPARTMENT OF HEALTH, EDUCATION, AND WELFARE

This department, created in 1953, spends more than $312,000,000 annually for health and medical services. Its major programs in this field are carried on by the Public Health Service and by the Food and Drug Administration.

Although the Commission found that the Public Health Service during the 152 years of its existence has had a "magnificent tradition of devoted service and leadership in world public health science," [9] it found that some of its programs need revision. By law it is charged with the task of "protecting and improving the health of the Nation." [10] In 1954 it spent $242,000,000 on this objective. Among its major activities are: the conducting of research into health problems through the National Institutes of Health, the operating of hospital facilities with 6,500 beds, the preventing of the introduction of communicable diseases into the United States, the administering of the Hospital Survey and Construction Act, and the providing for grants for hospital construction, as well as making grants-in-aid to the States for public health purposes.

The hospital facilities of the Public Health Service are used for several types of patients or cases, some of which the Commission felt should not be a Government responsibility. Of the 6,500 hospital beds under its jurisdiction, 3,600 are for general purposes. These provide service for 185,000 merchant seamen and for 91,000 per-

[9] *Ibid.*, p. 45.
[10] *Ibid.*

sonnel of the Coast and Geodetic Survey, Coast Guard, and Public Health Service Commissioned Corps, as well as their dependents. The remaining beds are used for the treatment of drug addicts and lepers. In 1954 it spent $32,000,000 on hospital and outpatient clinical care.

The Government should not have to provide medical care for merchant seamen, according to the Commission. The Government furnishes free to employees of the merchant marine a service which is normally the responsibility of industry itself or of its employees. This costs the taxpayers about $14,000,000 annually. Thus, the Commission found that the Federal Government "gives these employers what amounts to a form of Government subsidy."[11] There may have been a justification for this, it adds, when sailors' wages were low and their accommodations were poor, but today American seamen are among the most highly paid groups in industry. Many health insurance programs are open to them or to their employers. Similar aid is not given to the employees of international rail and air lines. Therefore the Commission recommended that the provision of hospital and clinical service to American seamen be discontinued.

The Public Health Service provides medical care for 44,000 members of the Coast and Geodetic Survey, the Coast Guard, and the Public Health Service Commissioned Corps, as well as for about 47,000 of their dependents. The Hoover Commission believed that the uniformed personnel of these services could get medical services from the hospitals of the armed services and that their dependents could also be served similarly, pending the development of a voluntary health insurance program for them.

Finally, the Commission recommended that the general-purpose hospitals of the Public Health Service be closed.

The grant-in-aid program for the building of hospitals should be reappraised, the Commission declared. Since 1946 the Federal Government has furnished financial assistance for the construction of non-Federal hospital facilities. It has paid out about $618,000,000 as against State and local contributions of $1,232,000,000. Since the inception of the program hospitals constructed with these grants constitute approximately one-third of all hospital construction. Despite its great utility this program needs reappraisal today, the Commission believes, especially in regard to its bed-ratio standards,

[11] *Federal Medical Services,* p. 47.

the regionalization of hospital services, and the relationship of small community hospitals to the total hospital program. Such a reappraisal, it says, should be made by the Federal Advisory Council of Health.

The grant-in-aid program for public health needs to be reexamined, according to the Commission. The Federal Government is spending annually $48,685,000 on grant-in-aid to the States for health purposes. The usefulness of these programs has been diminished by the rigid categories in which grants are made for specific purposes. If grants could be made for general health purposes a greater return might result from the Federal expenditure; but Congress by law has imposed this system of specific categories. Generally speaking, as a result too little reliance is placed upon the judgment of the States to determine the relative importance of different problems in the light of the special needs. The secretary of health, education, and welfare, the Commission asserts, should restudy the whole program of grants with special reference to its inflexibility.

The Food and Drug Administration performs an important role in maintaining the Nation's health by inspecting food and drugs. Actually, five Federal departments are wholly or partly concerned with health regulation or inspection. The Department of Health, Education, and Welfare and the Department of Agriculture have multiple regulatory duties costing annually several millions of dollars. In each of these agencies four distinct administrative units participate in regulation. The Department of the Treasury regulates narcotics, the Federal Trade Commission prohibits false and misleading advertising, and the Post Office Department has a small staff to take action against medical frauds perpetrated by mail.

The Food and Drug Administration is the most important of the agencies in this field. It has a good record, but according to the Task Force on Federal Medical Services, "the agency (1) tends to use punitive rather than educational methods of enforcement; (2) is so zealous in its work that it administers some activities no longer worth the time, effort, and money put into them; and (3) lacks enough staff to perform its proper functions." [12]

The Commission found that the Food and Drug Administration is

[12] Commission on Organization of the Executive Branch of the Government, *Task Force Report on Federal Medical Services*, February 1955 (Washington, D.C., U.S. Government Printing Office, 1955), p. 78.

carrying on activities that, in the present state of manufacturing and processing, are not worth the effort and that as a result, other important phases of its work, such as enforcing the food and drug laws, suffer. Its inspectors are able to visit annually no more than a small percentage of the 96,000 establishments that manufacture or distribute large quantities of products under its jurisdiction.

The Commission recommended that the President appoint a special committee consisting of representatives of the Bureau of the Budget, of the Department of Agriculture, and of the Department of Health, Education, and Welfare to study the inspection functions of these departments to determine which can be dispensed with and to eliminate conflicts and overlaps between agencies.

MEDICAL SUPPLY

Because of the chaos existing in the Federal medical-supply function, the Commission found that large savings can be attained through its improvement. The Federal Government buys more than $152,000,000 of medical supplies each year. Six departments account for $147,000,000, or 97 per cent of the total. The remaining 3 per cent are acquired by twelve other agencies. The armed services buy 35 per cent of the entire amount. Inventories of such material total $465,000,000, of which 99 per cent is held by five agencies. Further, there are 361 Government-operated facilities manufacturing medical supplies, frequently in competition with private industry. About 4,700 persons are engaged in these activities.

Little progress has been made in the development of an integrated system for storage and distribution of this material. Five separate catalogues of medical supplies are maintained by various agencies. The Commission believed that "the practice of medicine, dentistry, and the operation of hospitals, clinics, and research laboratories are so much the same regardless of the service or agency that medical supplies can be uniformly and commonly classified for all using agencies." [13] There is no warrant, it felt, for the maintenance of separate catalogue systems.

Nor is there any uniform system of stock accounting. The only joint operation in this area is conducted by the army and air force. The other agencies use a variety of methods or none for stock ac-

[13] *Federal Medical Services,* pp. 57–58.

counting or control. This evidence, the Commission believed, amply demonstrates that the Government should develop a uniform system of procuring, storing, and distributing medical supplies.

HEALTH INSURANCE

Despite the rapid growth of health insurance, the Federal Government makes no use of it to meet its medical responsibilities. Its use by the Government to discharge existing responsibilities, the Commission declared, would in some instances be in the public interest.

Various forms of health insurance now provide some protection against the cost of illness for more than 100,000,000 people. For 80,000,000 there is some assistance in meeting the cost of surgery, and for 42,000,000 there is some additional financial help for medical care. Yet the Federal Government, the largest employer in the free world, has no program of contributory health insurance for its employees.

Such programs should not be used, the Commission concedes, for groups for whom the Government's responsibility for medical care is reasonably justified, as for example, the men and women on active military duty or their dependents overseas, or for the veterans disabled in the course of duty; but the Commission recommends that the Federal Government develop a voluntary contributory program for medical care and hospital insurance to be administered through a pool of private health insurance agencies to cover its civilian employees. This insurance, it believes, should be financed through a form of payroll deduction with the Government contributing a portion of the cost.

Further, it says, the Government should also develop for dependents of military personnel within the United States a voluntary contributory plan for medical and hospital care to be conducted in a manner similar to that proposed for civilian employees. In this instance the Government, it feels, should pay a greater portion of the cost than it would pay for civilian employees. This plan, it adds, should also be extended to the dependents of uniformed personnel in the Public Health Service, Coast Guard, and Coast and Geodetic Survey.

The Hoover Commission asserts the program should be administered through some form of pooling arrangement with the private companies writing such insurance because

> medical and hospital care programs should not become a vehicle by which the Federal Government would enter or regulate all or part of the insurance industry. We believe rather that the Government approach should be through existing voluntary health insurance systems, through contribution to the purchase of insurance from voluntary systems rather than to have the Federal Government become a self insurer.[14]

Health insurance on a contributory basis for the dependents of military personnel is desirable, the Commission feels, because the direct provision of such care by the Government closely approximates socialized medicine and might be used as a pretext for its extension to other groups.

GENERAL PROPOSALS

The Commission recommended that the Armed Forces Medical Library should be reconstituted as a National Library of Medicine. For effective health research, there must be access to books and journals in medicine-related fields. The largest and best library of such material in the world is the Armed Forces Medical Library in Washington. No newly created library could hope to duplicate its matchless collections. "It is in fact the National Library of Medicine of the United States." [15]

For this library to function effectively, it must have a legal status and an administrative organization appropriate to its nature, as well as an adequate budget. There is no clear statutory authorization for the functions now served by this institution. It is ineffectively located from the standpoint of administration, inadequately housed, and too poorly supported to permit it adequately to continue its functions. Finally, the cost of its maintenance is hardly a fair charge on any of the military establishments.

The Commission recommended that there be established a National Library of Medicine as a division in the Smithsonian Institution, with its own board of trustees selected by that institution's regents. To this library should be transferred the medical collections and staff of the Armed Forces Medical Library.

[14] *Task Force Report on Federal Medical Services,* p. 31.
[15] *Federal Medical Services,* p. 63.

Despite the importance of measures for preventive health, the Federal Government spends only about $125,000,000 annually for this purpose, almost half by the Department of Defense. The Commission suggested that the proposed Federal Advisory Council of Health make recommendations to improve preventive health services.

On various forms of health research (including medical research) the Federal Government is now spending $119,000,000 annually as compared with only about $3,000,000 in 1941. Here again the Federal Advisory Council of Health should be given the responsibility, the Commission felt, for reviewing the Government's programs in this field and for making recommendations for improvements.

The problem of mental illness is awesome for the Federal Government as well as for the people as a whole. Most of the Nation's 650,000 mental patients receive care in State or Federal institutions and occupy half of the total available hospital beds. Too little attention is being given to the preventive aspects of mental illness. The armed services have an unusual opportunity for the early detection and prevention of mental illness among military personnel. The Commission recommended that the Federal Advisory Council of Health examine the means for establishing cooperative planning among Federal agencies providing psychiatric care and that the military services together with the Veterans' Administration give greater emphasis to preventive psychiatric services.

CONCLUSIONS

In addition to proposing recommendations that would result in a net annual saving to the Government of $290,000,000, the Commission in its study of Federal medical services raises for public consideration several fundamental questions.

First: Where is the line to be drawn between health services and programs that can appropriately be undertaken by the Federal Government and those which cannot? While the Commission made no general policy recommendations, several of the specific recommendations clearly point the way to the development of criteria for a redefinition of Federal responsibilities in this field.

Another way of putting this question is: If the Federal Government unreservedly takes on the responsibility for the medical care of

20,400,000 people, have we already taken a vital segment of medical care from the area of private responsibility and thereby gone a long way toward socialized medicine?

The Commission's recommendations recognize that the American public is willing to give some preferment to any veteran. However, it would require that veterans take responsibility for their own care when their disabilities are not service-connected. Thus, while the Government is the agent of the people in granting a special privilege for specified causes, there should be no assumption of the right of any group of citizens to receive such care at the expense of all the citizens.

The same principle is seen in the Commission's recommendations with respect to the use of health insurance instead of the direct provision of medical care for the dependents of military and other uniformed employees, and to the termination of medical care for American merchant seamen. The Government's responsibility relative to these groups should be limited not only for reasons of economy, but also for reasons of policy.

Second: How can we assure proper management of those health services which the Federal Government must continue to provide?

It was the Commission's belief that, as the initial step, the proposed Federal Advisory Council of Health would be the proper focal point for the review and evaluation of the Government's medical policies and activities.

4.

The Big Spender

CHAPTER 11

Big Defense, Big Business

Although the Department of Defense is a tremendous business enterprise, the world's biggest, in fact, it has neither the viewpoint nor the organization to operate as effectively as Americans have a right to expect. Its expenditures were about $35,000,000,000 in 1955, which is one-ninth of our national income. It employs 4,300,000 employees, which is 7 per cent of our active national labor force. This is twice as many workers as are employed by the ten largest American corporations. The original cost of the assets it uses was about $140,000,000,000, or approximately the value of all privately owned real property in the Nation. Among these assets are 30,973,247 acres of land that cost $28,700,000,000. It leases an additional 1,983,686 acres at an annual rental of $16,697,000. In addition, it owns 579,049,000 square feet of covered storage space. During 1955 it bought $20,000,000,000 of supplies and equipment.

Some 2,500 separate Government-owned business enterprises, with assets worth at least $15,000,000,000, are operated by this mammoth agency. Included among these are 210 passenger or freight ships and 536 passenger or cargo planes not used for tactical purposes. It spends more than $2,000,000,000 a year on research and development activities, or almost as much as the combined research expenditures of all private enterprise and endowed research institutions.

Thus, the Department of Defense itself is big business, and it is precisely because it is that the Hoover Commission studied its activities. Its business tasks, however, are complicated by the fact that the basic objective for its existence is national defense. This objective embraces the recruiting, training, and organization of armed forces for combat operations. It must be ready to defend the Nation at all times and at any cost.

UNBUSINESSLIKE ATTITUDES

The performance of its national role, almost of necessity, introduces into the Defense establishment a philosophy and an attitude that are inconsistent with sound business principles as well as with economy in Government. Essentially the military attitude is that it is much better to have a surplus of supplies and of personnel than to have too little, because deficiencies might cause defeat. Obviously, this is true, and obviously, also, it is unbusinesslike and wasteful. This philosophy is epitomized in the remark of a prominent flag officer:

> Our military people are not hired primarily to see how little they can get along with; they are hired primarily to seek to get enough material to meet their responsibilities.[1]

An assistant secretary of defense expressed the same view:

> It is not unreasonable to expect responsible military personnel to desire sufficient manpower and material at any place and at any time to minimize potential risks. Cost, even though given active and sympathetic recognition, tends to assume a secondary role.[2]

This anti-economy and unbusinesslike attitude is of fundamental importance, for it permeates the thinking of the entire establishment. Although civilian control of the Armed Forces is accepted as a principle of American Government, this approach of the professional soldier has influenced the thought and actions even of the responsible civilian officials. This type of influence is not easily eradicated by reorganization or by other simple means. Yet every reasonable step should be taken to make civilian control of the Defense Establishment a reality; otherwise we might end up with a military dictatorship.

PROGRESS OF REORGANIZATION

Recent reorganizations of the armed services have not attained significant results in improving their business activities, probably because these reforms have done little to eradicate this fundamental

[1] Commission on Organization of the Executive Branch of the Government, *Business Organization of the Department of Defense,* A Report to the Congress, June 1955 (Washington, D.C., U.S. Government Printing Office, 1955), p. 4.
[2] *Ibid.,* p. 4.

attitude of the military, although steps have been taken to reorganize and to improve the administration of the Armed Forces. These changes have been designed to attain unity, to increase civilian control, and thereby to promote economy and efficiency.

The National Security Act of 1947 set up a loose confederation of the army, navy, and air force in the National Military Establishment headed by a secretary of defense. All authority not granted to the secretary still remained in the departments. The joint chiefs of staff, made up of representatives of the three services, directed defense planning with little or no effective control by the secretary.

To strengthen civilian control and to implement unification, the first Hoover Commission proposed fundamental changes in the defense setup, most of which were embodied in the 1949 amendments to the National Security Act. These modifications constituted another short step in the direction of unification, and greatly strengthened the role of the secretary. In place of the National Military Establishment a Department of Defense was created. The Armed Forces were placed under the secretary's "authority, direction and control." The secretary of defense was made the principal military adviser of the President, thus reducing the heads of the three services to a subordinate position. A comptroller for the department and one for each of the services were provided, as was a full-time nonvoting chairman of the joint chiefs of staff.

In 1953 a further step was taken toward unification of the services and away from decentralized federation as envisaged in the original National Security Act of 1947. By Reorganization Plan No. 6 (1953), President Eisenhower strengthened the hand of the secretary of defense through the creation of a number of additional assistant secretaries, as well as by the abolition of the National Security Resources Board, the Munitions Board, and the Research and Development Board. The chairman of the joint chiefs of staff received a vote in its deliberations and received administrative authority over the Joint Staff. The joint chiefs of staff were divested of their unified command authority, and planning functions were declared to be their primary responsibility.

Despite these three major improvements the secretary still lacks effective control over the joint chiefs, as well as over the operations of the three services. Machinery for the efficient conduct of the business operations of the services is also lacking.

AREA OF APPLICATION OF BUSINESS METHODS

Business methods and attitudes are applicable only to a limited part of the work of the department. To determine that part it is necessary to consider the major functions of the department. These fall into three primary groups:

1. It must plan for national defense. This involves laying down the broad guidelines which must guide the several armed services.
2. It must organize and direct combat forces. On the basis of developed plans, such forces are organized for military readiness. These are directed and trained so as to make them effective in national defense.
3. It must provide support for the combat forces. Such support activities include procurement, production, distribution, research, personnel, and finance. These support functions are of two major types: combat-related support and supplier-related support.

Combat-related support includes activities closely related to the fighting men. As a result these are made physically a part of the tactical or combat forces. Their personnel must be interchangeable with the fighters, accompany them into combat, and have their point of view. The supplier-related activities are closely related to the facilities of production, service, and supply. The personnel require skills normally found in the civilian economy. The employees so engaged should be oriented toward business and the professions, and they do not accompany the troops.

It is with these supplier-related activities that the Hoover Commission dealt in its study of Defense because "studies show that the structure of the military departments has not kept pace with the vastly increased importance of support activities which has resulted from fundamental changes in the concept of military operations." [3] Added emphasis to this point was given in 1954 by the secretary of the army's plan for reorganizing that service. This stated: "For both major wars fought in this century, the Army has had to change its organizational structure radically in order to perform under wartime conditions. Each time the primary weakness was in the logistics area." [4]

[3] *Ibid.*, p. 8.
[4] *Secretary of the Army's Plan for Army Organization,* June 14, 1954.

With the increased complexity of war resulting from rapid technological change, these supplier-related activities are growing ever more important.

But even in this restricted area, as thus demarcated, the productive activities of Defense do not resemble any known business enterprise. The sources of these fundamental differences with private business are at least threefold:

1. The stupendous size of the enterprise, much larger than that of any other enterprise in the free world, makes it impossible to use ordinary yardsticks in appraising performance.
2. Since national survival is at stake, mere cost cannot be the sole or primary standard of value or of performance.
3. The dual personnel system, with both military and civilians working side by side, involves increased costs and difficult problems of management. This is made much more difficult because the uniformed personnel are expected to function on the basis of command while the civilian personnel are supposed to operate on the basis of sound management principles. These two dissimilar approaches are bound to clash.

Thus the department's business-type activities are unique, and as such the problems raised by them will require unique solutions.

METHOD OF STUDY

In approaching the problems of the Department of Defense, the Commission proceeded differently than in other areas. Its other studies were directed at a single function of the Government wherever it was found. The Defense Department was handled otherwise, first because of its magnitude, $35,000,000,000 out of a total budget of $64,000,000,000, and second, because many of the Commission's functional Task Forces uncovered unusual problems in the Defense area. At least eight of these groups touched upon Defense in a major way:

Budget and Accounting
Food and Clothing
Legal Services and Procedure
Medical Services
Personnel and Civil Service
Procurement
Real Property
Use and Disposal of Surplus Property

To coordinate the work of these groups and to study the structural organization of the Department of Defense insofar as it related to business activities, the Commission found it necessary to organize a special unit. Consequently, it established a Committee on the Business Organization of the Department of Defense. In coordinating the work of the Task Forces, this group found a number of important problems not being considered by the Commission. As a result, the following five Committees were organized to study special aspects of Defense:

Business Enterprises
Depot Utilization
Research Activities
Special Personnel Problems
Transportation

On the basis of these Committee and Task Force reports, as well as other studies, and the wide experience of the Commissioners, recommendations concerning the over-all organization of the department were formulated.

Before considering the problem of the over-all organization of the department, a number of its business-type activities will be surveyed. These will include food and clothing, transportation, depot utilization, research and development, and the disposal of surplus property. Earlier chapters also have touched on similar activities of Defense—medical services, legal services, business enterprises, real property, and budget and accounting.

Ever present in the consideration of these activities has been the desire to ease military attitudes and points of view incompatible with sound business principles and efficiency of operation, while preserving the supremacy of the armed services in their own appropriate sphere.

CHAPTER 12

Food and Clothing

The United States Government provides more than 10,000,000 meals each day and more than 7,000,000 complete outfits of clothing each year for the Armed Forces. Obviously this is a tremendous housekeeping job. In 1954 the Government directly spent $1,292,-000,000 for this food and clothing. Of this total $997,000,000 went for food and $295,000,000 for clothing. Not included in these figures were the cost of the huge management staff or of most of the transportation, storage, and other charges. The total expenditure involved is therefore much larger.

In addition, inventories of food exceed $200,000,000 and of clothing $2,700,000,000.

NATURE OF THE PROBLEM

Our soldiers and sailors are well fed and well clothed. Consequently, the major problem to be considered by the Hoover Commission was whether by an improved system of management the cost could be made to bear less heavily on our already overburdened economy.

The Commission stressed that its report on activities and problems of a business character in the Department of Defense must not be considered a general criticism of the military personnel or the civilian employees. "Our country enjoys a magnificent military personnel," it said, "and the civilian heads of the services are of great ability and fine devotion." [1]

Many of the weaknesses of the supply system, it found, are the result of war and emergency action. They are also an inheritance of legislation ill adapted to the new version of unification and more

[1] Commission on Organization of the Executive Branch of the Government, *Food and Clothing in the Government*, A Report to the Congress, April 1955, page ix.

modern business methods. "Their elimination often requires a revision of the laws in the light of growth, of new concepts, and of progressive business experience."[2] These weaknesses are the concern of more than one service and are beyond the capacity of any single official or department to correct or improve.

Progress has already been made in improving the efficiency of the individual department supply system and management functions. The Commission gave full recognition to the principle that the task of improvement is a continuing one and must reflect changing requirements, strategy, and other exigencies of the military situation.

The major responsibility for improving the administration of food and clothing is that of the secretary of defense. Congress has conferred on him all of the authority to unify, coordinate, and integrate procurement and supply management of the three services. This conclusion is supported amply by the policy statement contained in the National Security Act of 1947: "It is the intent of Congress . . . to provide for the establishments of integrated policies and procedures for the departments, agencies, and functions of the Government relating to the national security."

Further, Congress in 1949 positively stated that the secretary of defense "shall have direction, authority, and control over the Department of Defense, including the three armed services."[3]

Because Congress was disturbed by the secretary's slowness in developing a supply system, the Armed Services Appropriations Act for 1953, enacted in 1952, specifically directed, by the so-called O'Mahoney rider, that the secretary exercise his powers to set up a unified, coordinated, and integrated procurement system.

Former Secretary of Defense Robert A. Lovett clearly recognized this as the secretary's responsibility when he wrote to President Truman, on November 18, 1952, that the Secretary "clearly has authority to step in where necessary . . . in the field of supply, warehousing and issue." He went on to point out that difficulties have been encountered when "certain ardent separatists occasionally pop up with the suggestion that the Secretary of Defense play in his own backyard and not trespass on their separately administered preserves."

[2] *Ibid.*
[3] *Food and Clothing in the Government,* p. 2.

"From the text of these laws," the Commission report said, "it is obvious that Congress intended to have developed a coordinated, unified procurement and supply management system for the armed services, and that it conferred on the Secretary of Defense all the power necessary to accomplish this aim." [4]

However, there is little more semblance of unification now in the supply of food and clothing than before the National Security Acts and the O'Mahoney rider were passed. There still is waste, duplication, overlapping, and an unnecessary number of agencies concerned with food and clothing.

PROBLEMS COMMON TO FOOD AND CLOTHING

Congress has done much to improve procurement in the subsistence field. The Armed Services Procurement Act of 1947 permitted the agencies to depart from the long-existing practice of requiring competitive bidding on all purchases. Congress provided instances in which procurement by negotiation would be permitted, and established certain basic requirements for the use of that method. This law is used extensively for the purchase of perishable foods. The following benefits have resulted:

1. The requirements of the Government had grown to such dimensions that only a few firms or combination of firms could make bids, and the mere advertising for the purchase of such large quantities raised prices. The change of method permitted purchases from smaller establishments.

2. Previously, when bids were received for less than total quantities, the Government was compelled to fill its requirements by accepting commodities at higher prices than the price quoted by the lowest bidder; now it is possible to buy what the low bidder is able to supply.

3. Most bids contained restrictive clauses which could not be altered after the bids were opened; these are now subject to negotiation.

4. The administrative costs of the advertising-bid method were greatly increased by the necessary legal requirements, which resulted in voluminous paperwork in mailing, handling, printing, and checking by both the vendor and the Government.

[4] *Ibid.*, pp. 3 and 4.

It is significant that some nonperishable foods were purchased by negotiation under emergency powers granted to the President during the Korean War. The use of this method under these emergency powers resulted in savings of approximately $4,000,000 per annum in the nonperishable subsistence field. However, expiration of the emergency powers will necessitate a return to the "advertisement and bids" method. If existing law should be modified, savings in the same or larger proportions could be obtained on clothing as well as on nonperishable food.

"The cost of operation of the 'advertisement and bids' method has greatly increased with the growth of Government needs," the Commission pointed out; "moreover, the invitation to bid is a formal and voluminous document containing much legal detail, running as high as 25 pages, and involving much expense in administration and distribution." [5]

In one year, following advertisements for bids on clothing, 202,000 invitations, with specifications and terms as to requirements, were sent out. Only 28,483 were acknowledged, and 7,947 bids were received, or only about 3 per cent.

Another problem in the "advertisement and bids" method arises from the nature of the clothing manufacturing industry. The Chamber of Commerce reports that in New York City more than five thousand said establishments went out of business in one year and that five thousand new shops opened up. Many of the new ones were the old establishments under new names. By "advertisement and bids" the Government attracts the marginal operators, as many large manufacturers do not wish to disturb their civilian trade. Delinquencies in marginal shops are common, and bankruptcies force the Government to recover large quantities of cut cloth to be put together at a heavy cost and long delay. "The authority of the agencies to reject unreliable bidders is not clear in the law, and there is conflict in action by different agencies." [6]

FOOD

There is no unified system for procuring, distributing, and preparing food in the armed services. Responsibility for food supply in the army is assigned to the quartermaster general, in the air force to

[5] *Ibid.*, pp. 8 and 9.

[6] *Ibid.*, p. 10.

the deputy chief of staff, and in the navy to the Bureau of Supplies and Accounts.

From an organizational point of view, there are eight stages or functions in military food supply:

1. Determination of the ration.
2. Determination of requirements.
3. Purchase (or procurement).
4. Inspection at source and delivery points.
5. Storage (including refrigeration and surveillance inspection).
6. Inventories.
7. Distribution to consumption points or bases.
8. Inspection, preparation, and service at the mess level.

These functions vary somewhat between nonperishables and perishables. There also are differing patterns of these functions based on the nature of service, locality, and so on.

Some of these functions are cross-serviced, particularly inspection at point of origin and purchase, but the other functions are divided between the army, navy, and Marine Corps.

The quartermaster general of the army, through its Market Center System, has been procuring all foods for the armed services. It has been doing an excellent job and has made real progress toward unification. But it "cannot function with complete efficiency in the present situation of divided inventory, warehouse, and distribution systems." [7]

Nonperishable food of the military services is stored and distributed from about thirty depots, with each of the three services acting independently. In addition, the Quartermaster General Market Center stores perishable foods in six Government-owned refrigerator plants and has contracts with approximately 225 commercial refrigerator warehouses.

Lack of unified control of distribution and storage results in overlapping and duplication: "with minor exceptions few cases were found where storage space in a service depot, even when palpably in excess, was made available to the crying needs of another service." [8]

In the storage of food products the principle to be followed supposedly is "first in, first out." But in practice this is not applied, and as a result much material is kept in storage until it spoils.

[7] *Ibid.*, p. 16.

[8] *Ibid.*, p. 18.

For example: the fourteen naval supply depots in the United States (which held both mobilization reserves and operational stock) had on hand in 1954, 886,020 pounds of canned hamburger. Of these, 97,643 pounds were bought in 1950, 221,638 pounds in 1951, 289,658 pounds in 1952, and 277,081 pounds in 1953. At the 1954 rate of consumption of 1,233 pounds per month, this supply would be enough for 719 months. The same depots had 1,330,026 pounds of canned beef and gravy. This was bought as follows: 27,291 pounds in 1948, 1,989 pounds in 1949, 42,240 pounds in 1950, 794 pounds in 1951, 636,242 pounds in 1952, 479,670 pounds in 1953, and 145,800 in 1954. At the 1954 rate of consumption of 16,989 pounds a month, this would be enough for 79 months.

"The manual of the Bureau of Supplies and Accounts of the Navy states that the estimated keeping life of canned meats and poultry is 24 months at an average temperature of 40° F. and 12 months at 90° F." [9]

Departmental directives relative to food are not obeyed. A Defense Department directive of January 1953, for instance, established a four months' inventory of green coffee beans at each roasting plant. An inspection of the army roasting plant at Seattle showed an inventory of nine months' supply of green coffee and a three months' supply of roasted coffee. Fort Carson, Colorado, received from the Ogden General Depot a shipment of 90,000 pounds of dry white beans, with consumption less than 5,000 pounds of white beans per month.

RATIONS

There is also a wide difference between the services on the size and composition of rations. The Commission found that "the Army and Air Force have one ration, the Navy a different one, and the Marine Corps a third." [10]

Congress has long concerned itself with the size of rations. In the army the determination of the ration was delegated in 1901 to the President. The army ration is based on a monetary allowance. Congress in 1933 specifically determined the kinds and quantities of food that should go into the navy ration. This ration in kind was modified during World War II; but the earlier method has since been restored except for smaller bases and ships where it is issued

[9] *Ibid.*, p. 20. [10] *Ibid.*, p. 22.

on a monetary basis. The Marine Corps ration is under the same law as that of the navy. On the other hand, there is no legislative base for the air force ration, although by agreement it has adopted the army ration. However, in June 1948, the Congress authorized a supplemental ration to personnel in active air operations.

The Commission found that on a cost basis the ration of the navy exceeds that of the army and the air force. "Sampling of the two services at Corpus Christi showed that the Navy ration cost was $1.54 compared to $1.07 for the Army, and at Newport, R.I., the Navy ration cost was $1.34, whereas the Army's cost was $1.05." [11]

For every thousand rations the navy allows 824 pounds of potatoes for the army 552.60; the navy provides 109 pounds of eggs as against 237.70 for the army. Eighty-nine pounds of canned tomatoes are allowed by the navy and 36.68 by the army.

"Why the Navy allows about 50 percent more potatoes than the Army, or why the Army allows more than twice as many eggs as the Navy in rations is not understandable. Neither is it understood why the Navy includes twice the amount of canned tomatoes as the Army." [12]

FOOD PREPARATION

The entire purpose of the subsistence supply system is to provide proper meals for the armed personnel. "The actual preparation and serving of food is, however, the weakest link of the chain of subsistence activities. The cause of this weakness is traceable to an organizational misconception. It is predicated on the concept that at mess level, the preparation and serving of food is considered to be a command function and that this function can be divorced from all of the antecedent activities of the supply chain." [13]

Actually, the food procured for the Armed Forces is of good quality. "Although there has been much improvement over methods used at the close of World War II, the preparation and service of food in all the Services are still below acceptable commercial standards." [14] The reasons for this are: (*a*) there is no single authority responsible for the management, assignment, and training of personnel; (*b*)

[11] *Ibid.*, p. 23.
[12] *Ibid.*
[13] *Food and Cothing in the Government*, p. 24.
[14] *Ibid.*, p. 25.

there is a loss of nutritive value and palatability because food remains too long in storage; (*c*) there is inadequate preparation and service of food; (*d*) there is inadequate organization; (*e*) personnel is inadequate; (*f*) training is inadequate; and (*g*) facilities for food preparation are inadequate or poorly arranged.

PROPOSED ORGANIZATION FOR FOOD

Two methods of organizing the Department of Defense food-supply servicing were considered by the Task Force—cross-servicing and integration.

Cross-servicing is a system by which one military department provides goods or services to one or more other military departments within a specific geographic area. As a method of meeting existing problems this would not be a feasible solution because:

(*a*) About thirty distribution depots are controlled by three services that operate independent distribution missions, and that have differing requirements and independent storage management organizations.

(*b*) Consuming points in the continental United States alone, number in excess of five hundred for the services.

(*c*) Subsistence is stored in approximately 4,000 vendor warehouses in time of war, title to which is lodged independently with the services.

(*d*) The difficulty of obtaining teamwork among independent systems has already proved the impracticability of this method in time of peace, and the difficulty is much greater in time of war.[15]

As a consequence the Commission recommended a unified and integrated supply system for food. The secretary of defense, it declared, should designate some central agency to buy all food for the services on a negotiated contract basis. This agency should maintain central inventory controls and have charge of food warehousing and of supplying food to the bases. It should develop a uniform ration for all services, set up master menus, and provide training for personnel at the mess level.

CLOTHING

There is no unified or uniform system for the procurement and supply of clothing for the armed services. The responsibility for the army rests upon the quartermaster general of the army, in the air

[15] *Ibid.*, p. 29.

force upon the Air Force Materiel Command, in the navy upon the Bureau of Supply and Accounts, in the Marine Corps upon their own quartermaster general.

The Commission found that usually there are eleven stages in the provision of clothing:

1. Determination of requirements.
2. Advertisement and bids for most of the cloth, thread, buttons, and linings, as these materials differ from civilian supplies.
3. Award of contracts.
4. Inspection.
5. Advertisement and bids from manufacturers of apparel.
6. Award of contracts to these manufacturers.
7. Delivery from manufacturers to storage.
8. Inspection.
9. Storage.
10. Distribution to bases.
11. Issue to personnel.

"All the stages are independently conducted by the services except that the Quartermaster General of the Army does the purchasing and part of the inspection for the Air Force." [16]

The army and the air force purchases are conducted from the Quartermaster General Depot in Philadelphia. The navy purchases are conducted from the Navy Purchasing Office in Brooklyn, New York. The Marine Corps purchases are conducted from the Marine Corps Purchasing Office in Philadelphia.

Each service maintains its own system for the supply and distribution of clothing. The army operates seven "accountable distributing" depots with nine satellite depots. The Air Materiel Command operates two clothing supply depots, one serving the eastern United States, European, and African depots, and the other serving the western United States and the Far East. The Navy Bureau of Supply and Accounts operates sixteen primary "supply points." In addition, the navy has two redistribution points which store the overflow and ship only to the primary points. The Marine Corps has two major supply centers, one on the east coast and the other on the west coast.

"Some of the operations, such as the determination of requirements, design, and issue to personnel must be conducted by each

[16] *Ibid.*, p. 37.

Service separately. But the recitation of diversities indicates the lack of unification." [17]

On June 30, 1954, the army inventory of operating stocks of apparel came to $464,300,000 and its reserve stocks came to $837,-362,000. This is in large measure due to the fact that there are "too many depots and tremendous quantities of depot stocks which far exceeded the operating levels set by the services." [18]

Thus in 1954 the operational stocks (mobilization reserves are in addition) of the army had 10.6 years' supply of women's uniforms, the navy 9.3 years' supply of jumpers, and the air force 5.3 years' supply of blue jackets.

There are a number of reasons for these very large stocks:

a) Upon the cessation of hostilities in Korea, all of the services found themselves committed to continue to procure large quantities of clothing in the face of reduced demands. They found it cheaper to accept and store these goods than to cancel outstanding contracts.

b) The air force bought its new blue uniforms on a troop strength and replacement rate that never were realized.

c) The army bought women's clothing based upon a strength of 30,000, although this never has exceeded 15,000.

d) At the very time that the services were trying to reduce their excess stocks, the program for mobilization reserves was being developed.

The Commission found that there is "a complete lack of concern at depots over apparent excess stocks. At one very large depot the issues had never been analyzed by the depot staff." [19]

The mobilization reserve, referred to earlier, is based on the assumption that general mobilization will bring millions of men into uniform in a short period and that normal stocks and production will be insufficient to provide uniforms during the early months. By computing what the needs will be and deducting all available stocks and production, the services arrive at the maximum shortage that will occur, and stock a reserve supply designed to meet this shortage.

As of June 30, 1950, the services had more than $1,500,000,000 in clothing and equipage stocks identified as mobilization reserve, and yet as late as September 1954 the joint chiefs of staff had not yet

[17] *Ibid.*
[18] *Food and Clothing in the Government,* p. 39.
[19] *Ibid.,* p. 40.

completed their plan for the number and type of unit to be deployed. Similarly, the Joint Logistics Plan Group was still "developing the plan's broad logistics implications." "Yet the services are holding and even procuring mobilization reserves without this very basic foundation for computations." [20]

The Commission found that "with a clothing inventory in the Department of Defense of nearly $2,700,000,000 a reduction of $1,350,000,000 is possible, with an annual saving of about $30 million in interest and another $3 million in warehousing, etc., or a total of $33 million in this one category alone." [21]

Once the basic strategic plan is stabilized, the Department of Defense, the Commission declared, can apply its very comprehensive formulas and instructions for the computation of quantities required in reserve. Experience to date indicates a need for "tightening up" the instructions to eliminate wide variations in "judgment factors." [22]

The procurement of clothing now takes too long. Under the present methods of organization, the time from the determination of requirements through all of the various stages to the final delivery is 400 days for the army, 510 days for the air force, 300 days for the navy, and 247 days for the Marine Corps. The Commission believed that the procurement cycle, which in some cases runs as long as seventeen months, could be cut to not more than seven months for all services.

Although procurement plans normally call for replacement orders every three months, there are cases where such orders were being placed only every nine, or even every twelve, months, with the result "that the well-established clothing manufacturers look to private retail outlets for 'steady customers' and leave Government business to the marginal operators." [23]

These larger but less frequent orders also have a serious influence on prices. Under the practice of rigidly adhering prices and quantities in sealed bids, contracts are awarded to many manufacturers at a considerable range in unit cost. "A typical procurement action for cut, make, and trim for 343,665 overcoats was awarded to 12 different contractors with prices ranging from $7.25 to $8.92 and in quantity from 6,000 to 50,000. This complicates contract administra-

[20] *Ibid.*, p. 41. [21] *Ibid.*, p. 42. [22] *Ibid.*
[23] *Food and Clothing in the Government*, p. 43.

tion and inspection in addition to increasing the average cost of the item." [24]

The policies regarding adequate stock levels are not uniform among the services. Although Department of Defense in 1952 ordered that stock levels shall be maintained at the lowest practicable level and be uniform between military departments where similar conditions exist, two years later it was still the policy of the air force to maintain 270 days of stock of clothing and of the navy 240 days' supply.

Costly as is this peacetime "pipeline," it is even more costly in time of full mobilization. "Assuming that both the Air Force and the Army have a peacetime demand for 100,000 trousers a month, the Army would maintain 350,000 in the 'pipeline,' and the Air Force 900,000. Assuming that full mobilization would triple the monthly demand, including initial issue, the Army would carry a stock of slightly over 1,000,000, while the Air Force would require almost 3,000,000." [25]

But the stock levels proposed by the services pursuant to the directives of the secretary of defense are not enforced. Actually, the Commission found that at one base many of the common items of clothing were ten times the average monthly issue even though the authorized stock level was three months. At another base, winter clothing was being maintained through summer at the peak winter issue rate.

Certainly the badly organized machinery for the procurement and supply of clothing for the Armed Forces is urgently in need of improvement. In order to have an efficient, economical, and practical operation of the military clothing system, the Commission held that the Congress's desire for unification must be implemented.

The Commission's recommendation relative to clothing procurement and supply in the Armed Forces paralleled its proposal concerning food. The secretary of defense should designate, it said, a central agency to procure all clothing for the Armed Forces on their statement of requirements. These purchases should be on a negotiated contract basis. The agency should supply all clothing, have charge of all clothing warehouses and inventories, and standardize as far as possible clothing and the allowances for clothing.

[24] *Ibid.*
[25] *Food and Clothing in the Government,* p. 46.

CONCLUSION

These proposals for improving the procurement and supply of food and clothing would result in large savings to the taxpayers—probably as much as $340,000,000 a year. The centralized supply agencies operating under the secretary would also increase civilian control over these business-type activities.

This inquiry into food and clothing raises several fundamental questions that any citizen will want to have answered.

1. Are the members of the Armed Forces getting the best possible subsistence? The answer is no. Clothing offers a better picture than food. The Commission found that the "preparation and service of food in all services are still below accepted commercial standards."

2. Is the taxpayer getting his money's worth? Obviously if savings of $340,000,000 are possible, the taxpayer is not getting his money's worth.

3. How long can the bureaucrat continue to ignore the will of Congress relative to unification? Congress in 1947 decreed that unification of the Armed Forces should be attained in the supply field; but after eight years little has been done. This is of fundamental importance in the event of another war. Thus the Commission pointed out:

> In the event of another war, in all likelihood there will not be time, as in previous wars, for corrective adjustment. It is essential, therefore, that the Armed Services establish a plan of organization and definition of powers during peacetime that will be effective in a period of emergency without the necessity of disruptive change. In the final analysis, the sinews of war are provided by the civilian economy, and this vital power must not be unduly handicapped.[26]

[26] *Ibid.*, p. 28.

CHAPTER 13

Transportation

In the fiscal year 1953 the Federal Government spent approximately $3,000,000,000 on the transportation of its own freight and employees, including their dependents. The overwhelming portion of this sum was spent by the Department of Defense. More than 18,300,000,000 passenger miles of transportation were generated by the armed services at a cost of $400,000,000. About 76,400,000 tons of freight were transported at a direct cost of more than $1,373,-000,000.

In addition, the armed services had 221 merchant ships in the Military Sea Transport Services, 676 commercial-type airplanes operated by four separate air services, a commercial steamship line with three vessels, and an ordinary railroad in the Panama Canal Zone.

NATURE OF THE PROBLEM

The Commission found a general lack of modern traffic management in the Federal Government. The absence of over-all plans and policies resulted in duplication, inefficiency, and waste. Government agencies did not make the fundamental distinction between traffic management and traffic operational functions.

The Government's traffic problems are much the same as those of a commercial firm with multiple-plant operations where the general traffic manager and the traffic-control office perform traffic-management functions and, at the same time, traffic directors at various plants perform the operational functions incidental to the day-to-day handling of traffic. These operating personnel are responsible to the general traffic manager, even though such individuals are carried on the payrolls and are under the disciplinary supervision of local plant management. Because the Federal Government has a variety of traffic movements, the Government's traffic problems do not differ from those of private industry.

Centralized traffic management in Government, as differentiated from traffic operations, may be defined as the central determination of policy governing the movement of persons and goods, the determination of over-all costs, making studies of Government traffic movements, representation of the Government in proceedings before regulatory agencies and carrier-rate bureaus, the development of improvements in service, and the review of handling procedures.

Traffic managers in commercial business cannot be effective if procurement decisions are made without considering the cost of transportation, and if the warehousing and distribution blueprint is not geared to the least transportation expense. The same principles are also applicable in Government.

Many examples can be cited of the consequences of an absence of traffic management in the Government. The Munitions Board in 1953 showed that a pack of canned salmon was sent from the west coast to Bremerhaven, Germany, via the east coast at almost twice the transportation cost that would have been applicable had the same movement gone from the west coast to Bremerhaven by all-water shipment. Sugar was being purchased at refineries in New York, shipped to the army depot at Schenectady, only to have much of it backhauled. One particular carload was wanted for redistribution at Fort Totten, New York City, so quickly that it was not even opened and unloaded at Schenectady.

An example of disregard of the cost of transportation was the purchase of antifreeze in Philadelphia by one of the military services because the price quoted there was a half-cent per unit less than that in Oakland, California. The antifreeze then was transported from Philadelphia to Oakland for overseas shipment, with resultant waste of Government funds.

In 1951 the army shipped 807,000 pounds of tomatoes from California to New York while during the same period the navy moved 775,000 pounds from the east coast to California. From the standpoint of the Department of Defense the net effect of this traffic movement was that the armed services shipped twenty carloads of tomatoes from Sacramento to San Francisco via New York.

It is not to be assumed that such examples are the result of negligence; but they do indicate that our existing system has not provided for an integration of inventory control, procurement, warehousing, and management direction of transportation so as to avoid wastage of transportation and storage dollars. Someone is paying the cost of such failure, and obviously that is the taxpayer.

Thus the major problem is to develop adequate traffic management techniques for the Government so as to eliminate unnecessary expenditures.

DEPARTMENT OF DEFENSE TRAFFIC

The armed services moved 26,700,000 tons of freight in this country at a cost of $641,000,000 in 1954. They had a staff of 5,701 and a payroll of $21,300,000 to supervise such shipments.

In 1953 the Department of Defense established the office of Assistant Secretary of Defense for Supply and Logistics for the management of the traffic of the military services. Under this assistant secretary is a director of transportation and communications. Because the army, navy, Marine Corps, and air force continue separately to control their own traffic the Commission considered this arrangement inadequate.

During the fiscal year 1954 the Department of Defense and its component services provided for the transportation, in round numbers, of 14,450,000 passengers. Of these, roughly 6,540,000 were transported by land, 3,800,000 by air, 2,040,000 by sea, and 2,070,000 under the mileage allowance.

The identified travel expenditure for the fiscal year 1954 was $719,465,000, but there were further expenditures for construction, maintenance, and operation of Government equipment which would double that sum, or make a total of about $1,500,000,000.

There are four methods of providing passenger transportation in the armed services:

1. Special travel orders for personnel and dependents overseas.
2. The Government authorizes domestic transportation for groups and individuals by means of ticket-like transportation requests (TR's). The TR's may cover one individual or a group. The transportation companies accept TR's in exchange for tickets and present them to appropriate Government finance centers for payment. The total number of passengers traveling on TR's in 1954 is estimated at 6,500,000, and the total expenditure under this method for the fiscal year 1954 is estimated at $126,824,000.

3. Movement of groups of fifteen or more are arranged and routed by the service agencies, usually on contracts with the carriers. It is estimated that $46,700,000 was paid to the carriers in the fiscal year 1954 for such service—about $5,500,000 less than would have been the cost of moving the same number of persons individually.

4. A system of allowances of six cents a mile, not to exceed the official distance required to be covered by the individual to reach his destination. Out of this mileage the individual pays for his transport, meals, and berths. The cost of this form of service for the fiscal year 1954 was estimated at $128,443,000 and applied to 2,069,000 Department of Defense passengers.

Objections to this last method include the following: (*a*) The increasing use of the mileage allowance by the military "has defeated passenger traffic management and pyramided transportation costs to a serious extent, with higher costs yet to come." (*b*) The "six-centers" may hitchhike on the highways and aircraft; they may form share-the-cost groups to travel by automobile; they may pinch on meals, sleep in terminals, and cadge on the public. The purpose is, of course, to make money out of the allowances. (*c*) It has created a diversion of traffic from commercial carriers.

At least 50 per cent of the passengers on military aircraft within the continental United States are hitchhikers. The Commission found a lack of careful check of hitchhikers to determine whether they had already received a six-cents-per-mile travel allowance. The navy is more strict than were terminal offices of Military Air Transport Service in controlling air travelers who had received the six-cents-per-mile allowance and sought free rides.

The military control of passenger transportation in theory is located in the Transportation Division in the Office of the Assistant Secretary of Defense for Supply and Logistics. The responsibilities of this division in practice include only about 40 per cent of the domestic travel. The "six-centers" and travelers in Government-owned aircraft or highway vehicles comprise about 60 per cent of the domestic travel. These, as well as practically all of the overseas movement, are excluded from its jurisdiction.

The Department of Defense reports that the number of personnel assigned to the control and administration of passenger-traffic activities was 1,173, and that their payroll amounted to $4,364,895 in 1954. But probably this is not a complete tabulation of all employees performing passenger-traffic functions, because every military installation and office will have someone, perhaps only part time, issuing TR's. There is no central authority in any military service or in the Department of Defense effectively managing passenger transportation, and this absence of management results in waste of passenger transportation resources and in a weakening of the Nation's commercial transportation system.

In the Armed Forces the free storage and transportation of household goods and the transportation of private automobiles are considered by many to be among the "fringe benefits" provided by Congress. It is estimated by the Commission that the storage facilities within the continental United States required for household goods amount to 3,500,000 square feet. Almost 1,700,000 different movements of household goods took place in a single year. This probably costs in excess of $250,000,000 annually.

While the movement of household goods is a necessary service to personnel, there are many opportunities for economy:

1. Much of the crating is unnecessarily elaborate, and higher grades of lumber are used than are necessary. Crates and boxes are often made of the finest materials.

2. There is inflation of homebound household goods from overseas.

3. It would be less costly for the Government to provide quarters with adequate basic household effects in overseas installations than the two-way hauls across the oceans to Europe and to Asia.

4. Excessive payments for household-goods movement arises from short-term rotation policies.

The Commission recommended that the secretary of defense explore the opportunities of reducing the cost of this service.

SHIPMENT OF AUTOMOBILES

In 1954 the Military Sea Transport Service moved 71,667 automobiles for the private use of Armed Forces personnel at a total cost of $27,000,000. These cars occupied 916,400 measurement tons of shipping space, which is equal to one-third the capacity of the total nucleus-fleet dry-cargo traffic between United States and foreign ports. This has increased 15 per cent since 1953 despite the end of hostilities in Korea.

This traffic is authorized by an Act of 1949 which allows private automobiles belonging to service personnel under permanent change-of-duty orders to be transported on Government-owned vessels. This law has been interpreted by the Department of Defense to mean that only Government vessels can be so used. Aside from any other questions, this law creates a serious problem of ship-operating requirements. Automobiles are low-density cargo—large space and low weight. If a large number of cars is loaded aboard a vessel, weight cargo must be placed in the lower hold of the ship to provide stability.

Because the volume of automobiles cannot be accommodated on a space-available basis, entire ships are devoted to this movement. The number of vessels in this lift is such that the commandant of the Military Sea Transport Service stated: "We feel that if the private vehicle lift continues on the same scale as it is now . . . we will require all of these dry cargo ships for the movement of private vehicles."

The Commission recommended that the use of automobiles for official duties in foreign countries should be handled through regulated automobile pools, provided by the Government where feasible, and that automobiles for personal use be rented from the pool at a reasonable rate. If a car is desired for personal use abroad by military or civilian personnel, the owner, it held, should pay for its transportation.

Neither the military nor the civilian shipping agencies of the Government are conducting proper audits of freight bills, the Commission found. It is not clear whether the pre-audit of freight bills is the proper solution. Several agencies now successfully perform pre-audit work, such as the Tennessee Valley Authority and the Atomic Energy Commission, but in these cases pre-auditing is a relatively simple matter because limited types of cargoes and generally similar routings are involved. In contrast, the Department of Defense ships millions of different items to all points of the world, and both the rate structures and the task of pre-auditing would be highly technical and complex.

Furthermore, some believe that this work would require a large staff of tariff experts spotted in at least the major shipping points. Qualified personnel in sufficient quantity are simply not available. In addition, increased delays in making payments might result. The necessary duplication of tariff files would be enormous. Consequently, the Commission urged the secretary of defense to make a study to determine whether the pre-audit of Defense transportation bills would be feasible and economical.

MILITARY SEA TRANSPORT SERVICE

The National Security Act of July 1947 directed the unification of the various military sea transport services. In October 1949 the unified Military Sea Transport Service was organized by the secretary of defense. Under his directive the sea transport activities of the army and navy were consolidated under the direction of the chief of naval operations with an initial fleet of 140 ships. The MSTS performs carriage and space-booking operations only. Its functions begin when cargoes are accepted on board and end when they are unloaded. Authorization of passenger and cargo movements is the responsibility of the shipper services.

The directive of October 1949 stated that the policy is "to use privately owned and operated maritime vessels to the maximum practicable extent consistent with military requirements and prudent management," and that there should be a nucleus fleet composed of ships of suitable types, sizes, and speeds to "(*a*) carry out current logistic needs of military departments which cannot be met by commercial interests; (*b*) be available immediately in an emergency; and (*c*) allow for necessary expansion to meet mobilization requirements. . . ."[1]

The Military Sea Transport Service's total income in 1954 was $617,000,000. More than half was obtained from dry cargo, $136,100,000 from passenger service, and $110,000,000 from petroleum products. Its acknowledged expenses were $549,000,000, but many normal items of cost were not included. Out of a total of 221 ships used, 46 were privately owned and operated, 19 were government owned but privately operated, and the remainder were government owned and operated.

The MSTS dry-cargo traffic between the United States and overseas areas primarily moves along trade routes of heavy commercial use, mainly across the Pacific to and from the Far East (54 per cent), and across the Atlantic to and from Europe (28 per cent).

[1] Commission on Organization of the Executive Branch of the Government, report on *Transportation* (1955), pp. 29–30.

About 8 per cent moves on other established but less important commercial sea lanes. The balance, less than 10 per cent, moves to or from areas not served by American ships normally. More than 85 per cent of all MSTS traffic is "general" or "special" category merchandise which is very similar to commercial commodities and could be carried in commercial ships. Thus there appears not to be much cargo that cannot be handled by private carriers.

Twenty regularly scheduled ship operators have offered MSTS the annual equivalent of 8,000,000 tons of outbound space, only about 50 per cent of which has been used by MSTS. The unused outbound space offered was the equivalent of one and one-half times the volume of export tonnage carried on the MSTS nucleus-fleet ships.

It has been contended that commercial operators lack experience in handling certain types of military cargo, but these operators, the Commission asserts, are sufficiently able and experienced in all commodities except possibly larger assembled aircraft.

The failure of the MSTS to place larger amounts of available cargo in the space thus offered to it, as well as the uncertainty of its advance space commitments to ship operators, add to the economic problems faced by the shipping industry.

Although general policy statements of the Department of Defense and the Memorandum of Agreement between the secretaries of defense and commerce agree that the MSTS should perform no services which private industry can render, that agency's "freighters are performing services which could be performed, and have been offered, by private carriers but have not been fully utilized by Military Sea Transport Service." [2]

While Congress is endeavoring to establish a merchant fleet which will serve our commerce and also constitute a reserve for the military services in war, the Department of Defense "is competing unnecessarily with this subsidized fleet and in the end endangering the congressional endeavor to build up our merchant marine." [3]

Accurate cost comparisons between the nucleus fleet of MSTS and the privately operated ships under the United States flag are impossible. The total cost of nucleus-fleet ships would be increased greatly if several important unrecorded items of cost were included. Examples of these unrecorded items of cost are: (1) military pay and

[2] *Ibid.*, p. 36. [3] *Ibid.*

allowances, (2) vessel depreciation, (3) interest, (4) Panama Canal tolls, (5) free use of numerous Government facilities, and (6) insurance. The General Accounting Office has estimated that the first four of these would have added $100,000,000 to the $700,000,000 in MSTS operating expenses recorded in 1953.

The Commission found that there is no evidence that Government operation is more economical than private operation if all elements of cost are considered. It urged that MSTS include all items of cost in its accounts.

There is another element which would tend to reduce costs to the Government if it made larger use of privately owned shipping. Approximately 50 per cent of space on private ships used by MSTS in liner services is subsidized. Under the subsidy arrangements all profits in excess of 10 per cent on the "capital necessarily employed" by each company are shared equally by the company and the Government over the ten-year life of the contract. If such traffic should be increased, profits would increase. The amount of money that might thus be returned to Government through the greater use of subsidized vessels is difficult to estimate, "but the General Accounting Office notes that this is an important element to consider in comparing actual costs to the Treasury of Government versus private operation." [4]

In addition, Federal tax returns would increase when private ships are used in place of Government-owned vessels. Thus a larger use of private shipping lines under the United States flag would be advantageous. The Commission urged that Government-owned ships should not be operated when private facilities can render adequate service at reasonable rates, except for clearly established military security reasons, and that the shipping agencies and the MSTS should apportion more cargo to private carriers and reduce the amount of arbitrarily labeled "nonsusceptible" freight.

In the tanker field 16,200,000 tons of petroleum products were carried by the MSTS in 1954, 11,900,000 in Government-owned ships, and only 4,300,000 in privately owned vessels. If all costs such as the pay of military personnel, capital expenditures, interest, insurance, and other items were included in the MSTS costs, the Government operation costs of tankers would be considerably higher than the recorded figures.

[4] *Transportation*, p. 38.

Because the maintenance of a private tanker fleet is essential to defense, the Commission felt that greater use should be made of such ships. Their use "will prove more economical to the taxpayer, on the basis of current evidence, it said, particularly if all direct and indirect costs to Government are considered."[5]

The readiness of the navy to meet its basic long-term requirements with long-term commitments to private industry "should be encouraged as leading to tanker construction and enabling industry to improve and enlarge its facilities so as better to serve the military."[6] By encouraging the use of private tanker services to major destinations in time of peace, the Government will not only save in the cost of freight, but will build up its reserve tanker fleet for time of war.

The Commission concluded that "there cannot be two American merchant marines, one military and one civilian, operating independently and at times in competition with each other. Cooperation from the secretaries of defense and commerce, assisted by American ship operators and the Congress, is needed, it felt, to end this situation.

"The removal of certain vessels from the nucleus fleet, and their placement in ready-reserve status at Navy sites, will not seriously restrict their availability for emergency use."[7]

AIR TRANSPORT OF FREIGHT AND PASSENGERS

In 1954 the air services of the Department of Defense carried about 8,000,000 passengers. Of this number, approximately 4,800,000 should be classified as hitchhikers, or on "leave status."

The Department of Defense operates what amounts at least to three airlines:

1. The Military Air Transport Service (MATS) resulted from a merger on June 1, 1948, of the air force's Air Transport Command and the Naval Air Transport Service under the command of the air force chief of staff. It operates both in the domestic and in the international fields.

2. The primary mission of the Fleet Logistic Air Wings (FLOGWINGS) is the logistic support of navy fleets wherever and whenever called, with a secondary mission to provide auxiliary transport airlift to MATS when the latter is temporarily unable to meet prescribed lift requirements.

[5] *Ibid.*, p. 42. [6] *Ibid.* [7] *Transportation*, p. 46.

3. The primary mission of the Air Materiel Command (LOGAIR) is to procure and distribute aircraft and aircraft supplies for the air arm of the military services.

The purpose of MATS is to provide world-wide service under a single authority for the transportation of Government personnel and cargo. Its duties include maintaining certain types of airbases, ferrying aircraft, and providing technical services in the fields of communication, weather, air rescue, and aeronautical chart making. These technical services partly duplicate those of other branches of the Government.

In 1954 MATS had 103,268 employees, and their cost was $481,000,000. Because of the nature of MATS operations, there are necessarily many instances of planes loaded on the out journey and empty on the return flight. "Military Air Transport Service is aware of the inherent inefficiencies resulting from 'deadheading' its aircraft," the Commission declared, "and hopes to improve this situation by the relocation of bases now in process." [8]

Owing to the availability of planes this service has been used for moving cargo of a type which would be unthinkable in commercial operations and impracticable in wartime. For example, during July 1954 about 13,000 pounds of furniture was flown from Bermuda to the United States, and in September of that year 25,000 pounds of cement was flown to Bermuda.

An air-force band was flown about once a month from Westover, Massachusetts, to Bermuda, so that large open-air dances and concerts could be held as morale boosters. If this is necessary, the Commission said, "one of the two United States certificated airlines serving Bermuda with a number of daily flights could have readily accommodated the band in its regular scheduled pattern at a less cost to the Government." [9]

These air services, especially MATS, offer competition with the privately operated airlines. Almost 10,000,000 ton-miles of cargo and mail moved between the continental United States and world-wide destinations during July 1954 on MATS planes. Of this amount, 56.8 per cent was flown to terminal cities more than 6,000 miles distant, and 28.5 per cent to cities between 2,001 and 4,000 miles distant. The military mail tonnage moved by MATS in the fiscal year 1954 was outbound 9,856 tons and inbound 9,230 tons.

[8] *Ibid.*, p. 52.

[9] *Ibid.*, pp. 52–53.

The Commission found that in World War II and in the Korean War the commercial air carriers performed a dual service. In one role they, like the railways and industrial enterprises, were utilized to support the war economy. In the other role they served with the military transports to support strategic operations. About one-half of the commercial air transport was requisitioned during World War II.

To build a military air transport service capable of meeting all air transport needs in wartime would involve an enormous expenditure. The capital costs of new transport aircraft are about the same for military or civil use. Although the operating costs of MATS are reported as lower than those of private airline operating costs, these costs do not include depreciation, crew salaries, interest on Government funds used to purchase the aircraft, taxes, and other cost items of private operators.

Moreover, the great economy of the civil air fleet and their trained personnel lies in productive peacetime use while serving as an immediately available reserve for emergencies.

Related to this question of military carriage of passengers and freight are the subsidies paid by the Federal Government in part to maintain an adequate civilian reserve of aircraft. While United States domestic trunk airlines are now mostly free from mail subsidy, this is not yet true of the United States international air carriers. The subsidy to the United States international airline operations was designed to permit them to attain, among other things, "such stature in passenger and cargo capacity as to constitute in crisis an adequate logistical air arm of the National Defense Establishment." [10]

These carriers receive mail pay as provided by the Civil Aeronautics Act of 1938 whether or not full loads of mail are carried. When these military passengers or freight are not carried by the commercial airlines but are carried by military planes, the Government in effect pays the bill twice.

"To reduce the overall subsidy to the commercial international airlines, these airlines should be filled to their capacity with military traffic instead of being paid to haul 'imaginary' sacks of mail. Such action was recommended by the President's Air Coordinating Committee in May 1954." [11]

[10] *Ibid.*, p. 57.

[11] *Ibid.*

Should the United States international airlines obtain 25 per cent of the passenger volume and 50 per cent of the military mail moved by Military Air Transport Service in the fiscal year 1954, the Commission found that the subsidy to the international commercial carriers would have been reduced by $42,900,000, or almost 88 per cent. In addition, if MATS curtailed its operations proportionally the Government would have saved additional actual out-of-pocket expenditures. While the Commission's study was under way, the Department of Defense decided to take some steps to this end which it is estimated will result in an increase of about $18,000,000 in revenues for the international airlines, with a corresponding reduction in subsidy payments.

The Commission recommended that the various air transport services in the armed services be merged into the Military Air Transport Service and that its competition with the privately owned air carriers be curtailed.

GENERAL CONCLUSIONS

The Commission found that the organization of the Defense transportation function needs a "new look" in the form of strengthened central direction because of:

a) A lack of recognition of the key importance of transportation;

b) The failure to coordinate warehousing and procurement with transportation within and between the services;

c) The present organization plan which subordinates transportation;

d) The lack of review and improvement of operating performance;

e) Wide and unsupervised diffusion of technical functions;

f) The existence of too complete subservience to military control;

g) Supervision by inadequately trained officials;

h) The lack of adequate statistical and management control data;

i) The absence of adequate salaries for traffic management personnel.

For the fiscal year 1954, the cost of the staff engaged in traffic management represented for the army 2.2 per cent, for the navy, 6.6 per cent, for the air force 3.9 per cent, and for the Marine Corps 4.6 per cent of the amount paid for transportation. The number of personnel engaged in handling traffic management for the military services is excessive. Their salary is approximately $20,000,000 a year. If operating costs such as rent, travel, communications, and equipment were added, the total cost might well be doubled.

Much of this unnecessary expense, the Commission found, results from duplication of facilities and services. In some localities two or more of the military services operate field traffic offices; in some places such offices are maintained by all four services. "Not only are these duplicated efforts wasteful but they inevitably produce conflicts in policies and practices which confuse carriers and tend to lower the quality of transportation service furnished." [12]

The lack of coordination between the various services in their traffic and procurement activities is productive of expensive cross-hauling.

To remedy these defects the Commission recommended that the secretary of defense establish a director of transportation having no responsibilities other than traffic and transportation. This official should have authority to direct traffic-management activities, passenger and freight, in all the military services, including the coordination and consolidation of functions and facilities, to the extent that his office determines it to be necessary and practicable. He should be subject only to the authority of the assistant secretary of defense for supply and logistics.

The Commission declared that there is an excessive number of employees performing traffic-management functions. Contributing factors are: (*a*) the low quality of the personnel, (*b*) inadequate salaries, (*c*) present rotational policies, with respect to military officers, that adversely affect traffic management within the Department of Defense, (*d*) lack of recruiting of skilled civilians and lack of training.

The quality of personnel and inadequacy of pay, the Commission said, are partly due to classification standards set up by the Civil Service Commission.

Athough the Government can train personnel in the lower grades, it must, to have competent service, recruit top traffic-management personnel largely from commerce and industry. The Commission found that "this is difficult and frequently impossible, since the rates of pay for the same type of work in commerce and industry are so

[12] *Transportation,* p. 62.

much higher than permitted under Civil Service classification standards."[13]

The Task Force suggested that an increase in expenditures to obtain men of great qualifications at higher salaries would result in a reduction in the present number of traffic-management personnel as well as other economies.

The Commission urged the revision of classification standards for persons engaged in traffic management so that such personnel can be paid salaries comparable to those paid by private industry.

ACTIVITIES IN THE CANAL ZONE

When the Federal Government in 1904 acquired the assets of the French Panama Canal Company, it got a majority of the stock of the Panama Railroad Company which operated a rail line across the Isthmus of Panama and a steamship line between New York and Cristobal. In 1949 Congress created the Panama Canal Company as a Federal corporation to operate the canal, the Panama Steamship Line, and the Panama Railroad. The Governor of the Canal Zone is president of the company and reports to the secretary of the army. The Panama Canal Company is required by law to recover all its cost of operation, maintenance, depreciation, pay interest to the Treasury on the net Federal investment in its facilities, and reimburse to the Treasury the annuity payments to the Panama Government, together with all costs of the Canal Zone Government.

The Panama Steamship Line now owns and operates three 10,000-ton cargo passenger ships built in 1939 and runs a weekly service from New York to Cristobal via Port-au-Prince in Haiti. The employees number 477 persons. The cost of maintenance and repair of its vessels has averaged $285,000 a year over the past five years. The total number of passengers carried by the steamship line averaged about 12,400 annually during the past five years; but the passengers paying the full tariff have increased from 3,544 in the fiscal year 1950 to 6,866 in the fiscal year 1954. Other passengers have decreased from 9,422 in the fiscal year 1950 to 5,895 in 1954.

The Government in at least two ways offers competition to this service. Also during 1954, the air force and the navy conducted two hundred air flights between the United States and the Zone, carrying 4,966 passengers southbound and 6,904 northbound. This service

[13] *Ibid.*, p. 67.

also competes with the available commercial air services and private shipping.

The Government also competes with the Panama Steamship Line through the Military Sea Transport Service. In 1954 MSTS carried 45,883 tons of freight southbound from United States east coast ports to the Zone, as well as 33,632 tons northbound. In the same year MSTS carried 3,035 passengers and 5,545 troops southbound, and 3,746 passengers and 3,766 troops northbound.

The Commission believes that the Panama Steamship Line should be used by all Government agencies as the principal carrier between the United States and the Canal Zone.

The Panama Railroad has been operating for a full century. It is basically a single-track road, 47 miles in length, with 8 Diesel and 3 steam locomotives, 46 units of passenger equipment, and 578 freight cars. In 1954 it employed 463 persons. The freight tonnage handled by the railroad has steadily declined from 1,781,434 tons in 1943 to a low of 186,576 tons in 1954. The number of first-class passengers declined from 554,008 in 1943 to 146,000 in the fiscal year 1954. The carriage of second-class passengers shows a similar reduction. The Trans-Isthmus Highway was completed in 1943 at a cost of more than $9,000,000 and is accountable for much of this decline as well as the losses of the road.

The General Accounting Office, in its audit report for the year ended June 30, 1953, says, in part:

> The railroad reported a net operating income of $124,046 for 1953, before general corporate charges compared with a net operating income of $69,179 for 1952 before similar charges. After distributing general and administrative expenses, the railroad sustained a net loss for both years, although the presentation of the "Budget of the United States, 1955," by transferring the railroad's 1953 net loss to other activities, shows a break-even operation. From the standpoint of sound accounting and financial reporting, there is no justification for this action.
>
> We mentioned in our 1952 report that the military agencies were objecting to the Company's idea of closing down the railroad. Recently the Army declared that the railroad is a convenience but is not now required for defense purposes.[14]

Late in 1954 the Department of the Army stated that militarily the railroad has no significant defense value and could be discontinued.

[14] *Ibid.*, p. 79.

CONCLUSIONS

In addition to offering the possibility of annual savings to the taxpayer of about $151,500,000, this report of the Commission poses a number of important issues of public policy. Among these issues are:

First: Why has the Government-owned transportation system been permitted to compete with private industry, if it is the policy both of the Congress and of the Department of Defense to develop a strong, privately owned transportation system?

Second: In attempts to justify this duplication economically, should not Government-owned transportation systems record all their costs, when privately owned systems have to show full costs and then receive subsidies?

Third: Is not strengthening the administration of the program for moving military personnel preferable to tempting young men and women to "chisel" through lax supervisory practices?

Fourth: In view of the continued difficulty in recruiting and retaining military personnel, should Congress not reexamine "fringe benefits" in transportation? These do not strengthen the nation's military defense but do raise costs.

Fifth: When and how can the principle of unification in the Department of Defense's transportation system be translated into practice?

CHAPTER 14

Depot Utilization

The total storage space owned by the Federal Government would cover two Manhattan Islands with some to spare. It includes 696,000,000 square feet of covered storage and 668,000,000 square feet of improved open space. This is the equivalent of 31,000 acres. Each year the maintenance and operation of these facilities cost the Government approximately $3,500,000,000, or almost as much as it cost to run the entire Federal Government in 1930.

The Armed Forces own 83 per cent of all permanent Government-owned covered storage space and 94 per cent of the open space. The cost of operating their facilities is about $2,900,000,000 a year, or almost 85 per cent of all money spent by the Government on storage facilities.

Here, as in so many other situations, the problem before the Hoover Commission and also before its Task Force on Depot Utilization was to find through exhaustive investigation, conducted by experienced men, the most efficient and economical means of operating such of these facilities as are needed. Clearly, such an investigation had to indicate the weaknesses from which inefficiencies and waste arise. At the same time every effort had to be made to commend constructive, corrective action already taken. The Commission emphasized:

> It may be said at the outset that the deficiencies in Federal warehouse management are not the fault of individuals. They are the result of systems outmoded by the enormous growth of the Federal establishment, the failure of legislation to keep pace with needs, and the inherited traditions of certain agencies.[1]

[1] Commission on Organization of the Executive Branch of the Government, *Depot Utilization,* A Report to the Congress, May 1955 (Washington, D.C., U.S. Government Printing Office, 1955), p. ix.

DEPARTMENT OF DEFENSE

On the whole the armed services have done a relatively good job of managing their depots and warehouses. The major fault is that too often the housekeeping has been "excessively" good—more thorough than necessary and without regard to cost. Modern methods and equipment for handling material are in general use. The deficiencies of administration resulted from faulty and mostly outmoded management systems as well as obsolete legislation. According to the Commission, "There is, in consequence, great excess of storage space, duplication and consequent waste in the Department of Defense." [2]

Sad to say, the Armed Forces do not know how much storage space they have available. The Task Force on Depot Utilization found more than 100,000,000 square feet of storage space not listed in any of the departments' operating records. For example, it discovered that the Marine Corps had at least 2,000,000 square feet unlisted out of a total of 16,340,000 square feet. A large storage facility of the army, Cameron Station at Alexandria, Virginia, was not listed in tabulations of such space because it is called a station and not a depot.

About 170,000,000 square feet of the Armed Forces' storage space is not needed, the Commission found, and could be eliminated. This is well over 10 per cent of the total storage facilities owned by the Government. Although this sizable amount is unnecessary, the services are still constructing additional storage facilities. For example, the navy, which has more than 10,000,000 square feet of unoccupied space, is spending large sums on additions. In 1955 it made an outlay of $2,100,000 for the construction of 240,000 square feet of warehouse space at Port Hueneme, California, and for 1956 it requested another $2,259,000 to construct 347,300 square feet more.

Each of the three military services—the army, navy, and air force—owns and operates its own independent storage system. This unrealistic attitude, that each service should own its own facilities, is so firmly established that only in a few exceptional cases has excess storage space in one service's depots been made available to meet the needs of another service. Actually, there are sixteen different logistics systems in the Department of Defense, each with its own

[2] *Ibid.*, p. 3.

storage system. With each of these supply systems operating separately, effective control over location, construction, and efficient use of a depot system is impossible.

There is no way of obtaining complete utilization of depots in any area. A good example of this chaotic condition is to be found in the vicinity of Ogden, Utah. Here, situated within a few miles of each other, are four depots belonging to three services: the Utah Army General Depot, the Clearfield Navy Supply Depot, the Hill Air Force Base, and the Ogden Arsenal. Each is completely independent of the others, and each was constructed with apparent disregard for any possibility of interchange in the use of their space. Although the expanding air force is in dire need of more room for storage, the army and navy have surplus space which could be used advantageously by the Hill Air Force Base. Under a properly administered system, the Commission said, space would be made available and the air force would be required to use it. Nevertheless, this is not being done.

A similar situation exists in the area around Harrisburg, Pennsylvania.

Utilization of dehumidified warehouses, especially desirable for storing machine tools, constitutes another example of existing chaos. The navy has more than 8,000,000 square feet of such space, and at Spokane, Washington, it has 400,000 square feet that it considers to be excess and has offered to the army for the storage of machine tools. Several months after this offer was made the army had done nothing about accepting it.

The Commission considered it to be uneconomical to use more than 4,000,000 square feet of space for the storage of the household goods of military personnel. Under existing interpretation of laws, commercial storage facilities can only be used for the storage of such effects for periods up to six months. Space owned by the military services, on the other hand, can be used for nontemporary storage, that is, for periods in excess of six months, wherever such space is available.

To utilize available space, household goods of military personnel formerly stationed in the Washington, D.C., area, are being shipped to such distant points as Boston, Savannah, and even to San Antonio, Texas. This is done despite the availability of much usable space at Cameron Station at nearby Alexandria, Virginia. Obviously, this procedure often results in transportation costs in excess of the value of the goods being stored, since a large percentage of this furniture eventually is returned to the Washington area.

Movements over such long distances would not be necessary if there were proper cooperation and cross-servicing in the use of available space, or if commercial facilities could be used.

The cost of operating storage facilities in the Department of Defense is high by commercial standards. Because, according to the Commission, "cost is the acid test of efficiency in industry," [3] the cost of storing and handling materials should be reported on a uniform basis that would permit accurate interdepot comparison. This would also make possible comparisons with the cost of similar services in private industry.

The secretary of defense in the last few years has striven to integrate and coordinate the depot systems of the services. So far, satisfactory progress has been attained only in issuing the necessary directives and instructions; their implementation has been lagging at the levels below the bureaus and the technical services of the three military departments. This is because there are no regular procedures and staff to check on their implementation in the field, and it is in the field that the success of such programs will be determined.

For the development of an integrated depot and supply system there must be standardization of methods, record keeping, cost accounting, terminology, procedures, and reporting for the purpose of simplifying operations and facilitating controls. According to the Task Force, "The record shows that these objectives were prescribed and directives issued several years ago without material progress resulting." [4]

There are two ways in which the depot system of the armed services could be reorganized: through unification or by a system of cross-servicing. The first of these methods could be effected through the complete unification or integration of all of the supply systems for common-use articles. This would bring food, clothing, transportation, warehousing, and other services under a single adminis-

[3] *Ibid.*, p. 4.

[4] Commission on Organization of the Executive Branch of the Government, *Subcommittee Report on Depot Utilization in the United States Government,* June 1955 (Washington, D.C., U.S. Government Printing Office, 1955), p. 33.

trator handling all of these functions for the three services. The second method is cross-servicing. This would give one department the task of supplying specific designated needs of all of the military departments. For example, the army quartermaster general buys all perishable food for the three services.

There can be no doubt that Congress intended an integrated supply system for all of the armed services. Even if this integration is impossible, considerable improvement could be attained, the Commission felt, through cross-servicing of space requirements. One way to accomplish this would be to give area assignments for storage functions to one service, requiring it to fill the needs of the three in that specific area. Such a proposal would not involve the transfer of facilities from one service to another.

USE OF COMMERCIAL SPACE

Frequently the cost of building new storage facilities or of transporting goods to warehouses at distant points can be avoided through use of commercial storage space. Even now the Government is the largest user of privately owned storage facilities. The Department of Agriculture alone is paying an annual bill of $280,000,000 for such space. The army quartermaster general stores 80 per cent of its perishable food inventories in commercial cold-storage warehouses, and the armed services have another 7,000 carloads of supplies in such facilities. The General Services Administration spends at least $3,300,000 a year on rent for space to store the strategic stockpile.

During both World War I and World War II the use of commercial storage facilities was demonstrated to be essential for the military services. In World War II the Federal Emergency Warehousing Plan proved its worth. Under it, contracts were made for the use of warehouses in forty-one areas throughout the country. Since then the plan has been formalized as a Commercial Warehouse Service Plan operated by the Department of Defense through twelve field offices. The Commission found that "the plan has been demonstrated by experience to be the most practicable, economical, and flexible way of providing private storage services for the Department of Defense agencies." [5]

[5] *Depot Utilization,* A Report to the Congress, p. 10.

STRATEGIC STOCKPILE STORAGE

The Office of Defense Mobilization develops policies governing the storage, security, and maintenance of stockpiles of strategic commodities, while the General Services Administration manages their procurement and storage in conformity with such directives. Almost 19,000,000 square feet of covered space is used for such storage, 10,500,000 of which is supplied by the Department of Defense and 8,400,000 by the General Services Administration. In addition, 28,300,000 square feet of open space is used. Probably an additional 3,500,000 square feet of storage space will be required to meet expanding stockpile requirements.

The cost of storing and handling these materials comes to about $19,000,000 a year. The safeguarding of these stockpiles is most important because they contain approximately $6,000,000,000 of strategic materials that would be sorely needed in the event of war.

It is highly regrettable that no Government agency has an adequate inventory of the material in these stockpiles.

CONCLUSIONS

To correct the defects in the depot systems of the Armed Forces, the Task Force and the Commission joined in recommending that the secretary of defense establish positive control over the location, construction, assignment, and utilization of all armed service storage facilities. To do so, this official, together with the secretaries of the armed services, should maintain a current inventory of all storage space under their respective jurisdictions. His office should also review all proposals for the construction of new storage facilities. In that office there should be established a skilled staff to inspect storage installations to determine if the directives of the department are complied with.

Further, the Commission held that the secretary of defense should establish an economically justified policy for the use of commercial storage services so that the requirements for storing perishables and household goods can be met as far as possible through the use of commercial facilities. Close liaison should be developed, the Commission felt, between the assistant secretaries of defense for supply and logistics and for property and installations as well as with the comparable officers in the respective armed services. Congress, it added, should amend the law to permit the storage in commercial warehouses of household goods of armed service personnel for periods of more than six months.

The Task Force estimated that savings of $253,000,000 annually could be attained through the improved management of depot facilities of the Government. The proposals for their improvement that have been summarized in this chapter also would help to restore civilian control over the Armed Forces and congressional control over the purse.

CHAPTER 15

Research and Development

The Federal Government is spending at least $2,400,000,000 a year on research and development programs. The Defense agencies account for about $2,050,000,000 of this, leaving only $350,000,000 for the civilian departments. These programs are carried on by twenty-nine different agencies employing 124,000 civilian or uniformed workers.

In addition, private industry and nonprofit institutions, such as foundations and universities, expend more than $2,000,000,000 a year of their own funds for research in addition to money received from the Government to do research work on a contract basis.

NATURE OF THE PROBLEM

The American Government's program for research and development is, so far as known, the largest integrated scientific and technical endeavor that any nation has ever organized. The projects involved extend through the realms of abstract science, the evolution of scientific discovery, into the areas of practical inventions, technical improvements, and the development of weapons. In the military agencies the perfection of inventions and the improvement in weapons extend into the testing of these improvements, the standardization of design, and the development of production programs and methods. Finally, production must continually be accompanied by further research, and the utility of both weapons and equipment must be continually reevaluated.

The administrative organization of all Government research and development activities requires constant realignment to meet the problems presented by new discoveries in basic science and invention.

Basic research into nature's laws and materials is the very foundation on which scientific advancement is founded. These studies develop the raw material of applied science. "We owe to basic research the fabulous improvement in the health of the Nation," the Commission declared, "the greatest industrial productivity known to man; the weapons of defense which have protected our independence; and our knowledge of the laws which govern the Universe."[1]

The objective of the Hoover Commission's inquiry in the field of research and development was to seek improvements in organization and administration made necessary by the ever changing nature of the program. In the words of the Commission:

> Comments on secondary weaknesses in organization are not intended to disparage this enormous accomplishment but constructively to improve its management, whose major conduct has the approbation of this Commission.[2]

The investigation was limited to the examination of the management, organization, personnel, and the major programmatic areas. The subject matter of the research programs was not surveyed.

DEFENSE PROGRAMS

With expenditures in the fiscal year of 1956 for research and development for the Defense agencies in the neighborhood of $2,050,000,000, they will be seventy times as large as they were fifteen years ago. They were $29,000,000 in 1940. Such rapid growth has caused difficult problems of integrating military and civilian skills, and as a result the task of devising an adequate organizational structure has been far from simple. In 1954, 120 installations of the Armed Forces were engaged in research, on more than 8,200 separate projects, employing 39,000 military and 63,000 civilian personnel. About 40 per cent of the funds appropriated were spent directly by the military departments, 50 per cent were used for contracts with private industry, and 10 per cent were expended through agreements with academic and nonprofit institutions.

Practically all areas of physical and natural science, including chemistry, biology, mathematics, and physics, are represented in the

[1] Commission on Organization of the Executive Branch of the Government, *Research and Development*, A Report to the Congress, May 1955 (Washington, D.C., U.S. Government Printing Office, 1955), p. xii.
[2] *Ibid.*

basic and applied research programs. Aeronautical, chemical, electrical, electronic, mechanical, and metallurgical technologies all contribute to the development programs. Many of them are important components of every weapons-development project.

Although the high quality of the weapons systems that have resulted from these research programs indicates the outstanding nature of their attainments, nevertheless in some areas the Commission found that improvements can be attained and economies can be realized.

DEPARTMENT OF DEFENSE

As a part of the reorganizations of the Department of Defense the Research and Development Board was abolished in 1953, and in its stead two new assistant secretaries were installed, one to deal with research and development problems and the other with questions relative to applications engineering. Besides, there is a special assistant to the secretary handling the coordination of the atomic weapons program. These three high officials perform staff functions in their respective areas.

By their nature the research and development and the applications engineering programs in the Defense Department are inseparably interrelated. The recent integration of the staffs of these two assistant secretaries has improved operations. In the past two and a half years this has brought about reductions in personnel, but the separation of these two functions at the assistant-secretary level the Commission felt to be an unsound form of organization. Because the two areas should be administered, it said, by one assistant secretary, the Task Force and the Commission both urge their consolidation.

A step in the right direction, the Commission believed, was the establishment of a research and development policy council consisting of the assistant secretary covering research and development as well as the senior civilian and military officers dealing with research in the three armed services. This can become a major instrument for unification and coordination in research.

The Commission found that "a healthy evolution toward leadership, coordination, and integration of the programs of the three Departments is in progress." [3] At present, most of the research and development work is carried on by the three military departments.

[3] *Research and Development,* p. 8.

It is more desirable, it declared, to continue this arrangement with adequate measures for coordination than it would be to develop a unified, integrated research service.

But existing duplication of the research and development programs of the army, navy, and air force gives some cause for concern because it is wasteful and excessively expensive. Even now the secretary of defense has authority to correct this situation. The existing overlap is primarily a consequence of the emphasis on self-sufficiency of the three services. Nevertheless, some duplication is warranted, especially in areas such as weaponry where multiple approaches through parallel developments are essential.

Although progress is being made in the elimination of unwarranted duplication, the Commission believed that much still remains to be done. The situation could be greatly improved, it felt, if the secretary would utilize his authority to withhold or release appropriated funds from research and development programs so as to promote their integration and to prevent unwarranted duplication. In addition, the Office of the Assistant Secretary for Research and Development could do much to improve the situation.

In the development of weapons programs the Commission believed that the armed services have not been daring and imaginative enough, especially in producing new weapons and new weapons systems. The Research and Development Board, which was abolished in 1953, was responsible for most of the progress that was made in this field during World War II. Since then, the Commission found, most of the advances have resulted from informal proddings by civilian scientists and technologists.

The three military services have not distinguished themselves in the initiation of new approaches to weapons systems. Present procedures are inadequate for that purpose. The Commission believed that "it is desirable that the Department of Defense encompass this responsibility. Its present organization does not provide an adequate framework for such initiation."[4]

The Commission recommended that the assistant secretary of defense for research and development appoint a standing committee of outstanding scientists to canvass periodically the need for and opportunities presented by new scientific knowledge for the development of radically new weapons systems.

[4] *Ibid.*, p. 10.

In 1949 the joint chiefs of staff developed an organization of scientists to carry on weapons-systems evaluation. Because of the great value of the work of this group, it should be expanded, the Commission said, and strengthened at the level of the joint chiefs of staff. But to accomplish this, it is necessary to develop an environment that will encourage such work. This can best be created by placing weapons-systems evaluation in a position where it will be free from direct military control. Consequently, the Commission recommended that the weapons-systems evaluation group be handled as a contract operation by some university or nonprofit organization. After this has been done, this work should be expanded.

AT THE LEVEL OF THE SEPARATE ARMED FORCES

The Commission found the top-level civilian organization for research in the army, navy, and air force inadequate in numbers and training. The supervisory personnel largely has not been adequately trained in science. Great rewards to the public will follow, it felt, from the correction of shortcomings. In each of the armed services there should be an assistant secretary for research and development, it added, restricted in his area of operations to the research and development organizations in the specific department. This assistant secretary should be trained in science and technology.

Only through basic research, it stressed, can this country develop a long-range scientific and technical basis for new weapons systems. Basic research in the three military departments in 1954 received only $20,000,000, less than 1 per cent of their outlay for research. The Commission considered this amount inadequate, and it strongly recommended that expenditures for basic research be increased.

The amount of research done directly by the armed services has been on the rise. Of the $1,400,000,000 of appropriated funds used for research by them in 1954, roughly 40 per cent, or $560,000,000, was expended directly by the services on projects that they operated themselves, 50 per cent was spent through contracts with industry, and 10 per cent through agreements with academic or nonprofit scientific institutions. The Commission believed that this type of work can be performed best by civilian agencies, and therefore considered it regrettable that since the close of World War II the military departments have greatly expanded their facilities and personnel in this field.

"The operations performed there," it reported, "are generally at a lower level of effectiveness than could be realized if suitably placed in the civilian economy." [5]

The Commission recommended that these activities be performed at that place in the Nation where they can be done most effectively and with the greatest efficiency, that is, by private industry or non-profit foundations. It is estimated that $125,000,000 of the work now being done by the services could be shifted advantageously to civilian agencies.

The traditional organizations for research and development in the army or navy are not well suited, the Commission found, to the requirements of modern weaponry development. In these services it is distributed among many bureaus. A single integrated program is required in the promotion of weapons systems. "A single element of the system cannot be developed independent of the others," the Commission declared. "The 'system's' requirements and those of each of its elements must be jointly established and a continuing 'give and take' between the elements, their character and requirements must be made throughout the course of the development." [6]

Research in the army and in the navy is distributed among seven separate bureaus or corps in each service, while in the air force it is concentrated in a single command. Although the army has done something to integrate and coordinate its research activities, much remains to be done to develop an effective program. The Commission believed that there must be an adequate staff composed of competent personnel to integrate this work at the level of the secretary of the army.

Until recently the navy had no formal staff organization for coordinating and integrating the research programs of the seven separate bureaus. Here too the Commission asserted that some form of supervision at the secretary's level is required.

In comparison with the other two services, the air force has well integrated its research and development activities into the departmental structure. A separate command for this work was organized in 1950. All research operations throughout the department are a responsibility of this one command. The Commission found that

[5] *Ibid.*, p. 16.

[6] *Ibid.*, p. 17.

"this organization, of recent origin, is in a framework well suited to the needs of modern weaponry research and development." [7]

PERSONNEL

There are some 39,000 military personnel engaged in research and development activities. These uniformed personnel, especially at the officer level, are generally men of high personal qualities. Many of them have the professional training and equipment to fill these posts; but there is not a sufficient number of young officers now being trained, the Commission asserted, to provide for the increasing demands in the technical services.

Further, the Commission found that the armed services are not making adequate use of their existing uniformed personnel, largely because of rotation and assignment policies. The constant rotation of officers between research and development work on the one hand and operational assignments on the other ignores the urgent need for a high degree of specialization. On this basis, the Commission felt that it is impossible to develop officers expert in research and development fields. The officers with competence for such work must have the opportunity to pursue careers in this area, it added, and they should be excluded from the normal military cycle of rotations from research tasks to field assignments.

The Commission recommended that military officers assigned in the field of research should serve for longer periods and that they should receive the same preferment and promotions as if they were rotated on regular short-term service assignments.

The quality of the civilian personnel of the services suffers because of the inability to acquire and retain in the program enough men of adequate professional training and competence. The Commission believed that a higher level of compensation for civil service professional employees should be established that would be more nearly competitive with that in private industry, and that the number of higher-level civil service positions should be increased.

CIVILIAN AGENCIES

Research and development programs in the civilian agencies of the Government involve an expenditure of about $350,000,000 a year, or about 15 per cent of the total outlay. Here again the expansion

[7] *Ibid.*, p. 21.

has been rapid, rising from $68,000,000 in 1946 to $90,000,000 in 1950 and $291,000,000 in 1954. Most of this scientific work is performed in four departments: Agriculture; Interior; Commerce; and Health, Education, and Welfare. Between them, they employed 22,335 persons in 1954.

Only a small portion of the Federal program consists of basic research covering the laws of nature and the character of materials. About $130,000,000 was spent on such work by all agencies, of which $77,000,000 was spent by those in the defense field, leaving $53,000,000 for the civilian programs.

Of all the research activities inside and outside the Government, the Commission believed that the most beneficial to mankind are those related to health and medicine. Basic research in these fields covers such subjects as anatomy, physiology, biochemistry, bacteriology, and viruses. Despite this, the Federal Government spends on basic research in the medical field only about $18,000,000 annually, or less than 1 per cent of its research outlay.

A subject of concern, the Commission felt, is the tendency of privately endowed foundations to deemphasize their medical programs. Therefore the Commission recommended that the Government give larger support to basic research, especially in the medical field.

It is most significant that this Commission, dedicated to reducing Government expenditures, felt that it should urge increased appropriations in this field. This is evidence that the Commission put the national interest above economy.

In conclusion, the Commission paid this tribute to the men and women who have tirelessly administered the Government's research programs:

> There is no tribute great enough to express the Nation's obligations to its scientists, engineers, and military personnel, for their contributions to our constantly-increasing productivity and the strengthening of our national defense. And there can be no relaxation in this effort.[8]

[8] *Ibid.*, p. xii.

CHAPTER 16

Surplus Property

The Armed Forces estimated that during the fiscal year 1955 some $4,200,000,000 of their supplies will be reported as excess to their requirements. A substantial amount of this will become disposable surplus. In the previous fiscal year they actually disposed of $1,350,000,000 of personal property. From 1950 through 1953 domestic surplus valued at $2,400,000,000 was disposed of.

The amount of surplus property the Government will have at any one time is determined largely by the rate of acquisition of property, the size of inventories, and the changing patterns of use of Government supplies. If planes or tanks become obsolete, for instance, the amount of surplus to be disposed of will increase. Each year the Federal Government spends billions of dollars for new supplies and retires old, worn-out, or unneeded items. Between 1950 and 1954 the military agencies spent $107,500,000,000 for supplies, equipment, capital goods, real property, and construction. Estimated expenditures for supplies for 1955 amounted to about $23,900,000,000 for defense and $3,400,000,000 for civilian agencies of the Government.

Personal property in military warehouses ready for issue was estimated at $66,000,000,000 as of June 30, 1954. Civilian agencies of the Government reported a total of some $257,000,000 on December 30, 1953. Thus the Defense Department holds 99.6 per cent of the total Government inventories of personal property classed as current assets (other than agricultural surpluses).

In addition to these current assets, capital assets such as naval vessels, aircraft, weapons, movable industrial installations, vehicles, office equipment, and so on, are estimated to amount to $48,500,000,000. When one adds real property of more than $40,000,000,000, this total will swell to more than $155,000,000,000. This is the source of surplus. The estimate does not take into account the value of land in the public domain, of surplus farm commodities, or of stockpiles of strategic materials.

NATURE OF PROBLEM

Three basic terms need to be defined at the outset: "surplus," "excess," and "donable."

Although the term "surplus" conveys an obvious meaning, its technical use in law and administration is slightly different. When a Federal agency no longer needs a particular item of property, the item is termed "excess." Lists of excess items first are submitted to a central screening agency, and then these are circularized to other Federal agencies to determine if they have need for such items. After such a check, property that is not desired by any Federal agency is called "surplus."

Before surplus personal property is sold to interested buyers or otherwise disposed of, state health and educational institutions get a limited time to claim it to be used for specific purposes. Property thus transferred to them is called "donable." From 1946 to 1954 the Government donated to educational and public health institutions a total of $783,343,000 in personal property, $699,713,000 in real property, a grand total of $1,483,056,226.

The effective use or disposal of surplus property is an end function. If the accumulation of surplus is to be minimized, a whole chain of antecedent functions must be improved. These antecedent functions include:

1. The determination of requirements for property;
2. A knowledge of property on hand;
3. Procurement of the required property;
4. A determination of what is "excess" and what is "surplus" property.

Some of the basic factors that influence the creation of surplus will be considered next. Then the problems of excess, donable, and surplus property will be surveyed.

BASIC FACTORS

The disposal of surplus property is the end function in a whole chain of supply activities. "In a real sense, it measures the effectiveness of the supply system."[1] If large surpluses accumulate, requirements of goods to be procured were overestimated. Along the supply line military stocks pile up in warehouses only to emerge later as surpluses. Inadequate inventory controls and stocking of the same items under different names and identifications result in the creation of excessive stocks.

In large military establishments some surpluses are expected. Changes in strategical and tactical planning inevitably require changes in logistical support. Normal wear and tear, obsolescence, contract terminations, as well as other factors, all contribute to the creation of unneeded stocks.

However, the military services hoard supplies. They create layers of "reserves" to justify excessive stocks. They lack a common supply language. There are many duplications in supply activities and conflicts of authority. All of these factors lead to unnecessarily large surplus stocks.

The various layers of requirements, the diverse criteria of need of the different military agencies, and the normal tendency of the military to hoard against unknown demands make it difficult systematically and accurately to report excess.

Excessive inventories are the rule. Random selection by the Task Force of easily obtainable supply items in common use showed that military depots stock many of them in quantities sufficient for twenty or thirty years and even, in one case, for a 128-year supply!

For example, ten items were examined at the Raritan Army Stock Control Point in New Jersey. These were standard items with diverse uses, and easy to manufacture. The total inventory of the ten items amounted to about $1,000,000 and represented an average of 32.6 years' supply for this supply base. Of these ten items an inventory that cost $430,000 was determined to be excess.

Obviously, necessary stock levels have to take into account the possibility of great increases in demand in an emergency or in war. However, the need for holding in stock huge quantities of common-use items is highly questionable. These items are easily obtainable, even in times of war, through normal channels of civilian distribu-

[1] Commission on Organization of the Executive Branch of the Government, *Surplus Property,* A Report to the Congress, April 1955 (Washington, D.C., U.S. Government Printing Office, 1955), p. 4.

tion. The administrative costs of maintaining such inventories are enormous.

Even where items stocked or purchased reasonably reflect actual need, the authorized stock levels often are highly inflated. For example, the Army Signal Corps had an authorized stock level of 1,426,000 dry-cell flashlight batteries—an 8.6 years' supply of this item with a short shelf life. Although the stocks on hand of such batteries were below the authorized level, this unrealistic figure was the goal for procurement officers.

Despite the fact that inventory control is basic to effective property management in the multibillion-dollar Defense Establishment, many items in common use are stocked by the military under different names and numbers. This makes it difficult to maintain meaningful control over the procurement of new items or to make better use of the existing stocks of Government agencies.

For example, the Defense Department and eight civilian departments were asked by the Task Force to report the numbers under which twelve items were stocked by them, together with data on stock status and inventory activity. The Defense Department required eight weeks and the civilian agencies from three to eleven weeks to determine whether or not they carried these items, together with the stock numbers and the quantities for each item.

In the light of such facts as these, the Hoover Commission recommended that the secretary of defense direct the downward revision of authorized stock levels, especially for common-use items which are readily available from current production or which rapidly become obsolescent; require that stocks on hand not exceed authorized levels; and require the rapid elimination of present excess stock by redistribution to the maximum extent possible.

THE NEED OF A CATALOGUE

Cataloguing is a basic prerequisite of any system of inventory control. For at least forty years the development of a satisfactory catalogue has been a problem for the Federal Government. World War II supply difficulties revealed clearly the inadequacy of then existing stock catalogues. Thereafter, each of the military services developed its own system of stock identification.

The magnitude of the task of identifying and developing uniform descriptions for items in Government inventories can be seen by the fact that there are more than 4,000,000 items currently listed in agency records. A uniform catalogue applicable to all agencies is now being developed; but several more years will elapse before it is generally in use. By developing a uniform supply language and numbering system, and by weeding out duplicate terms and by standardizing many items, it is believed that the number of items in the Government supply system will be reduced to about 2,000,000, a cut of 50 per cent.

"The Commission commends the Department of Defense and the General Services Administration for their current efforts in carrying forward the work of establishing the Federal Catalog System." [2]

UTILIZATION OF EXCESS PROPERTY

The Federal Government is the greatest potential customer for its own excess property because it buys more supplies and materials than any other one buyer or large group of buyers in the world. Yet this buying is so distributed and its coordination is so poor that frequently one Government agency is disposing as surplus the very items being bought from outside sources by another agency.

The average financial return from the sale of surplus to the general public is extremely low in comparison with replacement value. Thus in 1955 the average return of the Defense Department was 10 per cent. Consequently, the Government and the taxpayers will derive the greatest benefit by transfers of excess property between its own agencies.

There have been only limited transfers of excess property among major organizations of any one department, as for instance the Department of Defense, or among the departments and agencies of the Federal Government as a whole. The utilization of excess property among the various Government agencies is hampered by the failure of agencies to report excess property as well as by their refusal to use material slightly at variance with the specifications of material to be procured.

A case in point is the Alaska Railroad, which after World War II acquired from the War Assets Administration several million dollars' worth of equipment purchased originally for army operations in

[2] *Ibid.*, p. 13.

Iran. This excess material fills seventeen warehouses, as well as large open areas at various points in the Territory. These supplies have remained in storage for more than seven years, and a physical inventory of them was lacking until recently when the General Services Administration got the task of preparing one.

The statutory basis for efficient utilization of excess property is the Federal Property and Administrative Services Act of 1949, as amended. By this Act the administrator of general services is responsible for prescribing policies and methods to promote the maximum utilization of excess property by the Government. Availability of such property is made known by a screening process. The administrator of the general services is nominally responsible for screening; but he can and has delegated his authority.

Various civilian agencies are entirely or partially exempted by law from reporting their excess property for screening, including the Department of Agriculture, the Housing and Home Finance Agency, the Tennessee Valley Authority, the Atomic Energy Commission, the Central Intelligence Agency, and the Federal Maritime Administration. The Commission felt that the exemptions should be individually reviewed.

The administration of the screening program within the Defense Department has been delegated by the Administrator of General Services to the secretary of defense. This is justifiable because more than 90 per cent of all excess property originates in the armed services. Some fifty military supply points prepare declarations of excess forwarded by owning units in approximately 1,200 different military locations. Each owning unit will file as many declarations as it has property falling into separate commodity classifications. This results in a spasmodic filing of declarations. Screening lists are a mixture of various classes of items. This makes efficient utilization practically impossible, and it also handicaps the preparation of catalogues by the various owning units in the process of advertising their commodities for sale.

The success of utilization efforts depends in large part upon the quality of screening. In 1954 the General Services Administration, in checking lists of excess property, supposedly already screened for military use, subsequently located an interested military agency and effected the transfer of $15,000,000 worth of property to armed services units.

To overcome administrative difficulties in the screening procedure, the Commission recommended changes designed to reduce the number of reporting units, to synchronize reporting of excess by commodity classes, and to effect consolidating lists of excess commodities on a regional and nation-wide basis.

A rather effective, direct, and simple method of utilizing excess property would be to require the supply-and-inventory control point of one military service to check its counterpart in the other two services before initiating the new procurement of any item. Such a "reverse screening" procedure would determine whether an item is available from Government-held excess inventories. Because of the vast possibilities this method holds for better utilization and for preventing duplications of procurement among agencies, the Commission recommended that it be put into effect for purchases of any item costing more than some designated amount.

DONATION OF SURPLUS FOR EDUCATIONAL AND HEALTH PURPOSES

Since World War I, Congress has made use of Federal surplus personal property as additional aids to the States for education. Since 1919 personal property that cost considerably in excess of $1,000,000,000 has been given away under this program. Of this amount, almost $800,000,000 has been disposed of since 1946.

The Federal Property and Administrative Services Act of 1949 authorizes the Administrator of General Services to donate surplus property to the States, without cost, for educational or public health purposes. The principal recipients are schools, colleges, universities, hospitals, clinics, and health centers.

At the conclusion of the screening process to determine whether any Federal agency can use the material, unclaimed personal property ceases to be excess and becomes surplus. At that point the property may be claimed by eligible State educational and public health institutions or by State surplus property agencies acting through the Department of Health, Education, and Welfare.

Because the Commission believed that the benefits to the public from the donation program far outweigh its defects, it recommended that the program continue with but small changes.

DISPOSAL OF SURPLUS

The Federal Government is now disposing of surplus personal property at an annual rate in excess of $1,000,000,000 (acquisition cost). The amount disposed of in recent years was:

1951	$399,500,000
1952	381,000,000
1953	581,200,000
1954	1,240,500,000
Total	$2,602,200,000

Ninety-five percent was disposed of by the armed services.

It can be expected, furthermore, that the annual volume will grow larger as our military-preparedness program continues. Obviously, rapidly changing technology increases the rate of obsolescence in military weapons. Rigorous control of inventories, if effected, will also uncover additional surpluses.

The Federal Property and Administrative Services Act of 1949, as amended, conferred on the administrator of general services "supervision and direction over the disposition of surplus property." [3] Disposal authority specifically has been delegated by the administrator to each agency, except those exempted by law from his authority. Although such agencies normally observe applicable General Services Administration regulations governing the disposal of their surplus property, they dispose of a variety of common-use items and other equipment in general use throughout the Government. As a result the Commission recommended that all disposal of excess and surplus personal property, except where the President otherwise directs, should be subject to the regulatory control of the administrator of general services.

The military services, which generate more than 90 per cent of Federal surplus property, dispose of their own surplus under authority the administrator of general services has delegated to them. When the Federal Property and Administrative Services Act of 1949 was passed, it was not foreseen that the military services would be faced with a surplus-property disposal program of the magnitude that resulted from the Korean War. In this unforeseen situation, the General Services Administration failed to maintain full authority and responsibility over the disposal program. For all practical pur-

[3] *Federal Property and Administrative Services Act of 1949*, Sec. 203(*a*).

poses it has permitted the armed services to operate outside its control.

The regulations of the General Services Administration have not been adequately formulated, the Commission found, to govern disposal operations, and the administration has not developed uniform procedures to establish standard practice among Government agencies. Moreover, the General Services Administration has not had an adequate staff to carry out these functions.

The Commission was of the opinion that Congress intended that the disposal of military surplus properties be subject to the control of the General Services Administration. It believed "that more aggressive efforts must be made by the General Services Administration to maintain effective policy control and administrative coordination of this huge merchandising function."[4] The primary objectives of the surplus-property disposal program, it felt, should be (1) to obtain the highest possible net return to the Treasury and (2) to clear warehouses of surplus supplies which necessitate millions of dollars in management costs.

However, the Commission believed that commercial-type activities such as surplus-disposal selling should be organized primarily to bring about the largest possible return.

Because properties become surplus wherever they happen to be in the supply system, they frequently are located at installations remote from normal commercial markets. Although potential purchasers will travel to distant places to buy if the bargain is attractive enough, the net return to the Federal Government will be reduced because this primitive method of sale on an "as is where is" basis takes on the aspect of a distress sale. The Commission recommended that surplus stocks be physically segregated from other stocks where economical and practical to do so for sales purposes. To encourage competitive participation by potential buyers of surplus property, the Commission urged that agencies carefully select the most effective advertising media to reach prospective markets; describe properties in terms of commercial use and conditions to the greatest practicable extent; allow ample time between announcements and closing dates of sales offerings to provide for inspection and preparation of bids by prospective customers; and display properties requiring inspection or evaluation of mixed-lot contents in a man-

[4] *Surplus Property*, p. 50.

ner to encourage sufficient inspection and evaluation by prospective customers.

The Federal Government today is selling surplus personal property by the following methods: formal sealed-bid sale, site- or spot-bid sale, auction sale, and negotiated sale. An analysis of the Defense Department's instructions concerning sales methods revealed that the auction method appears to be definitely preferred by it for the disposal of surplus machine tools and other production equipment. Although auction sales are a profitable sales method in selling many classes of commodities, the Commission found that this method will not yield the maximum return to the Government in the disposal of machine tools, nor in disposal of salvage, scrap, and certain other classes of commercially usable property.

This does not mean that the sealed-bid method should be used in preference to the auction sale. But it means that these commodities should be analyzed and offered for sale by whichever method will provide the highest return. Included among such methods might be sealed-bid sales, negotiated sales, and sales through service contracts with qualified distributors of specialized types of equipment.

When a Government production contract is terminated or cut back, or when significant changes are made in a product, varying quantities of Government-furnished materials remain unused and must be removed from the contractor's premises. The majority of such supplies were furnished either directly by the Government or purchased by the contractor subject to reimbursement or repurchase by the Government. When the contract is terminated, the disposal of this inventory becomes a Government problem. The Commission was particularly concerned with the problem of contractor inventories in aircraft production because of the continued upward trend of Government expenditures in this field.

The Commission believed that a real problem is presented by the excessive time involved in clearing contractors' plants of such inventories. The elimination of the Materiel Redistribution Division screening would offer only a partial solution because the nonreportable inventory is not subject to screening delay.

Sales of contract-terminated aircraft surplus have yielded low returns to the Government relative to acquisition cost. For example, contractor inventories in the amount of $9,800,000 sold by the sealed-bid method brought an average return of only 2.8 per cent.

Because of the nature of the materials and of the markets, expert merchandising knowledge is at a premium in this field. "It is too much to expect that the Government can employ specialists at salaries which compete with those in industry." [5]

Effective redistribution of contract-terminated inventories requires specialized knowledge of industry needs and of market demands. A strong incentive to accomplish this redistribution is an essential ingredient to its success.

The Commission believed that these problems can be solved in part by the use of service contracts with qualified civilian redistributors. Contractors of this type could embrace both the redistribution of excess materials to other military contractors, and disposal functions.

CONCLUSION

During the next several years, large amounts of supplies approaching $2,000,000,000 a year will be cleared from Government warehouses.

The return from the disposal of such property is low, averaging over a period of years 5 to 7 per cent of original cost. Many items are sold as scrap, destroyed, or abandoned. Often valuable items are sold in mixed lots with little regard for their possible commercial use.

"The huge savings to be gained from improved disposal procedures and methods are apparent when we consider that an additional one cent received on each dollar cost of property sold would yield an additional $20 million yearly." [6]

Much larger savings would result from more efficient property management throughout the Government, and especially within the Military Establishment, which accounts for about 99 per cent of all goods bought and stocked by the Government.

The Government has tremendous amounts of property which it never would have bought if it had had a good inventory system. "It is estimated that with proper inventory control and more realistic stock levels from $10 billion to $25 billion of supplies now in Government warehouses could be eliminated." [7] Removing from the supply system the large volume of obsolete stock on hand would also provide immediate savings through depot and warehouse clearance. This would substantially reduce overhead charges.

[5] *Ibid.*, p. 66. [6] *Ibid.*, p. xi. [7] *Ibid.*, p. xii.

CHAPTER 17

Business Organization of the Department of Defense

As the chapters "Food and Clothing," "Transportation," "Depot Utilization," "Research and Development," and "Surplus Property" have indicated, the Department of Defense is engaged in large-scale business activities. But as was indicated in Chapter 11, these business functions, although similar to those of private industry, differ from them in important ways, and require unusual treatment.

As a result of the Commission's studies many shortcomings have been uncovered in the management phases of the Defense Department, but the Commission hastened to indicate that these are not "the fault of individual officials." Rather the fault lies, it found, in outmoded systems of administration. Many weaknesses result from the expansion of the military departments in twenty years from a civilian personnel of about 140,000 to 1,180,000 and from a military personnel of 250,000 to nearly 3,000,000. Some defects are due to traditions. Other shortcomings arise from static laws enacted years ago which now create roadblocks to effective improvement. Some spring from practices that have not been modified to meet the new conditions that result from the National Security Act of 1947 and its amendments.

The Commission pointed out these defects for the purpose of illustration, and not to find fault with officials or agencies. Many public officials have struggled manfully with these tangles and have brought about improvements. "Considering the difficulties under which they labor," the Commission said, "the Defense Department is better administered than might be expected." [1]

In considering the problem of improving the over-all management

[1] Commission on Organization of the Executive Branch of the Government, *Business Organization of the Department of Defense*, A Report to the Congress, p. xvii.

of Defense, four major programs have been developed by the Commission.

1. Better organizational framework. Thereby civilian control will be made more effective, support activities will be better organized, and better opportunity for executive teamwork will be provided.

2. Integrate common supply and service activities. This will produce effectiveness in support activities, as well as increased efficiency and economy.

3. Increase tenure, motivation, and skill both of civilian and of military executives.

4. Establish better financial control throughout all levels of the armed services, thus enhancing the control of top management and facilitating greater economy of operation.

These will be considered in sequence.

BETTER ORGANIZATION FOR BUSINESS MANAGEMENT

The objectives that should be attained by improved organization include:

a) Clear and unchallenged direction of the entire Defense Establishment by the secretary of defense and the secretaries of the three military departments.

b) Logical delegation of responsibilities to the staffs of the secretaries so that each has a manageable set of duties as well as adequate authority to carry them out.

c) Close teamwork among all members of the top executive organization, including the members of the secretariats as well as officials responsible for the military command of the operating forces.

To attain these goals it is necessary to determine the roles of the principal members of the staff responsible for defense management and to indicate the primary obstacles to coordinating their activities. Then the needed improvements in management can be outlined.

ROLES OF PRINCIPALS

The secretary of defense and the secretaries of the three services have unquestioned responsibility, and full authority, in all matters relating to the Defense Establishment. All other members of the secretariats, as well as the military chiefs of staff, are responsible to one of these top managers.

Within the Office of the Secretary of Defense, the top personnel assisting the secretary include the joint chiefs of staff, who are responsible for military planning, and the deputy and assistant secretaries, who are responsible for planning, coordinating, and directing as assigned by the secretary. The role of the assistant secretaries is to provide a continuing review of the programs of the Defense Establishment and to help in instituting major improvements "without imposing themselves in direct line of responsibility and authority between the Secretary of Defense and the Secretaries of the Departments."

Within each of the armed services, the leading personnel assisting each secretary include the military chief of staff who has command of the specific force involved, and the under and assistant secretaries who assist the secretary in the over-all administration of the department.

MAJOR OBSTACLES

There are at least four obstacles to close and productive working relationships among top Defense executives:

a) Decisions and information do not flow freely from the joint chiefs of staff to the assistant secretaries of defense. As a result, the country is deprived of the benefits that should come from full civilian participation in the formulation and execution of national defense plans and programs.

b) The present assignment of responsibilities among the principal members of the staff of the secretary of defense impedes effective coordination. This is due to the numerous interrelationships among the functions for which these executives are responsible.

c) The responsibilities of the assistant secretaries in the military departments differ in nature and scope. This makes coordination difficult between the Office of the Secretary of Defense and the three services themselves.

d) Responsibility for the management of support activities is not clearly defined between the principal military and civilian executives.

IMPROVEMENTS IN MANAGEMENT

Important deficiencies exist in defense planning. The guide lines furnished the military departments for basic procurement planning are inadequate because of weaknesses in unified military planning. These weaknesses spring from the sheer difficulty of the task, from the inevitable service partisanship of the joint chiefs of staff, from their lack of time for planning, from their reluctance to share the planning task with the assistant secretaries of defense among others, and from the reluctance of civilian secretaries to assume responsibilities in the field of military planning.

For example, the computation of requirements in the departments suffers from excessive detail, inadequate knowledge of usage, and insufficient coordination with research and development activities. Or by way of another illustration, the secretary of defense and the three departmental secretaries are not conducting a sufficiently penetrating analysis and review of defense requirements.

The existing directives of the secretary of defense, if complied with, would improve greatly the operations of the joint chiefs of staff, but this of itself would not fully solve the problems mentioned. The desired relationship between the joint chiefs of staff and the assistant secretaries of defense can be attained only by the direct exercise of the secretary's authority. No other member of his present executive staff is in a position to achieve adequate coordination.

The Commission proposed that "the Secretary of Defense should create in his office a civilian position invested with sufficient stature and authority to insure the establishment and maintenance of effective planning and review of military requirements." [2] This official should maintain active liaison with the National Security Council and the joint chiefs of staff, as well as coordinate all guidance provided by the Office of the Secretary of Defense and the military departments covering the preparation of requirements programs.

The management job of the Office of the Secretary of Defense has been subdivided in a way which creates problems of coordinating the work of some of the assistant secretaries. Furthermore, the present organization results in awkward working relationships with the military departments because their top organization does not parallel that of the secretary of defense.

[2] *Ibid.*, p. 19.

The Commission urged that "the Secretary of Defense should emphasize the management areas of logistics, research and development, personnel and finance, and should regroup certain functions under Assistant Secretaries to strengthen coordination of these four principal management areas." [3]

In addition, it said, he should designate a principal career assistant for each assistant secretary of defense "of such stature and competence that continuity of administration will be improved." [4]

The responsibilities proposed for the assistant secretaries of defense charged with management would establish logical assignments for the administration of logistics, research and development, personnel, and finance. Corresponding assignments of responsibility to the assistant secretaries of the three military departments would facilitate greatly communication and working relationships between the departments and the Office of the Secretary of Defense.

As a result the secretary of defense should revise the assignments of the assistant secretaries in the three services so as to get a uniform grouping of responsibilities similar to that proposed for the four management assistant secretaries of defense.

It is of the greatest importance to have proper recognition of the support activities in the armed services. The history of the military departments reveals that the management of support activities has been one of the most controversial and difficult aspects of military organization. Thus, by tradition the bureaus of the navy and the technical services of the army have enjoyed a high degree of autonomy, because of legally established corps and separate appropriations. "In the Army, the pendulum has swung widely during and following two world wars, from the imposition of strong integration and direction of the technical services during wartime, to their return to autonomy during peacetime." [5] Throughout the navy the various bureaus have enjoyed a high degree of autonomy, but strong secretaries have exercised direct supervision, and the chief of naval operations has had a military command relationship. But the reorganization attained by the President in 1953 has resulted in revisions, and the three departments now are beginning to establish stronger management control over support activities.

Although some progress has been made, "there is still vagueness in the assignment of responsibility for support activities between the

[3] *Ibid.*, p. 21. [4] *Ibid.*, p. 24. [5] *Ibid.*, p. 28.

military Chiefs of Staff and the civilian executives."[6] As a result a much clearer blueprint is needed to clarify and strengthen the role of the assistant secretaries in each military department.

Regardless of the organizational structure developed, it must be recognized "that the ultimate purpose of the military departments is to keep our Nation in a state of preparedness for war and to conduct military operations in the event of war."[7] This means that the top military executives must plan and request the matériel, services, facilities, and specialist personnel they find necessary to support the operating forces. However, military requirements must be evaluated and given final approval by the departmental secretaries and the secretary of defense, the President, and the Congress. Furthermore, it is necessary that the military chiefs of staff have direct authority over tactical and combat-related support activities performed by their respective logistics organizations, including the training of personnel for tactical operations.

The Commission recommended that "the Secretary of Defense should define the relationship of the military Chief of Staff to the support activities as that of: (1) planning and requesting the matériel, services, facilities and specialized personnel required to support the operating forces subject to the review and approval of the Secretariat; and (2) exercising direct authority over tactical and combat-related support activities performed by the logistics organization."[8]

COMMON SUPPLY AND SERVICE ACTIVITIES

Since the enactment of the National Security Act in 1947, numerous efforts have been made to find ways to achieve coordination of common supply functions under the existing organization, but without an acceptable degree of success. Because of these failures the Commission reached "the conclusion that a definitive program must be outlined which will eliminate duplicate stocks, facilities, distribution and overhead personnel."[9] To devise such a plan, it is necessary to consider the various methods of achieving coordination of common supply and service activities.

There are at least three possible approaches:

[6] *Ibid.* [7] *Ibid.*
[8] *Business Organization of the Department of Defense*, p. 29.
[9] *Ibid.*, p. 40.

a) *Coordinated Purchasing.* At least thirty-five categories of items are now being procured through single-service and joint agency arrangements. Purchases under such arrangements amounted to $5,400,000,000 in 1954, of which $1,900,000,000 were purchases made by one service for another.

Although coordinated buying is sound in principle, "many of the arrangements were made in haste and without adequate planning, with the result that the potential benefits are not being achieved." [10] Furthermore, there are inherent limitations in this form of coordination. Planning of requirements is not coordinated, and the purchasing service is not informed of inventories and the current rate of consumption of the requisitioning services. Thus, the purchasing service is not able to evaluate procurement requests or to redistribute excess stocks. In addition, coordinated buying does not achieve integration of storage and distribution, and it is in these areas that there are glaring instances of duplication.

b) *Cross-Servicing.* Another form of coordination is known as "cross-servicing." This involves arrangements by one department to draw on the facilities, stores, or services of another within a specific geographic area. A number of cross-servicing agreements are now in effect at local levels covering such items as laundries, automotive maintenance, and commissary stores.

However, these arrangements are fragmentary, and, at best, cross-servicing is an expedient that depends on cooperation among three independent supply systems differing widely in their organization and procedures.

c) *Integrated Supply Systems.* A more complete form of coordinated supply would result from assigning to a single department full responsibility for the procurement, distribution, storage, and issue of common-commodity classifications.

The adoption of an integrated supply system for major items of common supply appears on the surface to be a practical means of eliminating overlapping supply within the existing military departments. Actually, such arrangements have the inherent weaknesses of the other types of coordination. These defects include:

I. Inertia or strong resistance on the part of the military departments in collaborating on such matters.

II. The difficulty of assuring equitable treatment for all services

[10] *Ibid.*, p. 41.

under tight mobilization conditions. In such a situation it is difficult for one service to meet its own needs and simultaneously furnish the degree of service desired by others.

III. The difficulty of eliminating duplicate staffs, facilities, and distribution systems. Long experience with single-service procurement assignments has not resulted in identifiable savings.

IV. Finally, much time still would be required to develop uniform requisitioning, purchasing, accounting, and inventory control procedures.

A SEPARATE SUPPLY AGENCY

As a result of these factors the Commission believed that "the highest degree of integration would result from the creation of a separate agency, within the framework of the Department of Defense, to serve all departments equally in purchasing, inventory control and distribution to the end of the wholesale pipeline." [11]

Such an agency would obviate interservice rivalries. It would be staffed by specialists. It would operate efficiently, like a commercial enterprise. It would provide advantages not easily evaded or destroyed by bureaucrats.

Any objections to the proposed agency can be avoided by carefully defining its role. In addition to its other advantages, such an agency would provide a supply system that would be quickly expandable in wartime without the need of drastic reorganization. It would remove commercial-type operations from the military departments, thereby freeing professional military personnel of unnecessary administration burdens.

The Commission recommended, therefore, that "Congress should enact legislation establishing a separate civilian-managed agency, reporting to the Secretary of Defense, to administer common supply and service activities." [12]

To implement this proposal it is necessary to do two things: first, to develop principles for selecting the items to be transferred, and, second, to devise a proper form of organization for the agency.

First, as a basis for developing principals for selecting the items to be transferred, it is obvious that matériel procured for the military falls into two major classes: military hard goods and common-use items mainly of a commercial nature. The separate agency here

[11] *Ibid.*, p. 43.

[12] *Ibid.*, p. 45.

proposed would be expected to assume supply responsibilities only for commercial-type items and services.

Second, it is imperative that well defined standards be established which would prevent the separate agency from performing any but service functions and prevent it from assuming responsibilities which would impair the services in carrying out their respective combat missions.

In order to obtain these objectives the Commission suggested four criteria:

a) In all cases requirements must flow from the military departments under policies established and reviews conducted by the Office of the Secretary of Defense.

b) Specifications for technical items also should flow from the customers to the service agency.

c) A buyer-seller relationship must exist.

d) The commodities and services that are placed in the separate agency should be of a commercial type commonly used in the civilian economy.

The Commission proposed that the new agency should be designated as the Defense Supply and Service Administration.

This administration would have the status of an additional operating arm of the Department of Defense, subject to policy direction and coordination by the Office of the Secretary of Defense comparable to that exercised over the three military departments. Its head, the Commission said, should be a presidential appointee, and its staff should be composed of career-trained support specialists; its initial organization should be formed by the transferring of necessary personnel and facilities from the military departments.

There are many commercial-type activities administered by the military departments which would qualify for inclusion in the administration. Studies indicate that it would ultimately encompass activities now employing about 150,000 persons and expenditures of $6,000,000,000 to $8,000,000,000, or about 20 per cent of the defense budget.

IMPROVING PERSONNEL

In addition to simplifying organizational structure and clarifying lines of authority in the Department of Defense, it is necessary, the Commission felt, to improve personnel by getting the right man for each management job, by improving his skills, and by keeping him in the job long enough so that he can make a genuine contribution.

Here attention would be directed, first, to ways in which the tenure of presidential appointees (like the secretaries and assistant secretaries) could be lengthened; and second, to steps to improve the performance of career-management personnel, both civilian and military.

PRESIDENTIAL APPOINTEES

Under our system of government, the secretaries, with their immediate assistants, are responsible to the President for ensuring that policies are in accord with the national interest; that programs for military readiness are kept in balance with the capacity of the economy to support them; and that national defense is adequate but economical.

It is imperative that these key posts be made attractive to able administrators.

Getting and holding presidential appointees involves real problems. During the past decade the average length of service has been sixteen months for assistant and under secretaries, and twenty-two months for secretaries.

To improve this situation the Commission recommended that Congress increase the pay of such officials and modify the conflict-of-interest laws.

SPECIALIZED PERSONNEL IN SUPPORT ACTIVITIES

"The importance of the support activities within each military department clearly requires more specialization of career management and technical personnel than now exists." [13] There are many obstacles to attaining such an objective.

Career civilian managers in support activities are denied adequate opportunities for advancement by the practice of filling top positions with military personnel, many of whom are not trained for such responsibilities. In addition, civilian personnel do not get the same opportunities for training and development as do military personnel.

Although the expenditures for training of military personnel are large, present career-management practices of the services do not utilize such trained personnel effectively in support activities. For

[13] *Ibid.*, p. 59.

example, such personnel are still rotated between military operations and support activities, and great emphasis is placed on the development of generalists in the military service. The three services operate on the principle that a military officer must be able to assume virtually any responsibility in a military activity. The cost of the excessive rotation of personnel is between $33,000,000 and $50,000,000 each year.

The Commission concluded that "it is clear that careers should be planned and developed, selections should be made, training conducted, and assignments and promotions controlled within specialized support areas, consistent with the abilities and interests of the personnel concerned and the needs of the service." [14]

In this area of personnel the strong traditions of the armed services can be uprooted only by legislation which will accord the same recognition to a career-management program in the support activities as has been given by the National Security Act to financial management.

It is desirable, the Commission felt, for Congress to provide a legislative basis for specialized management and technical personnel in the support activities.

DELINEATION OF CIVILIAN AND MILITARY ROLES

The demarcation of the relative military and civilian roles and the effective utilization of the two groups are problems peculiar to the Department of Defense. The only solution to these problems is to spell out the respective roles of civilian and military managers and technical personnel so as to provide opportunities and incentives for each.

The unjustifiable waste which results from duplicate military-civilian staffing is another factor that makes such demarcation imperative. There are 16,000 such duplicated assignments in the support activities today, the Commission found, representing an unnecessary cost of more than $110,000,000 per year to the taxpayer.

The Commission believed that Congress should by law establish criteria to distinguish clearly between the proper roles for civilian and military support managers and technical personnel and should direct the secretary of defense to apply them immediately.

[14] *Ibid.*, p. 61.

The implementation of such criteria would establish the number and types of positions requiring career-trained support managers and technicians, either military or civilian. "Since a large number of both groups will be required, and since the management skills are alike, members of both groups who pursue a career in support management should be governed by comparable personnel standards administered under the authority of the Secretary of Defense." [15]

The secretary of defense, the Commission recommended, should develop a personnel system for support activities which provides comparable standards for the selection, training, promotion, and compensation both of civilian and of military managers and of technical personnel. It is necessary for Congress to enact the necessary legislative changes to carry out this objective.

Accomplishment of such far-reaching changes in the personnel programs and procedures of the Department of Defense requires strong leadership by the secretaries and their staffs. Each assistant secretary responsible for a functional area (logistics, research and development, personnel, finance, legal, and so on) should be responsible, the Commission felt, for developing standards, formulating programs for training, assigning, rotating, and promoting personnel.

"Responsibility for coordinating the development of the career management program," it said, "should be assigned to the Assistant Secretary of Defense for Personnel who, with the departmental Assistant Secretaries for Personnel, should promulgate uniform policies to be applied in all functional areas, and oversee the administration of selection, training, assignment, and promotion programs." [16] The assistant secretary for logistics within each service should be supported by a personnel staff to assist him in his capacity as the top manager of supply and service activities.

THE TOOLS OF FINANCIAL MANAGEMENT

Because the Department of Defense spends more than sixty cents out of each tax dollar, it is imperative that it develop adequate controls over expenditures. The annual purchases of the armed services are almost twice as large as the total United States expenditures for public education.

[15] *Ibid.*, p. 65.

[16] *Ibid.*, p. 68.

It is not unreasonable for our military leaders to desire sufficient manpower and matériel to minimize potential military risks, but the public interest requires that the civilian leaders of the Defense Department counterbalance these natural tendencies of the military which, if not restrained, lead to waste in overbuilding, overbuying, and overstaffing. Thus, the heads of these departments have no more important task than that of guarding this large segment of our Nation's resources. In this area two major tasks must be performed: first, the tools of financial management must be perfected, and second, responsibility must be fixed for managing defense expenditures.

The most important tools of financial management to be perfected are budgeting and accounting. The defense budget essentially is a request for authority to incur obligations for goods and services, many of which will not be delivered during the year concerned. This system of budgeting is defective under present practice because it does not fully reveal either available resources or their cost.

Furthermore, this system has resulted in granting spending authority well in excess of total annual needs. For example, at the beginning of the fiscal year 1955, the Department of Defense had obligation authority of $50,000,000,000, whereas estimated obligations for 1955 did not exceed $36,000,000,000. Such an excess accumulation of obligation authority reduces the effectiveness of congressional control over the purse.

The Commission in its Report on Budget and Accounting recommended that obligation-type budgeting be discontinued and that, in its place, Congress authorize an "accrued expenditure budget." This would be based upon the value of goods and services estimated to be received during each year. In the case of items with long lead-times, such as weapons and major construction programs, Congress would also authorize contractual authority beyond the budget year. Actually, Congress would retain full control because it would approve only the funds to be spent each year. Thus Congress would have the opportunity of reviewing the program annually.

Accounting devices are also important for controlling expenditures. Expenditure control in the Government is largely based upon dividing congressional appropriations into a series of allotments to individual organizations which, in turn, make suballotments to their subordinate units and to service activities. This method of control results in an accounting system which assures that allotments and suballotments are not overexpended. The Task Force on Budget and Accounting characterizes this as "the primitive cash system of control which was relied upon in the early days of industry." The number of allotments has become tremendous (several hundred thousand in the Department of Defense alone). As a result no rational picture of expenditures in relation to performance can be obtained by top management. Furthermore, managers of large installations, such as some general depots and other multiple-purpose stations, are unable to determine their cost of performance. As a result one of the most potent incentives to economical operations is lacking.

To overcome these defects, the Commission in its Report on Budget and Accounting urged the adoption of business-tested systems of accrual accounting throughout the Government.

Although better financial tools are essential to effective control over defense expenditures, there is also an equally important need to recognize the part which every member of top management should play in managing defense assets and fiscal resources.

In the absence of adequate budgeting and accounting tools, primary reliance has been placed upon maintaining control through the budget justification and allotment processes. This process has placed an undue burden on the comptroller organization, especially in the Office of the Secretary of Defense. The assistant secretary (comptroller) has been placed in the position of exercising a definitive review of operating and procurement plans as developed in budget justification data.

To fix responsibility for managing defense dollars, each assistant secretary of defense should be responsible, the Commission said, for screening the requirement programs of each of the departments for his functional area and for advising the assistant secretary of defense for financial management as to the financial needs for such activities. It is also necessary that each departmental assistant secretary be held responsible for screening requirements and for participating in the formulation and review of the budget for those activities and programs under his jurisdiction.

Under such a system each assistant secretary would have to take an active part in reviewing and controlling programs and budgets in his functional jurisdiction. This would supplement the work of the assistant secretaries for financial management, who would continue to be responsible for the supervision and direction of budgeting.

CONCLUSIONS

This review of the management problems of the Defense Establishment is important because the recommendations on four phases of the organization of the Department of Defense—management organization, common supply, personnel, and finances—provide Congress and the public with effective solutions to crucial problems which have thus far eluded solution. This report poses a series of fundamental questions the answers to which are of great concern to Congress and the public.

1. Has civilian control over the nation's military organization been effective?

The Commission's stress on the need to reestablish civilian control over Defense indicates that the principle of civilian control over the military is recognized in form and not in practice. Throughout our history under the Constitution the mission of the armed services has been the same as it is now—national defense. There is no question that our national responsibilities and the technological character of warfare have both changed. The size and organization of the Defense Establishment have been enlarged to meet these new demands. The basic principle of civilian control of the Armed Forces never has been questioned.

Civilian control of business matters does not mean that military strategy and tactics are left to amateurs. Combat activities, even combat-related support, require individuals who can interchange with fighting forces, and no one would "civilianize" them. The management aspect of national defense, however, requires specialized skills and attitudes normally found among civilians.

2. Does Congress maintain effective control of the national purse in the field of defense?

The absence of inventories and the large carry-overs of unobligated funds indicate lack of such control. Without knowing what is owned and what is owed, control is impossible. The techniques of fiscal management, including proper inventory systems, must be adopted if the Congress is to regain control of national spending.

3. Is there compliance with the intent of Congress in the attainment of unification?

Supply systems have become an outstanding "horrible example" of the failure of the executive branch to comply with repeated congressional demands for unification, economy, and efficiency in the armed services. The recommendation for a new Supply and Service Administration developed from a recognition of the problems and viewpoints of the military services, as well as from a recognition of congressional conviction that real unification is imperative.

5.

Overseas Economic Operations

CHAPTER 18

The Kind Neighbor

From July 1945 through the fiscal year 1956 the United States Government will have spent $55,800,000,000 on various forms of foreign aid. Of this total about $4,300,000,000 was paid out in 1955, and approximately $4,700,000,000 will be disbursed in 1956. Of the $46,800,000,000 paid out from 1945 to 1954, $11,000,000,000 was in the form of loans and $35,800,000,000 went as grants. Of this amount only $12,100,000,000 was for military purposes. The grants are not repayable to the United States. The credits are presumably repayable obligations.

The United Kingdom got the lion's share of the foreign aid—$6,870,000,000. France followed with $4,982,000,000. Our former enemies fared well: Germany, $3,830,000,000; Italy, $2,653,000,000; and Japan, $2,490,000,000.

NATURE AND SCOPE

Because of its very size a program of this kind would deserve study by the Commission, but in addition many people contended that the program was wasteful and that it included many foolish projects. As a result, influential leaders demanded that the Commission examine thoroughly this huge spending program.

To cite only one of many examples of waste, a member of the Commission's Task Force on Overseas Economic Operations heard that the Foreign Operations Administration had taken a wretched group of Italians out of holes dug in a hillside that were almost caves, and moved them into a modern American-style village. Naturally he wanted to see it.

On the way he was amazed to see no craters from the bombs he thought had driven those people into caves. His guide explained that there had been no fighting in that region.

The new village was all that had been promised. Those people now had everything—even bathrooms. But he was told there might be one final item of expense. This would be for cement to plug up the caves to keep the people from moving back into them because, explained the young sociologist who acted as guide, they have got used to them.

"How long had they been living in them?"

The sociologist pondered. "About 2,000 years—give or take a few centuries."

Congress was highly concerned over the foreign-aid program and had itself looked into it repeatedly. The Commission said:

> This investigation in the field of mutual security was undertaken in response to the special wish of certain congressional members of the Commission. In this connection, the Congress determined by the Mutual Security Act of 1954 that the Foreign Operations Administration in particular should be ended as an independent agency on June 30, 1955. Therefore, a new method of organization must be found which will continue certain essential services, simplify others, and reduce Government expenditures. At the same time we seek to provide a program which will strengthen the countries of the free world militarily and economically, thereby sustaining the security of the United States and making available to the underdeveloped countries of the world the benefits of the technological advances enjoyed by the people of the United States.[1]

To survey this problem of foreign aid the Commission appointed an able Task Force. Headed by Henning W. Prentis, Jr., chairman of the board of the Armstrong Cork Company, it included Harry A. Bullis, board chairman of General Mills; Frederick C. Crawford, chairman of Thompson Products, Inc.; Ferdinand Eberstadt, investment banker; Arthur B. Foye, a leading accountant; Ernest Kanzler, vice chairman of Universal C.I.T. Credit Corporation; former Assistant Secretary of Commerce Julius Klein; former Secretary of Commerce Charles Sawyer, and Joseph P. Spang, Jr., president of the Gillette Company. All but one member had participated previously in the Government's foreign-aid programs or in official investigations of operations in that field.

[1] Commission on Organization of the Executive Branch of the Government, *Overseas Economic Operations.* A Report to the Congress, June 1955 (Washington, D.C., U.S. Government Printing Office, 1955), p. vii.

AMERICAN FOREIGN-AID ACTIVITIES

The Commission found thirty-four agencies in the Federal Government directly or indirectly engaged in or related to foreign aid. Apart from American military personnel, 115,250 persons were employed by the United States for work abroad, of whom 30,681 were Americans and 84,569 of other nationalities. Of this number, some 20,000 American workers and 74,000 citizens of other countries were retained by the Defense Establishment.

To understand the problem, it is imperative that the work of these agencies be described briefly. Before discussing the Foreign Operations Administration, the other related agencies in this field will be summarized.

EXECUTIVE OFFICE OF THE PRESIDENT

The President has the responsibility of determining and recommending to the Congress the policies, administrative methods, and expenditures for foreign aid. Under the Mutual Security Act of 1954, he had a special authority to assign or transfer the functions conferred on him by that Act to any agency of the Government, and to apportion the appropriations among them.

There are several councils, boards, committees, and special assistants who formulate advice for the President and who coordinate the various agencies in this field.

1. *The National Security Council* is the highest-level policy and advisory staff for the President with respect to domestic, foreign, and military policies relating to the national security.

2. *The Operations Coordinating Board* has the duty of implementing presidential decisions and those of the National Security Council through the departments and agencies. Its effectiveness is due to the stature of its members rather than to the adequacy of its facilities to make independent checks on the activities of the departments.

3. *The National Advisory Council on International Monetary and Financial Problems* is an advisory and coordinating committee dealing in part with foreign financial matters. This committee, in addition to determining the financial policies to be applied in the field of foreign aid, also determines the policies to be used relative to counterpart funds.

4. *The Economic Defense Advisory Committee* has two functions.

It assists the secretary of state in coordinating all economic defense programs of the Government and it advises on the major policy aspects of the control of East-West trade.

5. *The Council on Foreign Economy Policy* was established by the President on December 11, 1954, to help bring about improved organization of the executive branch of the Government for the development and coordination of foreign economic policy, including its relation to domestic economic policy.

6. *Special Assistants and Other Offices.*—In addition to those units of the executive offices that have been mentioned, important facets of foreign aid are included in the responsibilities of ten other committees and offices.

EXECUTIVE DEPARTMENTS AND AGENCIES

1. *The Department of State.*—Besides membership on most of the interdepartmental committees and councils, the secretary of state and the Department of State had wide and important responsibilities for foreign-aid activities even before the International Cooperation Administration was transferred to it. Subject to the President, the secretary of state determined the policies which control foreign aid in each of the recipient countries and assisted in developing foreign-aid programs to achieve policy objectives. He was responsible for negotiating the required foreign-aid agreements with each recipient country and for representing United States interests there. The State Department maintains embassies and missions in seventy-seven countries, including all countries receiving foreign aid. The State Department's overseas staff, as of June 30, 1954, totaled 14,640 persons, of whom 5,428 were United States citizens, and 9,212 foreign nationals.

2. *The Department of the Treasury.*—The secretary of the treasury is the chief fiscal officer of the Government and is a member of many of the coordinating agencies already listed. The foreign aid and economic functions of his department stem from his general financial and monetary responsibilities. The foreign and international responsibilities of the department are handled in Washington by the Office of International Finance within the Office of the Secretary of the Treasury.

3. *The Department of Defense.*—The secretary of defense, in addition to his responsibilities as a member of many of the above

coordinating committees, has important responsibilities in foreign-aid matters. The department has the major role in administering military aid and in building military strength throughout the free world. The expenditures of dollars for military assistance to the foreign countries indirectly affect economic aid.

The overseas activities of the department fall into two general categories. First, "military assistance" is extended to many nations, including offshore procurement (purchase of military supplies in foreign countries) and the support of the North Atlantic Treaty Organization. Second, the maintenance and support of United States military forces abroad is an important form of foreign aid.

Under the "military assistance" program, the department supplies arms, munitions, and military matériel needed by the armed forces of the cooperating free nations. Expenditures for these purposes were about $2,675,000,000 in 1955, not including outlays made directly by the Foreign Operations Administration.

While the bulk of the military supplies furnished friendly nations are obtained in the United States, "two phases of the program involve the actual spending of United States dollars overseas: Offshore procurement and North Atlantic Treaty Organization construction programs. In addition, the Foreign Operations Administration administers programs for Direct Forces Support and Defense Support." [2]

The offshore procurement of arms for military assistance programs under the Department of Defense involves important elements of economic as well as military aid, because this involves the expenditure of dollars abroad. The total of contracts let for such manufacture, mostly in western Europe, as of December 31, 1954, was $2,633,100,000. Of this amount, about $1,020,900,000 had actually been paid out; the balance represented uncompleted contracts.

The United States maintains large Armed Forces abroad, mainly in West Germany, Japan, Korea, the United Kingdom, and France. Overseas expenditures for 1955 to maintain these troops were estimated at $1,830,000,000. "These dollar expenditures have a great economic impact in these nations." [3] The Department of Defense also maintains military advisory groups and missions in many other countries throughout the world.

4. *The Department of Agriculture.*—This department maintains

[2] *Ibid.*, p. 11.

[3] *Ibid.*, pp. 13–14.

skilled staffs, both in Washington and abroad, to perform important functions such as the marketing of surplus agricultural products, the development of foreign markets for United States agricultural products, the administration of the agricultural attaché system, and the collection, analyzing, and dissemination of world agricultural data.

The department also provided technical advice and services to the foreign-aid program for which it was reimbursed by the Foreign Operations Administration. In 1955 the department received about $1,100,000 for this purpose. This included the cost of the services of agricultural experts both in the United States and overseas.

5. *The Department of the Interior.*—The Department of the Interior in conducting large irrigation and hydroelectric programs in the United States employs an experienced and skilled staff. It has furnished part of the staff of the Foreign Operations Administration for the survey and conduct of similar projects in foreign countries.

6. *The Department of Commerce.*—The Department of Commerce, charged with responsibility for fostering, promoting, and developing the foreign commerce of the United States, "has important responsibilities for collection, analysis, and dissemination of worldwide commercial data; administration of export controls; promotion of investment abroad; highway design and construction; and encouragement of travel."[4]

7. *The Export-Import Bank.*—This United States wholly owned corporation has a capital of $1,000,000,000 and an authority to borrow up to $4,000,000,000 from the Treasury. Thus it is able to lend up to $5,000,000,000.

On June 30, 1954, its loans outstanding to foreign governments and foreign enterprises were $1,333,643,000, and it had made loans of $1,428,000,000 to finance export-import trade. In addition, the bank had commitments to lend an additional $532,000,000.

Aside from financing American exports, the bank has made direct loans to governments to finance reconstruction (such loans to France at one time amounted to $1,300,000,000), loans to foreign countries to buy American agricultural and industrial products, loans to private foreign enterprises and to governments for resource development, as well as loans to foreign central banks to finance dollar

[4] *Ibid.*, p. 15.

exchange. It also acts as the fiscal agent for the Foreign Operations Administration and the International Cooperation Administration.

INTERNATIONAL ORGANIZATIONS

There are also numerous international organizations and agencies in which the United States participates. Though some of them do not have the primary purpose of providing economic aid to their members, in many cases the United States contribution results in substantial economic aid to the governments concerned.

The United Nations has several agencies engaged in economic and other services, some of which in effect give economic aid. Some are financed out of the general funds of the United Nations to which the United States contributed directly in 1954, $15,167,000, and in 1955 about $13,400,000. In addition, the United States contributes to various specialized agencies of the United Nations, including:

1. *United Nations Food and Agriculture Organization.*—"The Food and Agriculture Organization was established to raise the levels of nutrition and standards of living and to secure improvements in the efficiency of the production and distribution of all food and agricultural products by collecting and distributing information. The United States through the Department of State makes a direct contribution to this Organization."[5] In 1955 it contributed $1,650,435, or about 30 per cent of the UNFAO's budget.

2. *United Nations Educational, Scientific, and Cultural Organization.*—UNESCO's object is to contribute to peace and security by promoting collaboration among the nations through education, science, and culture. This country contributed about $3,150,000 in 1955 to UNESCO, or approximately 33 per cent of its budget.

3. *International Labor Organization.*—This is a specialized agency of the United Nations organized to aid in the raising of labor standards and the improvement of working conditions. It includes representation not only of governments but also of employers and workers as well.

4. *World Health Organization.*—This is another specialized agency of the United Nations having programs concerned with contagious and parasitic diseases, child health, nutrition, sanitation, mental health, and the training of public health personnel.

There are many other international agencies, like the World Bank,

[5] *Ibid.*, pp. 17–18.

the Monetary Fund, and the European Payments Union, to which the United States belongs or to which it gives financial assistance.

FUNCTIONS IN THE FIELD OF MUTUAL SECURITY

The Foreign Operations Administration was a large agency with a staff of seven thousand spending more than $2,000,000,000 annually. In order to make clear the Commission's proposals relative to this agency, it is first desirable to classify the various activities carried on by it. The Commission found that this organization performed nineteen different functions. Only the most important of these will be considered here.

1. *Military Assistance.*—The function of providing military equipment to friendly countries actually was administered by the Department of Defense, but in coordination with the director of the Foreign Operations Administration.

2. *Offshore Procurement.*—The function of purchasing arms and supplies in foreign countries for military assistance also was administered by the Department of Defense, but in coordination with the Foreign Operations Administration.

3. *Contributions to the Military Construction Program of the North Atlantic Treaty Organization* were likewise administered by the Department of Defense and coordinated with the Foreign Operations Administration.

4. *Korean Reconstruction.*—The Foreign Operations Administration has been responsible for programs of relief and reconstruction for Korea; but these were administered by a complex triangle involving the United Nations Relief Agency, the Foreign Operations Administration, and the United States Army, and the army has been providing the largest number of personnel. About $272,000,000 was alloted for this purpose in 1956.

5. *Defense Support and Direct Forces Support Programs.*—The Foreign Operations Administration, as well as its successor, provides money to supply American commodities through gifts or loans to designated foreign countries. The method of procurement takes two forms: purchase of materials for specific development projects and purchase of nonproject commodities. "The preferred procurement method is for the Government concerned to authorize purchases for its account through normal trade channels and make transporta-

tion arrangements subject to approval by the Foreign Operations Administration, which finances the transactions."[6] In other instances procurement is handled in part by the General Services Administration, the Department of Defense, and the Department of Agriculture, on behalf of the Foreign Operations Administration or of its successor. Little actual procurement has been done directly by the Foreign Operations Administration. But the programing and procurement of machinery and materials for industrial and other development projects has required technical and financial review by the Foreign Operations Administration.

A large part of the operations just mentioned are designated as "defense support" and "development assistance." Defense support comprises programs of economic assistance designed to support the military assistance given by the Department of Defense. The programs are developed separately for each country receiving such military assistance in cooperation with the Department of Defense. Expenditures for defense support in 1954 came to $1,057,800,000.

"Direct forces support" is difficult to distinguish from "defense support," as it also is designed to support military assistance. "Its purpose is somewhat more direct than Defense Support."[7] For instance, when a country is unable to supply items such as food, clothing, gasoline, and so on, for its civilian population at the same time as it furnishes them to its increased armed forces, the United States supplies such articles to the country's military forces under this program. One of the categories under this heading is called "Production for Forces Support." This includes, for example, the manufacture of artillery and ammunition in France for the use of its army and of certain aircraft in the United Kingdom for the use of its air force. Another category under this designation is the provision of direct assistance to free-world forces in Southeast Asia. The expenditures for 1954 for these were $180,000,000.

The Task Force pointed out:

> Generally speaking, both direct forces support and defense support aid have constituted budget support in a varying degree from country to country, and have involved activities, in most respects, which are indistinguishable from economic aid or technical assistance.

The term "defense support," it seems obvious, was originally introduced as part of an effort to win continued public and congressional support for

[6] *Ibid.*, p. 26.

[7] *Ibid.*, p. 27.

an economic aid program in Europe at a time when there was considerable opposition to additional economic aid grants. This, however, is not a commentary on the importance or necessity for such aid in developing the defensive strength of the free world.[8]

The introduction of such new terms to describe phases of the foreign-aid program does not facilitate public understanding of the program, especially when the terms used convey no real meaning in themselves.

6. *Technical Cooperation.*—The Foreign Operations Administration conducted programs of *technical cooperation* and *technical assistance* in many foreign countries for the purpose of promoting economic production and cultural improvement. Much criticism has developed concerning specific projects in these programs.

Technical cooperation, as defined by the 1950 Act for International Development, was primarily for the interchange of technical knowledge and skills, and for surveys, demonstration, training, and similar projects in the fields of economics, engineering, medicine, education, agriculture, fisheries, minerals, and fiscal matters.

Many of these projects have been badly planned. Several examples of such ill constructed projects are in order.

Because the Mutual Security Agency, the predecessor of the FOA, decided Indonesia should learn about the use of fertilizer, a quantity was taken there for "demonstration" purposes. Only then did this agency find out that Indonesian planters not only knew of fertilizer, but knew that the slight increase in yield did not justify its cost. We still have most of it on our hands at this writing.

Another badly handled project was the FOA's program of building seventy-five fishing boats for Indonesia. Although the boats were not delivered for months, no one bothered to train crews; therefore half of them remained idle another six months. To power them, the FOA over-ordered on engines, importing 340 Diesel marine engines from Japan. Because Indonesia was able to build but eight boats a month, this was a three-year supply.

Neutralist Indonesia is rich in rubber, oil, and tin. During the Korean War, when these products were in brisk demand, the Indonesians had hard money running out of their ears, and bought and

[8] Commission on Organization of the Executive Branch of the Government, *Task Force Report on Overseas Economic Operations* (Washington, D.C., U.S. Government Printing Office, 1955), p. 175.

paid cash for 700,000 yards of cotton sheeting. Nevertheless, immediately afterward FOA made Indonesia a free gift of another $620,000 worth of cotton cloth.

Liberia offers another illustration. FOA felt that Liberians should eat more fish, and its technicians encouraged them to build ponds to raise their own. The fact is that Liberian rivers and her Atlantic coast teem with fish which could be had for the trifling cost (in local funds) of nets and seines, if the Liberians wanted them. Actually, the people do not like fish, and the ponds were a wasted effort.

One of the worst planned projects was a pilgrim delousing station in Saudi Arabia. The king desired a delousing station to process pilgrims entering his kingdom to visit Mecca. FOA got the old gentleman to agree on an impressive setup including running water for baths for the pilgrims, and steam sterilizers for their robes and prayer rugs. A site was chosen and work was begun, but presently money ran low. Meanwhile, the United States Public Health Service recommended against the bath-steamer proposal which would have cost $300,000, pointing out that a setup for dusting the Faithful with DDT would cost only $10,000 and have better results.

But the king wanted the bath-steamer project because the pilgrims might take offense at a mere dusting. At about this point it was discovered that the FOA technicians in locating the project had failed to consult an expert on water: as a result there was not enough to run the steam sterilizers. The royal delousing station, planned to process the 1953 wave of pilgrims, still was not working at this writing.

7. *Development Assistance.*—The technical cooperation program has been expanded into an economic or development assistance program which provides additional funds to finance capital development and economic improvement in foreign countries. Funds are provided for constructing industrial projects such as steel mills, oil refineries, electric-power plants, and irrigation projects. Much of the funds for these projects are provided by the United States, but in most cases the receiving countries contribute part of the cost. One hundred and forty-three such projects in fourteen European countries have been completed or are in course of construction. These countries contributed about $2,200,000,000 toward their cost, while the United States granted directly about $600,000,000. This is not, however, the total amount contributed by the United States,

because technical staffs and counterpart funds used for these projects are charged to other accounts. "The variety of projects financed is indicated by $592,000,000 spent for iron, steel, automobile products, petroleum refining, chemicals, pulp, paper, glass, and other manufactures; $307,000,000 for mining and oil drilling; $72,000,000 for electric power, roads, air transport, communications, waterways, harbors, and ships; and $10,000,000 for irrigation and grain storage." [9]

The development assistance program, including industrial projects, is being expanded in Africa, the Middle East, Southeast Asia, the Far East, and Latin America. The appropriations available for development assistance in 1955 were $184,506,000.

REORGANIZING MUTUAL SECURITY

Obviously, military and economic assistance to the countries of the free world by the United States since the end of World War II has imposed a heavy financial burden upon American taxpayers.

Since 1945 numerous agencies have been responsible for administering this $50,000,000,000 program. The last of these (before 1955) was the Foreign Operations Administration, an independent agency created in 1953 to consolidate and coordinate all such activities. Congress had declared that this agency was to terminate on June 30, 1955, and the Commission was of the same opinion.

The primary purpose of the Commission in approaching this problem of reorganizing the administration of foreign aid was to strengthen the security of the United States. As a part of this basic policy the Commission emphasized:

(*a*) The United States foreign aid, despite many mistakes and waste, should be continued.

(*b*) There are great problems of economic and humanitarian advancement in many countries in the solution of which the United States should take part.

(*c*) The time has come, due to the increased economic strength of certain nations, when they no longer need extensive support from the United States.

(*d*) There are methods of organization of these efforts which will lessen their cost by elimination of duplication and greater efficiency in operation.

[9] *Overseas Economic Operations,* A Report to the Congress, p. 30.

(*e*) There are methods of organization which will bring about better coordination of these efforts at home and eliminate confusion among our representation abroad.[10]

Concerning the need for such a program, the Task Force said in its report:

Everyone will agree that there is great danger in the general world situation today and that the United States must do everything it can, within reason, to contain and limit the spread of communism. The post-war days of charity, however, are over, when the United States spent large sums for rehabilitation. Future foreign aid can be justified only if it is necessary for the defense of the free world; and we should certainly not plan our future course with the idea that is frequently advanced that foreign aid will have to be given permanently or for an indefinite period.[11]

To accomplish these objectives the Commission believed that the necessary administration could be organized in two ways:

1. The functions of the International Cooperation Administration in the Department of State could be established on an operational basis.
2. The Department of State, because of its primary duty of conducting our foreign relations, should be encumbered with the minimum of operational duties. On this basis as many as possible of the foreign-aid programs should be operated by other departments.

Under this latter concept, the director of the International Cooperation Administration would have in the main a coordinating and planning function and not an operational function. This could be accomplished by having existing line agencies perform many of the operating activities subject to central planning and coordination. The Commission embraced this second alternative.

The determination of over-all policies must rest with the President assisted by the secretary of state and the various advisory councils. "The President should always be in a position to react to world developments as they occur."[12]

The heads of the Government agencies concerned with administering aspects of these programs are members of these various

[10] *Ibid.*, pp. 39–40.
[11] *Task Force Report on Overseas Economic Operations*, p. 25.
[12] *Overseas Economic Operations.* A Report to the Congress, p. 45.

boards and committees on which the director of the International Cooperation Administration also serves. Therefore, there should be no difficulty in getting the necessary coordination and unity of action without large operational activities in the Department of State.

Nevertheless, the problem of staff for the contracting departments will arise. Each of the departments already has effective staffs in Washington, and many have staffs abroad experienced in these functions. The Commission believed that "great duplication of staffs can be avoided by using the staff and facilities of existing agencies." [13]

So that the Commission's recommendation relative to the organization for foreign aid will be clear, it is quoted in full:

> (*a*) That the Secretary of State, through the Director of the International Cooperation Administration, maintain strong control of the function of developing policies, objectives, and programs for nonmilitary foreign aid with respect to each country for which such aid is authorized, and, wherever advantageous and economical to do so, make full use of the staffs and facilities of the various departments and agencies of Government on a reimbursable basis to perform activities in connection with these programs. . . .
>
> (*b*) That the Director of the International Cooperation Administration should be responsible for the preparation of the budget and the accountability of all funds for non-military foreign-aid programs which should be appropriated to and expended by the Department of State, and should report to the Congress the expenditures made.
>
> (*c*) That the different agencies in many cases will be able to discharge their duties from their present staffs but if they should require additional staff, they should be free to obtain it from any quarter.
>
> (*d*) That the overseas nonmilitary personnel of United States agencies be subject to the line authority and direction of the United States Chief of Diplomatic Mission in each country.[14]

PRINCIPLES TO GUIDE THE ADMINISTRATION OF FOREIGN AID

As indicated earlier, the Commission believed that the United States must continue economic assistance to the free countries "to secure the maximum military security for ourselves and to take our part in the advance of the living standards of the free world. This

[13] *Ibid.*, p. 45.

[14] *Ibid.*, pp. 46–47.

does not mean, however, that the taxpayers' money should be spent without regard to receiving full value for the money spent." [15]

There are certain principles which should be followed in the administration of foreign economic aid which would make it more effective and which would effectuate a substantial reduction of expenditures.

In developing these principles the Commission divided these foreign-aid programs into three categories: (*a*) large manufacturing or industrial development projects, (*b*) small manufacturing projects, and (*c*) projects which increase food supplies.

The Commission stressed that industrial projects should not be undertaken in countries which do not already have an industrial background. "In these countries there is little local capital available for participation and the vast background of transport, marketing, technical, and executive skills is lacking. Large industrial projects cannot succeed against this background and in any event cannot affect the standard of living for many years to come." [16] Obviously, such projects are not the answer to unemployment. American industrial experience has demonstrated that for large manufacturing a capital investment of $100,000,000 or more is required to provide 10,000 jobs.

A recent report of the United Nations states relative to industrially undeveloped countries:

> There are numerous examples of countries embarking upon ambitious projects on the basis of no more than the general desire to industrialize and with astonishingly inadequate information concerning all the relevant technical, social, and economic data upon which success of the project so greatly depends.

It was the opinion of the Commission that "the most valuable contribution to world economic stability can be made by improvement of small manufacturing industries in nonindustrialized countries." [17]

The fundamental need of many of the countries in the "Asian-African arc" is increased food supplies. Therefore, sound irrigation projects and the introduction of improved agricultural methods constitute appropriate objectives for American aid programs.

[15] *Ibid.*, p. 49. [16] *Ibid.*, pp. 49–50. [17] *Ibid.*, p. 50.

METHOD OF FINANCING

The financing of foreign-development projects by the United States has taken four forms: (*a*) loans to Governments, (*b*) loans to private industries, (*c*) grants or contributions to Governments or private development projects, and (*d*) grants and loans to international organizations.

The Mutual Security Act of 1954 provided that foreign aid should be extended more largely in the form of loans and that the Export-Import Bank should make and administer such loans as directed by the Foreign Operations Administration.

It was the opinion of the Commission that "making loans to countries to support their defense, which they cannot repay, only creates future difficulties and misleads the American taxpayers, as they are not a recoverable asset. Where there is no prospect of repayment, outright grants should be made, and they can be better controlled." [18]

TECHNICAL ASSISTANCE

The original relatively modest objectives of the Point Four program of technical cooperation have been expanded tremendously. These activities now cover not only the importation of American industrial skills but also furnishing professors to universities, as well as bringing large numbers of persons to the United States for industrial and professional training, including labor relations, agriculture, commerce, trade, and public administration.

The idea that the standard of living in backward countries can be substantially increased by giving them consumption goods the Commission considered most illusionary. Some such supplies are necessary to replace local use of consumption goods by military-assistance programs and in case of famines. "But to try to spread over these huge populations in normal times any amount of consumption goods which the United States has the resources to expend would be so thin as to have no lasting effect." [19]

The Task Force emphasized:

It is frequently assumed that physical poverty is the primary cause of communism and that, therefore, communism can be cured by spending

[18] *Ibid.*, p. 51.

[19] *Ibid.*, pp. 52–53.

in an endeavor to raise the general standard of living. There is no convincing proof that this is universally true. Communism, for example, is strongest in the higher wage industrial centers of Italy. Most foreign economic aid programs seem to be based on emotions and opinions—not on hard facts. In fact, in many underdeveloped countries, economic indicia from which to draw intelligent conclusions are totally lacking. As has been previously indicated, so-called illustrative programs are of little practical value as a basis for appropriations, since they are based merely on individual judgments as to what aid may be desirable. Actual expenditures may prove to be for quite different purposes.[20]

The Commission's proposals relative to fundamental policy in this area follow:

(*a*) That as all the countries in the original North Atlantic Treaty Organization have the highest degree of technical proficiency, the technical assistance by American personnel in these countries should cease.

(*b*) That as the original North Atlantic Treaty Organization countries are well able to send technical staffs to the United States at their own expense, the United States should cease to pay for this service.

(*c*) That in the "Asian-African arc," with the possible exception of Japan, no large manufacturing projects be undertaken and no large industrial plants be constructed, except for production of strategic materials; that otherwise all industrial aid be confined to small industries.

(*d*) That special emphasis be placed on agricultural improvement and irrigation projects.

(*e*) That, except under unusual circumstances growing out of strategic considerations, technological cooperation and technical assistance programs be based upon organization of joint units of local and American personnel as set out above.

(*f*) That wherever assistance is necessary and there is no prospect of repayment of a loan, the assistance should be in the form of an outright grant.

(*g*) That economic aid of all types should be limited to such undertakings as can be staffed with qualified personnel.

(*h*) That no economic aid should be granted for projects or undertakings where private investment capital is available for such projects.

(*i*) That all economic aid should be contingent upon good faith efforts of the recipient country to improve the investment climate both for domestic and foreign capital of a private nature.

[20] *Task Force Report on Overseas Economic Operations,* p. 25.

(*j*) That, as recommended in our Surplus Property Report, we emphasize the desirability of using excess and surplus property in connection with our foreign assistance programs.[21]

FUNCTIONS TO BE GIVEN TO OTHER AGENCIES

Some phases of foreign aid, such as military assistance, must be continued for some time to come; but there are other activities of the Foreign Operations Administration which should be continued only on a reduced basis. The Commission urged that in many instances these aspects should be administered by designated permanent departments of the Government.

The President, by executive order of May 8, 1955, transferred all of the direct military-assistance functions to the Department of Defense. There were some other functions of a direct military aid character in the Foreign Operations Administration which should be analyzed to determine if they should not also be delegated to the Department of Defense.

The functions of the Export-Import Bank in connection with foreign aid should be expanded, the Commission felt. This bank now investigates and makes loans on its own responsibility to foreign governments and enterprises for the development of industrial and natural resources. It also has made loans as fiscal agent for the Foreign Operations Administration. As a result this bank is in a position to cooperate with the International Bank for Reconstruction and Development to relieve much of the burden now imposed upon the United States. It also is equipped to review all proposed loans for economic aid to determine whether or not the projects involved are susceptible of private investment projects.

The Commission proposed that "all United States Government loans, where there is assurance of repayment, for industrial and natural resource development, whether to private institutions or governments, be made and managed by the Export-Import Bank." [22]

Similarly, many other functions of the International Cooperation Administration should be transferred to departments such as Interior, Commerce, Labor, Agriculture, and Treasury. In addition, many of the staff of the ICA might be transferred to these agencies.

[21] *Overseas Economic Operations,* A Report to the Congress, pp. 53–54.
[22] *Ibid.,* pp. 56–57.

The problem of providing for the qualified remainder is not one of great proportions because the annual turnover of Federal employees exceeds 500,000 a year.

CONCLUSIONS

For a number of years there have been large carry-overs of foreign-aid funds from appropriations for earlier years. On June 30, 1955, there was an unexpended balance of approximately $7,900,000,000 in this account. In addition, there was available as of December 31, 1954, in foreign currencies the equivalent of $973,000,000 in counterpart funds, some of which remained unspent at the end of 1955. An additional $2,700,000,000 was appropriated for mutual security for 1956. Thus the total sum available for 1956 would be about $11,500,000,000. A large part of this total is committed by contracts for the purchase of arms, for foreign assistance and off-shore procurement. Other sums are committed for industrial projects now under construction and to universities for technical assistance and other purposes. Through the recapture of unobligated funds, future appropriations can be reduced.

The Commission believed that important savings in administrative costs can be attained through the organization and principles of action proposed by it while at the same time the foreign-aid program can be made more effective.

"We realize," it said, "that some of the money spent on this program in the past has been spent unwisely and in some cases the taxpayers have not received full value for their money. We believe that the recommendations for eliminating the duplication of staffs and overlapping programs," previously summarized, "together with adherence to the basic principles contained in this report which should govern the conduct of our mutual security program, will result in substantial savings in the amount of money required to meet our needs in making the free world strong." [23]

The Task Force estimated that if its recommendations were adopted, a minimum of $360,000,000 could be saved each year from the mutual-aid nonmilitary programs without hindering the attainment of their objectives.

The Foreign Operations Administration was transferred to the

[23] *Ibid.*, p. 64.

State Department by the President in May, 1955, effective at the end of June. As the head of this new organization, called the International Cooperation Administration, the President appointed John B. Hollister, the executive director of the second Hoover Commission. In making appropriations for 1956, Congress reduced the original budget request for this agency by about one billion dollars.

6.

A Job Well Done

CHAPTER 19

A Few Words in Conclusion

A reading of the findings of the Commission on Organization of the Executive Branch of the Government should certainly convince most people that these constitute a painstaking and penetrating analysis of the major functions of the Federal Government. In all, the Commission made thirty-nine reports to the Congress, counting Commission and Task Force reports separately, and these offer a durable and comprehensive record of a sincere and honest appraisal of the Government by conscientious and capable American citizens. They represent, in fact, the most thorough and objective examination of the workings of our Federal system since the founding of the Republic.

In almost infinite detail these studies present a documented picture of a sprawling and voracious bureaucracy, of monumental waste, excesses and extravagances, of red tape, confusion, and disheartening frustrations, of loose management, regulatory irresponsibilities, and colossal largesse to special segments of the public, of enormous incompetence in foreign economic operations, and of huge appropriations frequently spent for purposes never intended by the Congress. It is not a pretty picture no matter how you view it.

The Commission did not paint it that way to discredit the Government. These citations of horrible examples of waste and extravagance —the Task Force reports abound with them—were solely to stir the people, the Congress, and the executive into taking remedial action.

Not once in its reports did the Hoover Commission mention an individual except to praise him. Again and again it cleared Federal workers of blame for deplorable or undesirable conditions. Many of them it found hard-working, sincere, and competent. Many of those consulted were as disturbed about conditions as were the members of the Task Forces, and as eager to remedy them, but they were helpless to do so. Instead, the Commission blamed the system.

The vast labyrinth of overlapping agencies and activities that is the American Government grew so fast and so big that it overflowed the bounds of reason and made over-all control and intelligent direction impossible. Bureaucratic methods that were satisfactory for a small Government did not meet the needs of a Government that had become a big business. That is largely why the system is at fault. That is also why it is vitally important that from time to time some independent, capable, and patriotic group of citizens like the Hoover Commission take a long look at it and its operations and, after determining its weaknesses and its failures, offer recommendations for improvements.

The Commission's reports make it clear that the Federal Government should be required to serve the interests of all the people all the time, and not just segments of the population. The Commission always concerned itself with the whole population of the United States and not with just fractions of it, and in so doing it offended many of the self-serving pressure groups, the organized, vociferous minorities who favor economy and efficiency for everyone else as long as it does not curtail their own vested interest in waste and extravagance. As was to be expected, these greedy, noisy pressure groups have been the most vocal of the Commission's critics, and the most unreasonable. They have distorted and misrepresented the Commission's actions, and this was to be expected too, for they flourish only when the public is uninformed, misinformed, or misled.

Of course, there will be honest differences of opinion, in Government and out of it, on some of the Hoover Commission's recommendations. A few of them are controversial in nature. There were differences of opinion within the Commission, and dissents resulted; but these were not more numerous proportionately than are those of the Supreme Court of the United States. They are but an expression of democracy in action. No one on the Commission expected its recommendations to be accepted as a whole and without discussion. Moreover, the Commission did not act for one session of the Congress. The great mass of information it gathered and its recommendations are available to the public, to students of government, and to the members and committees of Congress for consideration and action. It is difficult to conceive of any action by the Congress in any of the areas that it surveyed without reckoning with its findings.

THE COMMISSION'S OBJECTIVES

In Chapter 1 we stated that throughout the Commission's reports there run a number of basic ideas or objectives. The Commission's purpose in presenting them was to protect and to improve our constitutional Republic and the society on which it rests. Now that we have detailed the major problems with which the Commission dealt and how it tried to solve them, let's consider briefly how it developed these ideas or objectives in its recommendations.

They follow, with examples of specific recommendations designed to implement them.

1. Is the activity so conducted as to maintain the separation of powers and to preserve the rule of law?

The Hoover Commission itself is as good an expression of the working of the principle of the separation of powers in the American Government as could be found. It was set up by the legislative branch of the Government to investigate the operations of the executive branch and was instructed by law not to investigate the judicial branch. This it observed in all its inquiries and carried out in all its recommendations. One obvious fault of Big Government is the inevitable inclination of the Executive to override the legislative and the judicial and to dominate State governments as well. The whole Hoover Report is aimed at cutting Big Government down to its proper and constitutional size, and making it abide by the rule of law. The Commission recognized at all times that this is a Government of law and not of men, and at all times it strove to protect the individual citizen against the overreaching and autocratic bureaucrat.

The Commission also strove to restore the rule of law to Government. Repeatedly it returns to this principle in its recommendations. This is clear in the reports on Budget and Accounting, on Business Enterprises, on Depot Utilization, on Federal Medical Services, on Personnel and Civil Service, on Real Property, on Surplus Property, on Transportation, and on Water Resources and Power, and it is spelled out in detail in the report on Legal Services and Procedure. For instance, in Recommendation No. 30 of that report it said:

Authority delegated by the Congress to Federal administrative agencies should be clearly and precisely defined in the legislation, and agencies should strictly adhere to the letter and intent of the law.[1]

2. Does the present method of conducting the activity impair congressional control over the purse?

As a creature of the Congress, set up by it and reporting to it alone, the Hoover Commission in examining every activity of the executive branch was conscious of the rights of the legislative branch and never ceased to protect them. Four members of the Commission were members of the Congress and were always ready to fight for its prerogatives. Moreover, all the members of the Commission knew that the history of all Anglo-Saxon peoples, as well as that of the United States, shows that control of the purse by the representatives of the people in the legislature is their most effective control over the executive. Many times it has been the only control. The refusal to vote funds can halt most national activities.

This theme runs through all the Commission reports. It is fortified especially in the report on Budget and Accounting. Again and again it comes up in other reports. Whenever the opportunity presented itself, the Commission required prior authorization from the Congress for the spending of every cent of the public money. Repeatedly it also called for an annual review by the Congress of expenditures in all fields. As a policy it opposed the voting, even by the Congress, of large sums of money with discretion for the spending of it by bureaucrats. It especially opposed the accumulation of large sums in certain agencies like the Department of Defense and Foreign Aid of appropriated but unspent and uncommitted monies. A typical recommendation is No. 5 in the Commission's report on Water Resources and Power. It reads:

That the revolving funds be abolished and all monies payable into these funds be covered into the general fund of the Federal Treasury and all project funds be appropriated by the Congress.[2]

[1] Commission on Organization of the Executive Branch of the Government, *Legal Services and Procedure,* A Report to the Congress, March 1955 (Washington, D.C., U.S. Government Printing Office, 1955), p. 50.

[2] Commission on Organization of the Executive Branch of the Government, *Water Resources and Power,* A Report to the Congress, June 1955 (Washington, D.C., U.S. Government Printing Office, 1955), I, 55.

3. Is the activity so conducted as to transgress on civil control of the Government?

As our survey has clearly indicated, one of the major studies of the Hoover Commission was devoted to the business activities of the armed services, and in turn one of the major attacks on its reports is that they tried "to centralize even more authority in civilian management at the Department of Defense level and would reduce the authority of the military personnel even in command fields." [3] The Commission members knew, of course, of the steady resistance offered by generals and admirals to civilian reforms in the armed services. They knew that the military had tried to block and later to vitiate unification of the military services under a civilian secretary of defense. They also knew that the definite orders of Congress to provide an inventory of what they own and a catalogue of common-use articles so that business principles could be applied to the services had not been obeyed, or had been delayed. They also knew that civil control of the armed services is a basic American principle, written into the Constitution, and given effect by General Washington, when he became our first President.

Therefore the principle of civilian control of the armed services was maintained by the Commission's recommendations where it existed and strengthened where it was weakened. Yet the Commission did not impinge on the purely military prerogative of deciding needs in the areas of strategy, morale, and logistics. The Commission was as deeply concerned over personal liberty as it was over national defense, for with loss of the former the latter would not be important, and so it did not encourage military domination of national policies, not even in the field of national defense. In this respect a typical recommendation is No. 24, in Budget and Accounting:

> That the Comptrollers in the military departments be responsible only to the Secretary of their respective services, and that concurrent responsibility to a Chief of Staff or equivalent be discontinued.[4]

4. Does the activity as organized and operated interfere with or transgress upon the free enterprise system?

[3] Hanson Baldwin, *New York Times,* Aug. 9, 1955.

[4] Commission on Organization of the Executive Branch of the Government, *Budget and Accounting,* A Report to the Congress, June 1955 (Washington, D.C., U.S. Government Printing Office, 1955), p. 56.

Even a casual reading must make it clear that the Commission's reports give the American public for the first time the extent of the Federal Government's ventures into commercial-type business. For instance, they reveal that there are 2,500 such businesses in the Department of Defense alone, with an investment estimated at $15,000,000,000. They ask that at least 1,000 of them be terminated. They also show the vast expenditure of public money in water-power projects, with 10 per cent of the people benefiting from subsidies paid by 100 per cent. One report after the other discloses some activity or other of the Government striking a blow at the free enterprise system on which our high standard of living is based and undermining the economy which pays a large share of the taxes on which the Government itself functions. Scores of the Commission's recommendations are aimed at taking the Federal Government out of commercial-type businesses or at preserving the free enterprise system. One of the more specific is Recommendation No. 7 in the report on Business Enterprises. In part it reads:

(*a*) That the following commercial-type facilities operated by the Department of Defense, except when located in isolated or overseas areas, be closed:

Bakeries
Meat cutting plants
The Army and Marine Corps clothing manufacturing plants
The Navy custom tailor shop
Laundries (except those needed to perform hazardous operations)
Dry-cleaning plants [5]

5. Is the activity conducted in the most efficient and economical manner?

Efficiency and economy were prime targets of the Hoover Commission in its study of Government activities, and every one of its reports presents evidence that its work in these areas was effective. It was so effective, in fact, that the Commission's enemies have tried to use it as a basis of attack. Some of them charge that the Commission put a dollar value, and that alone, on all Federal activities. The fact is that the Commission did point out waste and extravagance, inefficiency and incompetence, where they existed. That was

[5] Commission on Organization of the Executive Branch of the Government, *Business Enterprises,* A Report to the Congress, May 1955 (Washington, D.C., U.S. Government Printing Office, 1955), p. 34.

its duty, and it did it. Its sponsors in the Congress, and the Commission itself, felt that the American taxpayer should have the truth about the business of Government, and the reports give it to him in detail.

One point should be stressed here. The Commission did not seek savings purely for the sake of saving a few million or a few billion dollars, important though that might be. In all instances it also gave full consideration to the importance of the activity in terms of service to the American people and to the security and defense of the nation. For instance, the Commission's report on Research and Development recommended a large increase in expenditures so that a more efficient job for the defense of the country and the welfare of the people might be done.

ESTIMATE OF SAVINGS

Most of the Task Forces made estimates of savings that would result from implementation of their recommendations. Not all of these recommendations were accepted by the Commission, and in many instances the Commission made recommendations that went beyond those of the Task Forces. It is difficult, therefore, to give an exact figure for possible savings.

Following are annual savings estimated by the Task Forces, with one item, that of Lending Agencies, a Commission estimate:

Budget and Accounting	$4,000,000,000
Depot Utilization	253,000,000
Federal Medical Services	290,000,000
Lending, Guaranteeing, and Insurance Activities	200,000,000
Overseas Economic Operations	360,000,000
Paperwork Management–Part I	255,000,000
Paperwork Management–Part II	33,300,000
Personnel and Civil Service	48,500,000
Real Property Management	185,000,000
Special Personnel Problems–Department of Defense	388,800,000
Subsistence (Food and Clothing)	400,000,000
Transportation	151,500,000
Use and Disposal of Federal Surplus Property	2,000,000,000*

* For the first 4 years; thereafter $1,000,000,000 per annum.

The following Task Forces indicated that great savings could result from their recommendations, but made no dollar estimates:

Business Enterprises

Business Organization of the Department of Defense

Intelligence Activities

Military Procurement

Water Resources and Power

The Commission was careful to point out that it did not add up these savings for the reason that the total would be an overestimate. Some of these savings overlap others, particularly the savings estimated for Budget and Accounting and for the Use and Disposal of Surplus Property. Some of them also represent savings based on business practices that are not entirely applicable to procedure required by law of Government agencies.

"In any event," the Commission pointed out with pride, in its final report to the Congress, "with all such discounts there are enough possible savings to enable the balancing of the budget and reduction of taxes."

The Commission's investigations also indicated that large amounts of capital tied up in various Government-sponsored operations could be returned to the United States Treasury. Among these are:

1. The Government could recover some or all of the capital that it supplied to start various lending and financial agencies that have since gained the operational experience and financial strength to stand on their own feet. Among such agencies are: Federal Housing Administration, Federal intermediate credit banks, Federal National Mortgage Association, and the Rural Electrification Administration.
2. Agencies to which the Government has given authorization to draw funds from the Treasury in larger sums than are needed for their activities.
3. Lending agencies that can be liquidated more rapidly.
4. Speedy disposal of all surplus personal and all unneeded real property.

Altogether the return of such assets would exceed $10,000,000,000, according to the Commission's report. This is on the conservative side, however, and Mr. Hoover has estimated that they might total $15,000,000,000. Certainly they would provide funds to make a substantial cut in the national debt.

The Commission's own statement of the scope and purposes of

its studies and recommendations is expressed in its final report. There it says it sought six objectives:

First —To preserve the full security of the Nation in a disturbed world.

Second —To maintain the functioning of all necessary agencies which make for the common welfare.

Third —To stimulate the fundamental research upon which national security and programs are based.

Fourth —To improve efficiency and eliminate waste in the executive agencies.

Fifth —To eliminate or reduce Government competition with private enterprise.

Sixth —and perhaps the most important of all—to strengthen the economic, social, and governmental structure which has brought us, now for 166 years, constant blessings and progress.

PUBLIC OPINION

The implementation of the Commission's program of reform must await the development of full public awareness of the importance of its recommendations in terms of the well-being of all American citizens. The educational program is well advanced and is being pushed by the Citizens Committee for the Hoover Report. History provides comforting evidence that the facts upon which national judgment ultimately rests can be obscured only for brief periods of time. Lincoln's adage that you cannot fool all the people all of the time still is well founded.

ATTACKS BY PRESSURE GROUPS

Most of the attacks on the Commission's recommendations have come from spokesmen of selfish pressure groups. When these could not face the facts produced by the Commission's reports in their areas of special interest, they resorted to generalizations that misrepresented the Commission and its intentions. They have shouted that the Commission "sought to turn back the clock," that it proposed the "virtual liquidation of the Rural Electrification Administration," that it urged the "stopping of crop loans to farmers" and the "sabotaging of the whole field of public power." Nothing could be further from the truth.

On the contrary, one will search in vain for a recommendation in a Commission report that would discard any meritorious or efficient Federal activity, or, for that matter, that would halt the wholesome evolution of the functions of the Government. Over and over again the Commission tried to reinforce all Federal activities in the public interest. It did recommend that certain agencies that have reached maturity and that perform significant public services be required to stand on their own feet and to finance themselves instead of being a continuing burden on the taxpayer. It did recommend that certain agencies of demonstrated merit and financial success be mutualized as are such other agencies as the Federal Reserve banks, the home-loan banks, and the Federal Deposit Insurance Corporation. This constitutes a compliment to their good management and financial integrity, and certainly it is not an attempt, "snide" or otherwise, to abolish them.

In the final analysis, the continuance of any Government agency or activity must depend on its demonstrated value to the people. If it is essential, and if the services supplied are better or cheaper than can be provided by private industry, it deserves to be continued. If not, it does not deserve to survive, and pressure groups, as well as citizens in general, should realize that. In any case, the accounts should be kept in an honest manner and cover all costs. There should be no hidden subsidies. And the charges should relate to the cost of the service.

The constructive reforms recommended by the Commission for some of the Federal agencies that were created during the depression and that have survived since on subsidies from the Treasury might well be the very means of giving them a long and healthy life. Some of these agencies not only serve a useful purpose but are financially sound. Some of them, however, not only give service to their beneficiaries below true cost, but also give them refunds or dividends, while making little or no effort to repay the Treasury or to end their subsidies. Naïve indeed would be the person who would believe that all the people are going to keep on forever providing services below cost and thus giving subsidies to minorities that can well afford to pay for the service. Inevitably the true facts must come out, and the majority that has been milked through the years will revolt and end that activity.

On the other hand, consider the Federal agencies that have been organized on the basis suggested by the Commission. Take the Federal home-loan banks, for instance. They were created in 1932, during the Hoover Administration. Their initial capital was supplied by the Treasury. Since then they have repaid the capital; they have been mutualized; their stock is owned by member concerns; and the management is in the hands of the owners, subject to regulation by the Home Loan Bank Board. Up to 1954 they had advanced $5,500,000,000, declared dividends of $63,152,000 and built up a surplus of $39,362,000. They are financially independent, serve their members well, and will of course go on indefinitely helping Americans to build and to own homes.

The Federal home-loan banks are not alone in this respect. There are a half-dozen other Federal agencies that have followed similar methods and are similarly successful. Experience with such agencies influenced the Hoover Commission to recommend that other agencies that could do so be required to free themselves from being supported by the taxpayer.

Another method of attack by spokesmen of pressure groups is to distort the Commission's proposals. An example of this is the charge, often repeated, that the Commission recommended a raise in parcel-post rates in disregard of the needs of poor people and for the benefit of the Railway Express Agency. Reference to the Commission's report would reveal that it merely pointed out that Congress in 1950 (Public Law 643, 64 Stat. 1050) required the postmaster general to increase rates to cover the cost of parcel post but that present rates had failed to provide an adequate return. It recommended that he obey the law. That and nothing more. The distorters of this simple recommendation fail to point out that present parcel-post rates constitute a hidden subsidy to the large mail-order houses and other business firms, because the rates charged to them do not cover the total cost of delivering their packages.

Still another trick of spokesmen for antagonistic pressure groups is to attack the Commission as a body or its recommendations as a whole when in fact their opposition is to one or two or at most a few recommendations that expose or would reform their own racket. They would sacrifice the good of the whole community rather than reveal their own pet interest. Actually, the vast bulk of the Commission's recommendations are noncontroversial and have aroused no opposition, either in Government or out of it.

ALL ITS GOALS MET

Thus it will be seen that the Hoover Commission met all its goals. It made a frontal attack on Big Government and all that it means, but it did not recommend the elimination of any one activity required for the security or the welfare of the American people. All its recommendations stood firmly on American principles of Government. It reaffirmed the rule of law. It supported civil control of the Government. It strengthened control of the purse by Congress. It kept in mind at all times the basic fact that the American Government is for the benefit of all the people and not just for fractions of them, no matter how noisy and insistent these fractions may be in presenting their selfish demands. It served the cause of States' rights by asserting and reasserting that the Federal Government should not do what can be done equally well by State or local governments. It helped to renew the vigor and prosperity of the free enterprise system by exposing the Government's colossal business ventures and by demanding that it stop its unfair competition.

Apart from all else, the Commission's investigations and studies have been of great educational value, and this fact alone would make them definitely worth while. Mr. Hoover pointed this out at the final session of the Commission. Intelligent discussion, he said, is vital to the success of our Republic. The Commission assembled the greatest mass of facts on Government ever gathered at one effort in our history. Its recommendations have caused discussion throughout the Nation. This, added Mr. Hoover, is good for the Nation.

A reading of these chapters should make it clear that implementation of the Commission's 314 recommendations, or the bulk of them, would have a salutary effect for all American citizens. Not only would it bring greater efficiency and economy into Government; it would also retard, if not halt, the steady trend toward Big Government, which if it goes on might well be disastrous. Above all, it would protect the American citizen in all his rights.

Appendix A

Following are the Task Forces and Committees of the Commission on Organization of the Executive Branch of the Government and their personnel:

Budget and Accounting

This Task Force studied budgeting, accounting, and auditing processes to bring about adequate congressional control over finances as well as full public reporting.

Chairman: J. Harold Stewart
Members: Dudley E. Browne, H. E. Humphreys, Jr., Christian E. Jarchow, Gwilym Alexander Price, Kenneth C. Tiffany, J. David Wright
Staff Director: Joseph M. Sullivan

Intelligence Activities

This Task Force studied the operations of the Central Intelligence Agency and other major intelligence activities.

Chairman: General Mark W. Clark
Members: Richard L. Conolly, Ernest F. Hollings, Henry Kearns, Edward V. Rickenbacker, Donald S. Russell
Staff Director: James G. Christiansen

Legal Services and Procedure

This Task Force studied the legal services and procedure of the executive branch of the Government.

Chairman: James Marsh Douglas
Members: Herbert Watson Clark, Cody Fowler, Albert J. Harno, James McCauley Landis, Carl McFarland, Ross L. Malone, Jr., David F. Maxwell, Harold R. Medina, David W. Peck, Reginald Heber Smith, E. Blythe Stason, Elbert Parr Tuttle, Edward Ledwidge Wright

Special Consultants: Robert H. Jackson
George Roberts
Arthur T. Vanderbilt
Staff Director: Whitney R. Harris
Research Director: Courts Oulahan

Lending Agencies

This Task Force studied the operations of Federal lending agencies and the agencies engaged in guaranteeing and insuring loans and deposits.

Chairman: Paul Grady
Members: Paul Bestor
George L. Bliss
Henry T. Bodman
William W. Campbell
Albert Leslie Cole
Clifford D. Cooper
Gardner Cowles
Preston Hotchkis
Arnold B. Keller
Staff Director: Theodore Herz

Medical Services

This Task Force studied the more than sixty Federal agencies which are of importance to the health of the nation.

Chairman: Chauncey McCormick *

Assistant Chairman: Dr. Edwin L. Crosby
Members: Dr. Francis J. Braceland
Dr. Otto W. Brandhorst
Dr. Edward D. Churchill
Dr. Michael DeBakey
Dr. Evarts A. Graham
Dr. Alan Gregg
Dr. Paul R. Hawley
Dr. Theodore George Klumpp †
Dr. Hugh Rodman Leavell
Dr. Basil C. MacLean
Dr. Walter B. Martin
Dr. James Roscoe Miller
Dr. Dwight L. Wilbur
Dr. Milton C. Winternitz
Consultants: Joseph G. Noh
Marion A. Stephens
Staff Director: Dr. James P. Dixon

Subcommittee on Health Insurance

Chairman: Msgr. Donald A. McGowan
C. Manton Eddy
Jay C. Ketchum
Dr. H. B. Mulholland
Elmer A. Van Steenwyk

Subcommittee on Dentistry

Chairman: Dr. Otto W. Brandhorst
Dr. Rudolph H. Friedrich
Dr. James P. Hollers
Dr. Leo J. Schoeny

* Deceased, September 8, 1955.
† Appointed to replace Mr. McCormick as Chairman, September 26, 1954.

Overseas Economic Operations

This Task Force studied the Government's activities in the international economic field.

Chairman: Henning W. Prentis, Jr.
Members: Harry A. Bullis, Frederick C. Crawford, Ferdinand Eberstadt, Arthur B. Foye, Ernest Kanzler, Julius Klein, Charles Sawyer, Joseph P. Spang, Jr.
Staff Director: Bernard S. Van Rensselaer

Paperwork Management

This Task Force studied paperwork in the Government and that imposed upon private individuals and business enterprises having dealings with the Government.

Chairman: Emmett J. Leahy
Members: Herbert E. Angel, Thomas F. Conroy, Edmund D. Dwyer, Berchel H. Harper
Staff Director: Matson Holbrook

Personnel and Civil Service

This Task Force studied Government personnel and personnel management problems.

Chairman: Harold W. Dodds
Members: Frank W. Abrams, Chester I. Barnard, Lewis B. Cuyler, Devereux C. Josephs, Don G. Mitchell, Willard S. Paul, Robert Ramspeck, William Hallam Tuck, Leonard D. White
Staff Director: George A. Graham

Procurement

This Task Force studied all procurement activities of the Government, with emphasis on the problems involved in military supply management.

Chairman: Robert Wilson Wolcott
Vice Chairmen: Ira Mosher and George P. F. Smith
Members: Frank M. Folsom, William T. Golden, Horace Babcock Horton, Carl A. Ilgenfritz, Mervin J. Kelly, George Houk Mead, Frank H. Neely, Mundy I. Peale, Robert Proctor, George A. Renard, Franz Schneider, Charles J. Stilwell
Staff Director: Valentine B. Deale

Real Property

This Task Force studied the real property holdings of the Federal Government being utilized or potentially useful for commercial, industrial, or institutional purposes, or which were acquired for purposes of national defense.

Chairman: John R. Lotz
Members: James M. Barker, William V. Burnell, John Anthony Hill, Thomas D. Jolly, Glenn McHugh, William C. Mullendore, Benjamin H. Wooten
Staff Director: Ben P. Gale

Subsistence Services

This Task Force studied the functions of all agencies of the Federal Government which provide food and clothing.

Chairman: Joseph P. Binns
Members: Vallee O. Appel, George H. Coppers, Andrew J. Crotty, Howard B. Cunningham, James McBrayer Garvey, John L. Hennessy *, Clifford E. Hicks, Ollie E. Jones, John H. Kraft, Herbert F. Krimendahl, Joseph A. Lee, John T. McCarthy, George M. Mardikian, Perry M. Shoemaker, Gordon A. Stouffer
Staff Director: C. D. Bean

Subcommittee on Depot Utilization

Chairman: Clifford E. Hicks
Vallee O. Appel, Leroy D. Greene, Theodore G. Klumpp, Perry M. Shoemaker, George P. F. Smith
Staff Director: Hulon O. Warlick, Jr.

Use and Disposal of Surplus Property

This Task Force studied the use and disposal of surplus property owned by Government agencies.

Chairman: General Robert E. Wood
Members: Harry Erlicher, Leroy D. Greene, Thomas D. Jolly, Carl Kresl, James D. Mooney, George A. Renard, Edward Starr, Jr., Walter W. Tangeman
Staff Director: Gerald S. Wise

* Deceased, July 2, 1955.

Water Resources and Power

This Task Force studied all agencies having to do with water resources and power, including navigation, flood control, drainage, irrigation, reclamation, domestic water supply, and the generation, transmission and distribution of electric energy produced by Government agencies.

Chairman: Admiral Ben Moreell
Members:
Charles L. Andrews
William B. Bates
Pope F. Brock
Carey H. Brown
Charles Edison
James P. Growdon
Julian Hinds
Wesley W. Horner
John Jirgal
Edward A. Kracke
J. Bracken Lee
Albert Chester Mattei
Leslie A. Miller
Harry Winford Morrison
Lacey V. Murrow
Frank H. Newnam, Jr.
Malcolm Pirnie
Harry E. Polk
Roscoe Pound
John Wallace Reavis
Donald Randall Richberg
Arthur B. Roberts
Robert William Sawyer
William D. Shannon
Royce J. Tipton

Staff Director: Charles D. Curran

Committee on Business Organization of the Department of Defense

This Committee studied the business organization of the Defense Department. Its purpose was to coordinate the work of several Task Forces insofar as they were concerned with that Department. Among these cooperating Task Forces were Subsistence Services (including its Subcommittee on Depot Utilization), Budget and Accounting, Lending Agencies, Real Property, Overseas Economic Operations, Medical Services, Use and Disposal of Surplus Property, and Paperwork Management.

Chairman: Charles R. Hook
Members:
Joseph P. Binns
George C. Brainard
Howard Bruce
Michael DeBakey
Frank M. Folsom
Joseph B. Hall
Mervin J. Kelly
Arthur Franklin King
John R. Lotz
George Houk Mead
Frank H. Neely
Willard S. Paul
Thomas R. Reid
Reuben B. Robertson, Jr.
Franz Schneider
Perry M. Shoemaker
Robert Wilson Wolcott
Robert E. Wood

Liaison Assistant: Frank Upman, Jr.

Subcommittee on Business Enterprises in the Department of Defense

Chairman: Joseph B. Hall
C. D. Bean
George P. F. Smith
Leroy D. Greene

Assistant to the Chairman: Frank J. Andress
Staff Director: Bernard F. Zuccardy

Subcommittee on Research Activities in the Department of Defense

Chairman: Mervin J. Kelly
Frederick L. Hovde
Robert M. Kimball
C. Guy Suits
Clyde E. Williams
Staff Director: G. Terrell Selby

Subcommittee on Special Personnel Problems in the Department of Defense

Chairman: Thomas R. Reid
Vice Chairman: John J. Corson
Frederick G. Atkinson
Frederick J. Bell
George C. Brainard
Samuel L. H. Burk
Raymond S. Livingstone
Willard S. Paul
Reuben B. Robertson, Jr.
Robert J. Smith
Staff Director: Cecil E. Goode

Subcommittee on Transportation Activities in the Department of Defense

Chairman: Perry M. Shoemaker
Consultant: Selig Altschul
Alvin Shapiro. Clifford E. Hicks
Director of Passenger Study: James K. Knudson
Director of Freight Study: John B. Keeler
Acting Director of Freight Study: John R. Staley

Appendix B

Biographical Sketches of Commissioners and of Task Force Members

Abrams, Frank W., Mattituck, New York. Syracuse University. Retired Chairman of the Board of Standard Oil Company (New Jersey). Member of Task Force on Personnel and Civil Service.

Andrews, Charles L., Memphis, Tenn. Lafayette College. President or member of various cotton associations. Partner in the C. L. Andrews Cotton Company. Member of Task Force on Water Resources and Power.

Angel, Herbert Edmund, Bethesda, Md. George Washington University. Director, Records Management Division, National Archives and Records Service, General Services Administration. Member of Task Force on Paperwork Management.

Appel, Vallee O., Chicago, Ill. University of Chicago and Harvard University. President of Fulton Market Cold Storage Company, Chicago, Ill. Member of the Secretary of War's Food Commission in 1946, and of the Advisory Committee, Research and Marketing Administration. Vice President and Director, National Quartermaster Association. Member of the Task Force on Subsistence Services, and of the Subcommittee on Depot Utilization of the Committee on Business Organization of the Department of Defense.

Atkinson, Frederick G., New York, N.Y. Columbia University. With R. H. Macy & Co., Inc., as Vice President in charge of personnel. Wartime Chief of Personnel, United States Air Transport Command. Member of Subcommittee on Special Personnel Problems in the Department of Defense.

Barker, James M., Chicago, Ill. Massachusetts Institute of Technology. Chairman of the Board, Allstate Insurance Co. Former financial Vice President and now Director and Adviser to Sears, Roebuck & Company in connection with world-wide retail store development. Member of Task Force on Real Property.

Barnard, Chester I., New York, N.Y. Harvard University. Formerly President, Rockefeller Foundation and General Education Board. Now Chairman, National Science Board; Director, National War Fund. Member of Task Force on Personnel and Civil Service.

Bates, William B., Houston, Tex. University of Texas. Chairman of the Board, Second National Bank of Houston, and in active practice of law. Member of Task Force on Water Resources and Power.

Bell, Frederick J., Washington, D.C. Rear Admiral U.S.N. (Retired). United States Naval Academy. Author of books on naval and management matters. Now Executive Vice President, National Automobile Dealers Association. Industry Member, President's National Labor-Management Manpower Policy Committee. Member of Subcommittee on Special Personnel Problems in the Department of Defense.

Bestor, Paul, Glen Ridge, N.J. Tarkio College and Yale University. Formerly President, Federal Land Bank of St. Louis, and Federal Intermediate Credit Bank; and Farm Loan Commissioner. Now President, Trust Company of New Jersey. Member of Task Force on Lending Agencies.

Binns, Joseph P., New York, N.Y. Cornell University. Managing Director, the Waldorf-Astoria, and Vice President, Hilton Hotels Corporation, in charge of operations in the East. Chairman of the Task Force on Subsistence Services and a member of the Committee on Business Organization of the Department of Defense.

Bliss, George L., Mount Vernon, N.Y. University of Pennsylvania. President, Century Federal Savings and Loan Association, New York. Member of Task Force on Lending Agencies.

Bodman, Henry T., Grosse Pointe Farms, Mich. Princeton University. General Vice President, National Bank of Detroit. Member of Task Force on Lending Agencies.

Braceland, Francis J., Hartford, Conn. La Salle College and Jefferson Medical College. Chief psychiatrist, U.S. Navy in World War II. Now Psychiatrist-in-Chief, Institute of Living, Hartford, and Clinical Professor of Psychiatry, Yale University. Member of Task Force on Medical Services.

Brainard, George C., Cleveland, Ohio. Cornell University. Chairman of the Executive Committee, Addressograph-Multigraph Corporation. Member of Committee on Business Organization of the Department of Defense and the Subcommittee on Special Personnel Problems in the Department of Defense.

Brandhorst, Otto W., St. Louis, Mo. Washington University. Dean, Washington University School of Dentistry since 1945. Member of Task Force on Medical Services, and Chairman of the Subcommittee on Dentistry.

Brock, Pope F., Atlanta, Ga. University of Georgia. General Counsel, Coca-Cola Company, Atlanta. Member of Task Force on Water Resources and Power.

Brown, Carey H., Scottsville, N.Y. University of Chicago, U.S. Military Academy. Corps of Engineers, 1910–1930. Manager, Engineering and Manufacturing Services, Kodak Park Works, Eastman Kodak Company. Member of Task Force on Water Resources and Power.

Brown, Clarence J., Blanchester, Ohio. Washington and Lee University and Wilmington College. Member, U.S. House of Representatives, 76th to 83d Congresses, 7th Ohio District. President of the Brown Publishing Company. House sponsor of legislation by which Congress created both the first Hoover Commission and the present one. Member of the Hoover Commission.

Browne, Dudley E., Burbank, Calif. University of California (Los Angeles). Comptroller, Lockheed Aircraft Corp. Member of Task Force on Budget and Accounting.

Brownell, Herbert, Jr., New York. University of Nebraska and Yale Law School. Attorney General of United States. Member of the Hoover Commission.

Bruce, Howard, Baltimore, Md. Virginia Military Institute. Chairman of the Board, Worthington Corporation, N.Y. Member of Committee on Business Organization of the Department of Defense.

Bullis, Harry A., Minneapolis, Minn. University of Wisconsin. Chairman of the Board of General Mills, Inc. In 1953 headed Government team to Formosa evaluating Mutual Security operations. Member of Task Force on Overseas Economic Operations.

Burk, Samuel L. H., White Plains, N.Y. University of Pennsylvania. Director of Personnel Administration, General Foods Corp. Member of Subcommittee on Special Personnel Problems in the Department of Defense.

Burnell, William V., Belmont, Mass. Tufts College. National President, American Society of Appraisers. Formerly Vice President, Stone & Webster Engineering Corporation, in charge of Appraisal and Valuation Division. Member of Task Force on Real Property.

Campbell, William W., Forrest City, Ark. University of Arkansas. President, National Bank of Eastern Arkansas. Member of Task Force on Lending Agencies.

Churchill, Edward D., Boston, Mass. Northwestern and Harvard universities. Chief Surgeon, Massachusetts General Hospital in Boston. Member of Task Force on Medical Services.

Clark, Herbert Watson, San Francisco, Calif. University of Michigan. Chairman, Committee of Bar Examiners, State of California; member, American Law Institute. Member of Task Force on Legal Services and Procedure.

Clark, Mark Wayne, Charleston, S.C. General, U.S. Army (Retired). United States Military Academy. President, The Citadel. In World War II commanded Allied ground forces in Italy. In 1952–1953 Commander in Chief, Far East Command. Chairman of the Task Force on Intelligence Activities.

Cole, Albert Leslie, Greenwich, Conn. Director and General Business Manager, Reader's Digest Association. Member of Task Force on Lending Agencies.

Conolly, Richard Lansing, Brooklyn, N.Y. Admiral, U.S.N. (Retired). In World War II, Commander in Chief U. S. Fleet. Now President of Long Island University. Member of Task Force on Intelligence Activities.

Conroy, Thomas F., New York, N.Y. Manager of New York Office for

Pan American World Airways, Inc. Member of Task Force on Paperwork Management.

Cooper, Clifford D., Covina, Calif. Pasadena City College and University of Texas. National Chairman of the Committee for Young Men in Government. President, Horning-Cooper, Inc. Member of Task Force on Lending Agencies.

Coppers, George H., Englewood, N.J. Fordham University. President, National Biscuit Company. Governor, American Bakers Association, and Director, Grocery Manufacturers Association of America. Member of Task Force on Subsistence Services.

Corson, John J., Arlington, Va. University of Virginia. Management consultant with McKinsey & Company. Vice Chairman of Subcommittee on Special Personnel Problems in the Department of Defense.

Cowles, Gardner, New York, N.Y. Harvard University. President of Cowles Magazines, Inc.; also President or Chairman of Board of Directors of several publishing companies. Member of Task Force on Lending Agencies.

Crawford, Frederick Coolidge, Cleveland, Ohio. Harvard University. Chairman of the Board, Thompson Products, Inc. Vice President and a Governor of Aircraft Industries Association. Member of Task Force on Overseas Economic Operations.

Crosby, Edwin L., Winnetka, Ill. Union College, Albany Medical College and Johns Hopkins University. Director, American Hospital Association. Assistant Chairman and Director of Research of Task Force on Medical Services.

Crotty, Andrew J., Boston, Mass. Boston College. Career in mass feeding techniques and now President of Crotty Bros., Inc. Past President of the National Restaurant Association. Member of Task Force on Subsistence Services.

Cunningham, Howard B., Englewood, N.J. Vice President in Charge of Procurement, National Biscuit Company, New York, N.Y. Member of Task Force on Subsistence Services.

Cuyler, Lewis B., Princeton, N.J. Princeton University. Vice President in charge of Personnel, National City Bank of New York. Member of Task Force on Personnel and Civil Service.

DeBakey, Michael, Houston, Tex. Tulane University. Chairman, Department of Surgery, Baylor University, College of Medicine. Member of Task Force on Medical Services and Committee on Business Organization of the Department of Defense.

Dodds, Harold W., Princeton, N.J. Grove City College, Princeton University, and University of Pennsylvania. Adviser to foreign governments. President of Princeton University. Chairman, Task Force on Personnel and Civil Service.

Douglas, James Marsh, St. Louis, Mo. Washington University. Formerly Chief Justice, Supreme Court of Missouri. Chairman of the Board of Washington University. Chairman, Task Force on Legal Services and Procedure.

Dwyer, Edmund D., Falls Church, Va. St. Bonaventure College and Georgetown University Law School. Control Engineer with Federal Works Agency. Director of Office Methods Staff for Navy Department. Member, Board of Directors of Armed Forces Management Association. Member of Task Force on Paperwork Management.

Eberstadt, Ferdinand, Huntington, N.Y. Princeton University. President and Chairman of Eberstadt & Company, Inc., and of Chemical Fund, Inc. In 1946, Assistant to Bernard Baruch on U.S. Delegation to UN Atomic Energy Commission. Member of Task Force on Overseas Economic Operations.

Eddy, C. Manton, Hartford, Conn. Brown University. Vice President and Secretary, Connecticut General Life Insurance Company. Formerly Chairman of the Joint Group Committee of the Life Insurance Association of America and American Life Convention. Member of Medical Services Task Force Subcommittee on Health Insurance.

Edison, Charles, West Orange, N.J. Massachusetts Institute of Technology. With Thomas A. Edison, Inc., since 1914; President, 1926, Chairman of the Board, 1950. Assistant Secretary of the Navy and Secretary of the Navy from 1936 through 1940. Governor of New Jersey 1941–1944. Member of Task Force on Water Resources and Power.

Erlicher, Harry, Schenectady, N.Y. Public Schools. Formerly General Purchasing Agent and Vice President, General Electric Company; President and Director, Loughborough Mining Co. Now Special Assistant to the Under Secretary of the Army. Member of Task Force on Use and Disposal of Surplus Property.

Farley, James A., New York. Former Postmaster General of United States. Organized James A. Farley & Company which merged with five other firms to form General Builders Supply Corporation of which he became President. Formerly Chairman, New York State Athletic Commission, and Chairman, Democratic National Committee. Now Chairman of Board of Directors, Coca-Cola Export Corporation, and Chairman of Board, Coca-Cola Bottling Company of Boston. Member of Hoover Commission.

Ferguson, Homer, Detroit, Michigan. Former United States Senator. Now Ambassador to the Philippines. Member of the Hoover Commission.

Flemming, Arthur S., Delaware, Ohio. Ohio Wesleyan University. Director, Office of Defense Mobilization (on leave as President of Ohio Wesleyan University). Member of the United States Civil Service Commission, 1939–1948. Served with the Office of Production Management, War Manpower Commission, Navy Department, Department of Labor, and the Atomic Energy Commission, in connection with national manpower and personnel problems. Member of both Hoover Commissions.

Floberg, John F., Chicago, Ill. Loyola University (Chicago) and Harvard Law School. Assistant Secretary of Navy for Air, 1949–1953. Now partner in Kirkland, Fleming, Green, Martin & Ellis. Member of Advisory Committee to Task Force on Procurement.

Folsom, Frank M., New York, N.Y. President, Radio Corporation of

America. Member of Task Force on Procurement and of the Committee on Business Organization of the Department of Defense.

Fowler, Cody, Tampa, Fla. Cumberland University. Formerly President, American Bar Association. Member of Task Force on Legal Services and Procedure.

Foye, Arthur B., New York, N.Y. New York University. Senior partner, Haskins & Sells. President, American Institute of Accountants; President, Far East-America Council of Commerce and Industry; Vice President, American Asiatic Association. Member of Task Force on Overseas Economic Operations.

Friedrich, Rudolph H., Plainfield, N.J. Northwestern University. Chairman of Council on Federal Dental Services, American Dental Association. Member of Medical Services Task Force Subcommittee on Dentistry.

Garvey, James McBrayer, Cincinnati, Ohio. Princeton University. Career with American Laundry Machinery Company, becoming President in 1950. Also President of Garvey Brothers Company, Fort Myers, Fla. Member of the Task Force on Subsistence Services.

Golden, William T., New York. University of Pennsylvania and Harvard University. Chairman, Executive Committee, the National Radiator Co. Reviewed for the President and the Director of the Budget the Government's military-scientific research organization. Member of Task Force on Procurement.

Goubeau, Vincent dePaul, Philadelphia. De la Salle Institute, New York City. Vice President, Director of Materials, Radio Corporation of America. Member of Advisory Committee to Task Force on Procurement.

Grady, Paul, New York. University of Illinois. Partner in firm of Price Waterhouse & Company. Chairman, Task Force on Lending Agencies, first and second Hoover Commissions.

Graham, Evarts A., St. Louis, Mo. Princeton University and Rush Medical College. President, American College of Surgeons. Editor, *Year Book of Surgery* since 1929. Professor of Surgery, Washington University School of Medicine. Member of Task Force on Medical Services.

Greene, Leroy D., Bethlehem, Pa. Formerly with Bethlehem Steel Company, in charge of buying and selling of scrap and demolition activities; member of Somervell Mission to Europe on disposition of war scrap; also member of E.C.A. missions in 1949 and 1949 looking into disposition of German scrap. Now Consultant to Office of Defense Mobilization. Member of Task Force on Use and Disposal of Surplus Property; Committee on Business Organization of the Department of Defense, and its Subcommittees on Depot Utilization and Business Enterprises in the Department of Defense.

Gregg, Alan, New York. Harvard University. Staff, International Health Board of the Rockefeller Foundation; Associate Director and Director Medical Sciences of Rockefeller Foundation and Vice President of the Foundation. Chairman, Advisory Committee for Biology and Medicine, Atomic Energy Commission. Member, Health Resources Advisory

Committee, Office of Defense Mobilization. Member of Task Force on Medical Services.

Growdon, James P., Pittsburgh, Pa. University of Nebraska. Engineer of Navy's underground oil storage installations at Pearl Harbor. Member of Task Force on Water Resources and Power.

Hall, Joseph B., Cincinnati, Ohio. University of Chicago. President of the Kroger Company. Chairman of Board of Trustees, Ohio University. Former Chairman, Commercial Activities Subcommittee of Advisory Committee on Fiscal Organization and Procedures, Department of Defense. Member of the Committee on Business Organization of the Department of Defense, and Chairman of Committee's Subcommittee on Business Enterprises in the Department of Defense.

Harno, Albert J., Urbana, Ill. Dakota Wesleyan, Yale universities. Formerly President, Association of American Law Schools; President, National Conference Commissioners on Uniform State Laws. Dean, College of Law, University of Illinois. Chairman, Board of Directors, American Judicature Society. Member of Task Force on Legal Services and Procedure.

Harper, Berchel H., Omaha, Neb. University of Nebraska. Secretary of Northern Natural Gas Company. Member of Task Force on Paperwork Management.

Hawley, Paul R., Chicago, Ill. Major General, U.S. Army Medical Corps (Retired). Indiana University and University of Cincinnati. Head of Blue Cross and Blue Shield commissions. Director, American College of Surgeons; President, Health Service, Inc. Member of first Hoover Commission's Task Force on Federal Medical Services. Member of Task Force on Medical Services.

Hennessy, John L., New York. Hotel and Restaurant Executive. Former Chairman of the Board, Statler Hotels. President of J. L. Hennessy Associates, Inc., food consulting firm. Member of the Task Force on Subsistence Services.*

Hicks, Clifford E., New York, N.Y. New York University. President New York Dock Company and New York Dock Railway. Member of Task Force on Subsistence Services, Committee on Business Organization of the Department of Defense, and Chairman of the Subcommittee on Depot Utilization.

Hill, John Anthony, Armonk, N.Y. Amherst College and Columbia Law School. President and Director of Air Reduction Company, Inc. Chairman, National Security Industrial Association. Member of Task Force on Real Property.

Hinds, Julian, Los Angeles. University of Texas. Formerly with United States Bureau of Reclamation; engineer in charge of Calles Irrigation Project and Dam, Mexico; engineer, Department of Water and Power, City of Los Angeles; General Manager and Chief Engineer (Retired), Metropolitan Water District of Southern California. Member of Task Force on Water Resources and Power.

* Deceased, July 2, 1955.

Hollers, James P., San Antonio, Tex. Tulane University. Member, American Dental Association, formerly Chairman of its Army and Navy Committee, and formerly Chairman of Reference Committee, Federal Government Dental Services. Member of Medical Services Task Force Subcommittee on Dentistry.

Holifield, Chet, Los Angeles. Member, U.S. House of Representatives, 78th to 83d Congresses, 19th California District. Owner of a men's apparel store in Norwalk, Calif. Member of Hoover Commission.

Hollings, Ernest Frederick, Charleston, S.C. The Citadel and University of South Carolina. Lieutenant Governor, State of South Carolina. Member of Task Force on Intelligence Activities.

Hollister, Solomon C., Ithaca, New York. University of Wisconsin. Dean of the College of Engineering at Cornell University. Formerly civil engineer on municipal, structural, and flood-control projects in the States of Washington and Oregon. Chairman or member of numerous engineering associations and advisory groups. Member of Hoover Commission.

Hook, Charles R., Middletown, Ohio. With Armco Steel Corporation since 1902. Advanced from Night Superintendent to President and now Chairman of the Board. Served in various Government activities. Chairman of Committee on Business Organization of the Department of Defense.

Hoover, Herbert, New York. Stanford University. Thirty-first President of the United States. Formerly Chairman of the Commission for Relief in Belgium, United States Food Administrator, Member of the War Trade Council, and Director of Relief and Rehabilitation of Europe on behalf of the Allied Governments. Secretary of Commerce under Presidents Harding and Coolidge. At the request of President Truman, undertook coordination of the world food supplies of thirty-eight countries in the famine of 1946, and in 1947. Chairman of the first and second Hoover Commissions.

Horner, Wesley Winans, St. Louis, Mo. Washington University. Formerly Chief Engineer, City of St. Louis; Member, National Resources Planning Board; Member, Engineering Advisory Committee of Atomic Energy Commission. Now engineering consultant. Member of Task Force on Water Resources and Power.

Horton, Horace Babcock, Chicago, Ill. University of Chicago and University of Illinois. President, Chicago Bridge & Iron Company. Member, War Labor Board, World War II. Member of Task Force on Procurement.

Hotchkis, Preston, San Marino, Calif. Universities of California and Southern California, College of Law. Now Chairman of the Investment Committee of Founders' Insurance Co.; President of Central Business Properties, Inc.; Executive Vice President of the Fred H. Bixby Ranch Company. Member of Task Force on Lending Agencies.

Houston, John C., Jr., Washington, D.C. Yale University. Formerly

Executive Vice Chairman, Munitions Board, Department of Defense; Commissioner of Civilian Production; served on White House staff, and as Director, Program Controls Bureau, War Production Board; formerly Treasurer, R. P. Adams Company, Inc., Buffalo, New York, and Vice President, Stacom Industries, Inc., Long Island City, New York. Member of Advisory Committee to Task Force on Procurement.

Hovde, Frederick L., Lafayette, Ind. University of Minnesota and Oxford. President of Purdue University. Member of Research Advisory Board of National Research Council. Member of the Subcommittee on Research Activities in the Department of Defense.

Humphreys, H. E., Jr., Scarsdale, N.Y. University of Pennsylvania. President and Chairman of the Board of United States Rubber Company. Member of Task Force on Budget and Accounting.

Ilgenfritz, Carl A., Pittsburgh, Pa. Public schools. Vice President for Purchases and Director, United States Steel Corporation of Delaware; member, Advisory Committee to Task Force on Federal Supply, first Hoover Commission. Member of Task Force on Procurement.

Jackson, Robert H., Washington, D.C. Albany Law School. Successively Assistant Attorney General, Solicitor General, and Attorney General of the United States. Appointed Associate Justice of U.S. Supreme Court in 1941. Named Chief of Counsel for U.S. to conduct prosecution of trials of European Axis War Criminals. Consultant to Task Force on Legal Services and Procedure.*

Jarchow, Christian E., Chicago, Ill. University of Illinois. Formerly Auditor, Comptroller, and now Executive Vice President of the International Harvester Company. Member of Task Force on Budget and Accounting.

Jirgal, John, Chicago, Ill. University of Wisconsin. Specialist in utility economics. In active practice as a specialist in appraisal, financial investigation, and rate making; has done extensive business reorganization, recapitalization, and liquidation work. Member of Task Force on Water Resources and Power.

Johnson, Earl D., Washington, D.C. University of Wisconsin. Assistant Secretary of the Army for Manpower and Reserve Forces, 1950–1952; and Under Secretary of the Army, 1952–1953. Participated as Defense Department Representative in negotiations for Japanese Peace Treaty and Administrative Agreement with Japan. Now President of the Air Transport Association and Air Cargo, Inc.; Director and Chairman of the Board, Panama Canal Company. Member of Advisory Committee to Task Force on Procurement.

Jolly, Thomas D., Pittsburgh, Pa. Carnegie Institute of Technology. Served in U.S. Army in World War I. Former Chief Engineer and Director of Purchasing, now Vice President, Aluminum Company of America. Member, Advisory Committee on Federal Supply, first Hoover Commis-

* Deceased, October 9, 1954.

sion. Member of Task Force on Use and Disposal of Surplus Property and Task Force on Real Property.

Jones, Ollie E., Chicago, Ill. University of Illinois. With Swift & Co. since 1912, now Executive Vice President (his duties include sales and advertising) and Director. Served as member of the Food Industry War Commission. Director of the Grocery Manufacturers of America. Member of Task Force on Subsistence Services.

Josephs, Devereux C., New York, N.Y. Harvard University. Formerly Chairman, Teachers Insurance and Annuity Association; former President, Carnegie Corporation of New York. Now Chairman of Board, New York Life Insurance Company. Member of Task Force on Personnel and Civil Service.

Kanzler, Ernest, Detroit, Mich. Universities of Michigan and Harvard. Chief, Automotive Branch and Director for Operations, War Production Board, during World War II. Vice Chairman of the Board, Universal C.I.T. Credit Corporation. Member of Task Force on Overseas Economic Operations.

Kearns, Henry, La Verne, Calif. University of Utah. President and General Manager, San Gabriel Valley Motors. Director and member of several committees of the United States Chamber of Commerce and active in numerous California State and local civic organizations. Member of Task Force on Intelligence Activities.

Keller, Arnold B., Hobart, Ind. Mount Morris College. Formerly with the Rutland (Ill.) Bank and the Gary (Ind.) State Bank. Formerly Vice President and Treasurer, now Senior Consultant and Director, International Harvester Company. Member, Advisory Committeee, Task Force on Lending Agencies, first Hoover Commission. Member of Task Force on Lending Agencies.

Kelly, Mervin J., Short Hills, N.J. Missouri School of Mines and Metallurgy, University of Kentucky, and University of Chicago. Formerly physicist with Western Electric Company. Member of several technical societies and institutes; served on various governmental committees. Formerly physicist, now President, Bell Telephone Laboratories. Member of Task Force on Procurement, Committee on Business Organization of the Department of Defense, and Chairman of Subcommittee on Research Activities in the Department of Defense.

Kennedy, Joseph P., New York. Harvard University. Former Ambassador to Great Britain. Formerly President, Columbia Trust Company of Boston; President and Chairman, Film Booking Offices of America; Chairman of Keith, Albee, Orpheum Theatres Corporation; President and Chairman, Pathé Exchange, Inc. Served as Chairman of the U.S. Securities and Exchange Commission and U.S. Maritime Commission. Member of both Hoover Commissions.

Ketchum, Jay C., Detroit, Mich. Now Executive Vice President and General Manager, Michigan Medical Service (Blue Shield). Member of Board of Directors, Health Service, Inc., Chicago, Ill. Senior Vice President, Medical Indemnity of America, Inc., Columbus, Ohio. Member of Medical Services Task Force Subcommittee on Health Insurance.

Kimball, Robert M., Cambridge, Mass. Secretary, Massachusetts Institute of Technology. Administrative Associate Director, Los Alamos Scientific Laboratory, N.M., 1948–1950. Member of Subcommittee on Research Activities in the Department of Defense.

King, Arthur Franklin, San Francisco, Calif. Ohio Wesleyan University. Formerly with McGraw-Hill Publishing Company, and President, King Publications. Member of Committee on Business Organization of the Department of Defense.

Klein, Julius, Washington, D.C. Harvard University. Formerly Chief of Latin American Division, Department of Commerce; U.S. Commercial Attaché, Buenos Aires; Director, Bureau of Foreign and Domestic Commerce; Assistant Secretary of Commerce; and Consultant to various governments. Member of Task Force on Overseas Economic Operations.

Klumpp, Theodore George, New York, N.Y. Princeton and Harvard universities and Philadelphia College of Pharmacy and Science. President of Winthrop-Stearns, Inc., N.Y., and Winthrop Products, Inc., of New Jersey; and Vice President of U.S. Pharmacopeia. Chairman of Task Force on Medical Services (appointed Chairman, September 26, 1954).

Kracke, Edward A., Montclair, N.J. Harvard University. Formerly President of New Yok State Society of Certified Public Accountants; served on many committees of the American Institute of Accountants, as a member of the Board of Examiners of the Institute. Partner, Haskins and Sells. Member of Task Force on Water Resources and Power.

Kraft, John H., Chicago, Ill. Long career with the Kraft Foods Company and its operating head since 1937, when he became Executive Vice President. Retired recently as Chairman of the Board. Vice President and Director of National Dairy Products Corporation and Director of the National Cheese Institute. Member of the Task Force on Subsistence Services.

Kresl, Carl, Hinsdale, Ill. University of Chicago. Formerly Merchandise Supervisor, Sears, Roebuck & Company. Member of Task Force on Use and Disposal of Surplus Property.

Krimendahl, Herbert F., Indianapolis, Ind. Formerly President of Crampton Canneries, Inc., Celina, Ohio. President of Stokeley-Van Camp, Inc., of Indianapolis. In 1942 was Tin Administrator for the War Production Board. Since 1942 has been Member of the Advisory Committee on Research and Marketing Act, Department of Agriculture. Member of Task Force on Subsistence Services.

Lack, Frederick R., Southport, Conn. Harvard University. Vice President, Western Electric Co., Inc., New York. Member, Advisory Committee to the Task Force on Procurement.

Landis, James McCauley, New York, N.Y. Princeton and Harvard universities. Chairman, Securities and Exchange Commission; Dean, Harvard Law School; Chairman, Civil Aeronautics Board; Member, Commission on Uniform State Laws, Massachusetts. Member of Task Force on Legal Services and Procedure.

Leahy, Emmett J., Darien, Conn. Catholic University. Founded Management Consultants Service, the Business Archives Center in New York, and the Security Records Center in New Jersey, now consolidated in Leahy & Company, of which he is President. Chairman of the Task Force on Records Management, first Hoover Commission. Chairman of Task Force on Paperwork Management.

Leavell, Hugh Rodman, Boston, Mass. Universities of Virginia, Harvard, and Yale. Formerly Medical Director, U.S. Public Health Service. Professor of Public Health Practice, Harvard School of Public Health. Member, first Hoover Commission's Task Force on Federal Medical Services. Member of Task Force on Medical Services.

Lee, J. Bracken, Salt Lake City, Utah. Governor of Utah. Formerly in insurance business and Mayor of Price, Utah. Member of Task Force on Water Resources and Power.

Lee, Joseph A., Greenwich, Conn. Yale University. First Vice President of Standard Brands, Inc. (recently retired). Trustee, American Bakers Foundation; Treasurer, Director, and member of Executive Committee, American Institute of Baking. Member of Task Force on Subsistence Services.

Livingstone, Raymond S., Cleveland, Ohio. Case Institute of Technology. Has been with Thompson Products, Inc. since 1929 and is now Vice President in charge of Personnel. Member of Subcommittee on Special Personnel Problems in the Department of Defense.

Lotz, John R., New York, N.Y. University of Illinois. Former Chairman of Board, Stone & Webster Engineering Corporation. Consultant, E.C.A. Industrial Advisory Committee for revision of reparations and dismantling plants in Germany. Chairman of Board, Overseas Consultants, Inc.; retained by Secretary of War to report on impact of reparations on Japan, and by Government of Iran to study necessity for, and implementation of, its seven-year development plan. Chairman of Task Force on Real Property, and member of Committee on Business Organization of the Department of Defense.

McCarthy, John T., St. Paul, Minn. President, the Jersey Bread Co., Toledo, Ohio. Served as Chairman and President of the American Bakers Association, now Chairman of its National Affairs Committee. Member of Secretary of War's Food Commission in 1946. Member of the Task Force on Subsistence Services.

McClellan, John L., Camden, Arkansas. United States Senator. Former Member, U.S. House of Representatives, Sixth Arkansas District. Member, law firm of Gaughan, McClellan and Gaughan. Member of the first and second Hoover Commissions.

McCormick, Chauncey, Chicago, Ill. Yale University. Director, American Relief Commission in eastern Poland, later in Romania. Formerly member, Illinois Child Welfare Commission; Chairman of the Board, Illinois Children's Home and Aid Society; Trustee, Chicago Foundlings

Home. President, Art Institute of Chicago. Chairman of Task Force on Medical Services.*

McFarland, Carl, Missoula, Mont. Universities of Montana and Harvard. Formerly Assistant to Attorney General of the United States. President of Montana State University. Member of Task Force on Legal Services and Procedure.

McGowan, Donald A., Arlington, Va. Roman Catholic Priest (Rt. Rev. Msgr.). North American College, Rome, Italy. Formerly Superintendent, St. Elizabeth's Hospital, Boston; President, New England Hospital Assembly; and Vice President, Massachusetts Hospital and American Hospital associations. Now Director, Bureau of Health and Hospitals, National Catholic Welfare Conference. Chairman, Medical Services Task Force Subcommittee on Health Insurance.

McHugh, Glenn, New York, N.Y. Columbia Law School. Vice President of the Equitable Life Assurance Society, in charge of Real Estate Operations. Former Assistant Counsel, Office of Legislative Counsel, U.S. Senate, and Special Assistant to the Administrator of the Export-Import Bank. Member of Task Force on Real Property.

MacLean, Basil C., New York. McGill and Johns Hopkins universities. Formerly Superintendent of Montreal General Hospital and Touro Infirmary of New Orleans; Past President of American College of Hospital Administrators; Director, Strong Memorial Hospital and Professor of Hospital Administration, University of Rochester. Commissioner of Hospitals, New York City. Member of Task Force on Medical Services, and Member of Subcommittee on Depot Utilization of the Committee on Business Organization of the Department of Defense.

Malone, Ross L., Jr., Roswell, N.M. Washington and Lee University. Formerly City Attorney, Roswell, N.M.; Deputy Attorney General of United States. Trustee, Southwestern Legal Foundation. Member of Task Force on Legal Services and Procedure.

Mardikian, George M., San Francisco, Calif. Long career in food business, including operation of two restaurants. In charge of feeding delegates to 1945 United Nations Conference in San Francisco. Made studies resulting in substantial improvement of U.S. Army feeding programs in United States, Europe, and Far East. Now food consultant to Quartermaster General. Member of the Task Force on Subsistence Services.

Martin, Walter B., Norfolk, Va. Johns Hopkins University and Virginia Polytechnic Institute. Chief of Medicine, St. Vincents Hospital, and Attending Specialist, U.S. Public Health Service Hospital, Norfolk. Civilian Medical Consultant to Army Surgeon General. President, American Medical Association. Member of Task Force on Medical Services.

Mattei, Albert Chester, San Francisco, Calif. Stanford University. President, Honolulu Oil Corp. Member, National Petroleum War Committee, World War II. Member of Task Force on Water Resources and Power.

* Deceased, September 8, 1954.

Maxwell, David F., Philadelphia, Pa. University of Pennsylvania. Member, Pennsylvania and American Bar Associations (Chairman, House of Delegates, 1952–1953). Member of Task Force on Legal Services and Procedure.

Mead, George Houk, Dayton, Ohio. Hobart College and Massachusetts Institute of Technology. Member and Chairman, Business Advisory Council, U.S. Department of Commerce. Chairman of the Board, Mead Corporation. Commissioner, first Hoover Commission. Member of Task Force on Procurement and of the Committee on Business Organization of the Department of Defense.

Medina, Harold R., New York, N.Y. Princeton and Columbia universities. Judge, U.S. District Court, Southern District of New York. Now Judge of the Court of Appeals for Second District. Member of Task Force on Legal Services and Procedure.

Miller, James Roscoe, Evanston, Ill. Universities of Utah, and Northwestern. Formerly Medical Director, Chicago-Northwestern Railroad. Member, Commission on Veterans' Medical Problems, National Research Council. Director, Northwestern University School of Medicine. President, Northwestern University. Member of Task Force on Medical Services.

Miller, Joseph L., Washington, D.C. Haverford College. Member of various Government boards and commissions dealing with labor problems. Member, Advisory Committee to Task Force on Procurement.

Miller, Leslie A., Cheyenne, Wyo. Formerly Member, House of Representatives and Senate, State of Wyoming. Collector of Internal Revenue, Wyoming District. Former Governor of Wyoming. Chairman of Task Force on Natural Resources, first Hoover Commission. Member of Task Force on Water Resources and Power.

Mitchell, Don G., Summit, N.J. Cincinnati, Florida, and Northeastern universities. Now Chairman of the Board, Sylvania Electric Products Company; Chairman of the Executive Committee and a Director of American Management Association; Member, Board of Trustees, National Industrial Conference Board. Member of Task Force on Personnel and Civil Service.

Mitchell, Sidney A., New York. Yale. Formerly Member, Bonbright & Co., Inc. Served with the Navy Department in Washington, D.C. (distinguished civilian service award) and with the Department of State. Treasurer, Belgian American Education Foundation. Former Chairman of the Citizens Committee for the Hoover Report. Executive Director of the first Hoover Commission. Member of the Hoover Commission.

Mooney, James D., New York, N.Y. New York University, Case Institute of Technology. Formerly Vice President, and Member, Board of Directors, General Motors Corporation; formerly President and Chairman of the Board, Willys Overland Motors, Inc. Member of Task Force on Use and Disposal of Surplus Property.

Moreell, Ben, Pittsburgh, Pa. Washington University. Admiral U.S. Navy (Retired). Served in Navy 1917–1947. During World War II, Chief, Bureau of Yards and Docks, and employed in many other governmental activities. Now Chairman of the Board, Jones & Laughlin Steel Corporation. Chairman of Task Force on Water Resources and Power.

Morrison, Harry Winford, Boise, Idaho. University of Idaho. Formerly Superintendent, U.S. Bureau of Reclamation, Boise, Idaho. In active practice, engineering and contracting. Director of Six Companies, Inc., builders of Hoover and Parker dams. Member of Task Force on Water Resources and Power.

Mosher, Ira, Longmeadow, Mass. Began career as certified public accountant in 1913; became successively Comptroller, Treasurer, Vice President, and General Manager of American Optical Company. Chairman of the Board, Russell Harrington Cutlery Company. Now President of Ira Mosher Associates, Inc. Former President, National Association of Manufacturers. Vice Chairman of Task Force on Procurement.

Mulholland, H. B., Charlottesville, Va. University of Toronto; University of Virginia, Department of Medicine. President of the American Diabetes Association. Vice Chairman, Council on Medical Service, American Medical Association. Member of the Medical Services Task Force Subcommittee on Health Insurance.

Mullendore, William C., Los Angeles, Calif. University of Michigan. General Attorney, Executive Vice President, President, now Chairman of the Board, Southern California Edison Company. Member of the Task Force on Real Property.

Murrow, Lacey V., Washington, D.C. Washington State College. Director of Transportation and Research with the Association of American Railroads. Member of Task Force on Water Resources and Power.

Neely, Frank H., Atlanta, Ga. Chairman of the Board of Rich's in Atlanta. Chairman, Federal Reserve Bank of Atlanta. Member of the Task Force on Procurement and of the Committee on Business Organization of the Department of Defense.

Newnam, Frank H., Jr., Houston, Tex. Texas A. & M. College. Formerly Engineer with Texas Highway Department. Chief Engineer for Headquarters S.O.S. China Theater; Chief of Engineering Division, Galveston District, Corps of Engineers. Now in practice as engineering consultant. Member of Task Force on Water Resources and Power.

Owens, Frederick E., Port Washington, N.Y. Republic Aviation Corporation, Farmingdale, N.Y. Member, Advisory Committee to the Task Force on Procurement.

Paul, Willard S., Oklawaha, Fla. Lieutenant General U.S.A. (Retired). Clark University, Dartmouth College, Johns Hopkins and American universities. Now Assistant to the Director, Office of Defense Mobilization and Consultant to the Assistant Secretary of Defense for Manpower and Personnel. Member of Task Force on Personnel and Civil Service, Committee on Business Organization of the Department of Defense, and the Subcommittee on Special Personnel Problems in the Department of Defense.

Peale, Mundy I., Garden City, N.Y. University of Chicago. President, General Manager, and Director of Republic Aviation Corporation. Chairman, Board of Governors, Aircraft Industrial Association, 1953; Chairman, Industrial Consulting Committee, National Advisory Committee for Aeronautics, 1954. Member of the Task Force on Procurement.

Peck, David W., New York, N.Y. Wabash College, Harvard Law School. Now Presiding Justice, Appellate Division, First Department, Supreme Court of New York. Member of Task Force on Legal Services and Procedure.

Pirnie, Malcolm, New York, N.Y. Harvard University and Rensselaer Polytechnic Institute. Now in general practice as consulting engineer and consultant to various Government agencies. Member of Task Force on Water Resources and Power.

Polk, Harry E., Williston, N.D. University of North Dakota. Owner of *Williston Herald* and other weekly papers in North Dakota and Montana. State Director, National Reclamation Association. Member of Task Force on Water Resources and Power.

Pound, Roscoe, Watertown, Mass. University of Nebraska and Harvard Law School. Formerly Professor, Harvard University; Dean of Harvard Law School. Member of Task Force on Water Resources and Power.

Prentis, Henning W., Jr., Lancaster, Pa. University of Missouri and University of Cincinnati. President, Armstrong Cork Company, 1934–1950; Chairman of the Board since 1950. Past President, National Association of Manufacturers. Chairman, Pennsylvania Post-War Planning Commission. Headed survey group to evaluate Mutual Security operations in the United Kingdom. Chairman of Task Force on Overseas Economic Operations.

Price, Gwilym Alexander, Pittsburgh, Pa. University of Pittsburgh. Captain, U.S. Army, World War I. President of Westinghouse Electric Corporation. Member of Task Force on Budget and Accounting.

Proctor, Robert, Boston, Mass. Dartmouth College and Harvard University. Member, firm of Choate, Hall and Stewart, Boston, Mass. Member of Task Force on Procurement.

Ramspeck, Robert, Washington, D.C. Atlanta Law School. Member of 71st–79th Congresses; Vice-President, Air Transport Association of America; Chairman, U.S. Civil Service Commission. Now Vice President, Eastern Air Lines, Inc. Member of Task Force on Personnel and Civil Service.

Reavis, John Wallace, Cleveland, Ohio. Cornell University. Now in active practice of law. Member of Task Force on Water Resources and Power.

Reid, Thomas R., Dearborn, Mich. University of Arkansas. Director of Civic Affairs, Ford Motor Company. Member of Committee on Business Organization of the Department of Defense and Chairman of the Subcommittee on Special Personnel Problems in the Department of Defense.

Renard, George A., New York. University of Illinios. Formerly practiced law in Illinois; Executive Secretary-Treasurer, National Association of Purchasing Agents; Member, U.S. Navy Advisory Committee on Procurement, and U.S. Munitions Advisory Board on Stockpiling Materials. Member of Task Force on Use and Disposal of Surplus Property, and Task Force on Procurement.

Richberg, Donald Randall, Washington, D.C. Universities of Chicago and Harvard. General Counsel, National Recovery Administration. Now in active practice of law. Member of Task Force on Water Resources and Power.

Rickenbacker, Edward Vernon, New York. International Correspondence School. In World War I commanded 94th Aero Pursuit Squadron and personally credited with twenty-six victories. World War II activities included special missions for Secretary of War to nine foreign countries and areas. U.S. and foreign Government awards include the Congressional Medal of Honor. Since 1933 with Eastern Air Lines, Inc., as General Manager and President; now Chairman of the Board. Member of Task Force on Intelligence Activities.

Roberts, Arthur B., Cleveland, Ohio. Case Institute. Formerly Director of City Public Utilities, Cleveland. Member of Task Force on Water Resources and Power.

Roberts, George, New York. Yale and Harvard universities. Formerly Special Counsel to Reconstruction Finance Corporation, and member of Secretary of War's Advisory Board. Consultant to the Task Force on Legal Services and Procedure.

Robertson, Reuben B., Jr., Cincinnati, Ohio. Yale University. Served in U.S. Army during World War II. Former President, Champion Paper and Fibre Company. Now Deputy Secretary of Defense. Member of Committee on Business Organization of the Department of Defense and the Subcommittee on Special Personnel Problems in the Department of Defense.

Russell, Donald Stuart, Spartanburg, S.C. University of Michigan. Formerly member, Price Adjustment Board, War Department; Assistant to Director of Economic Stabilization; Assistant to Director of War Mobilization; Deputy Director, Office of War Mobilization Reconversion; Assistant Secretary of State. Now President, University of South Carolina. Member of Task Force on Intelligence Activities.

Sawyer, Charles, Cincinnati, Ohio. Oberlin College and University of Cincinnati Law School. Formerly member of Cincinnati City Council; Lieutenant Governor of Ohio; Ambassador to Belgium; Minister to Luxembourg; U.S. Secretary of Commerce. Now senior member of Dinsmore, Shohl, Sawyer & Dinsmore, Cincinnati. Member of Task Force on Overseas Economic Operations.

Sawyer, Robert William, Bend, Ore. Harvard University. Formerly practiced law in Boston; member, Oregon State Highway Commission; President, Oregon Reclamation Congress; member and President, National Reclamation Association; Oregon Economic Council. Now Chairman, Oregon Capitol Planning Commission; Editor-Publisher of *Bend* (Oregon) *Bulletin.* Member of Task Force on Water Resources and Power.

Schneider, Franz, New York, N.Y. Formerly Financial Editor of *New York Post, New York Evening Star.* Deputy Administrator of War Shipping Administration during World War II; Special Adviser to the Director of Office of War Mobilization and Reconversion. Now Executive Vice President of Newmont Mining Corporation. Task Force on Procurement and of the Committee on Business Organization of the Department of Defense.

Schoeny, Leo J., New Orleans, La. Loyola University. Past President and Secretary of Louisiana State Dental Society. Formerly Chairman of Louisiana State Dental Society's Bureau of Dental Health Education. Member of Medical Service Task Force Subcommittee on Dentistry.

Shannon, William D., Seattle, Wash. University of Michigan. Connected with engineering staff of Detroit River Tunnel and other projects. Washington State Senator since 1950. Member of Task Force on Water Resources and Power.

Shoemaker, Perry M., Summit, N.J. University of Michigan and Yale University. With Pennsylvania, Erie, and New York New Haven & Hartford railroads until 1941, when he became Transportation Assistant to the President, Delaware, Lackawanna & Western Railroad; now President; Member and former President, American Association of Railroad Superintendents. Member of the Task Force on Subsistence Services; Committee on Business Organization of the Department of Defense, and its Subcommittee on Depot Utilization, and Chairman of the Subcommittee on Transportation Activities in the Department of Defense.

Smith George P. F., Chicago, Ill. With Borg-Warner Corporation, Chicago, since 1938, where he is now Vice President. Member, Board of Governors, National Electric Manufacturers Association; Board of Directors, National Association of Manufacturers; Procurement and Production Industry Advisory Committee of the Department of Defense. Vice Chairman of the Procurement Task Force; member of the Subcommittees on Business Enterprises in the Department of Defense, and on Depot Utilization of the Committee on Business Organization of the Department of Defense.

Smith, Reginald Heber, Boston, Mass. Harvard University. Vice President, National Legal Aid Association. Assistant Editor of the *Journal* of the American Bar Association, and Director, Survey of Legal Profession in America for American Bar Association. Member of Task Force on Legal Services and Procedure.

Smith, Robert J., Dallas, Tex. Jefferson School of Law. President and Director of Pioneer Air Lines, Inc. Formerly Vice Chairman, National Security Resources Board. President of National Air Council and Air Transport Association. Member of Subcommittee on Special Personnel Problems in the Department of Defense.

Storey, Robert G., Dallas, Texas. University of Texas. Dean, School of Law, Southern Methodist University; President, Southwestern Legal

Foundation; former President, American Bar Association; now President, Inter-American Bar Association; Member, International Bar Association. U.S. Executive Trial Counsel to Justice Jackson in Nuremberg trial of major Axis war criminals, 1945–1946. Member of the Hoover Commission.

Spang, Joseph P., Jr., Boston, Mass. Harvard College. President, the Gillette Co., Boston. Headed mission to France to study Mutual Security operations, February–March 1953. Member, business mission to Yugoslavia, June 1954. Member of Task Force on Overseas Economic Operations.

Starr, Edward, Jr., Philadelphia, Pa. Yale and Pennsylvania universities. Member of a committee for disposal of overseas surplus in the Pacific area after World War II. Now partner, Drexel & Company. Member of Task Force on Use and Disposal of Surplus Property.

Stason, E. Blythe, Ann Arbor, Mich. Universities of Michigan and Wisconsin and Massachusetts Institute of Technology. Formerly Michigan Commissioner in National Conference on Uniform State Laws; member, Michigan Constitution Revision Study Committee. Dean of Michigan University Law School. Member of Task Force on Legal Services and Procedures.

Stewart, J. Harold, Boston. Mass. Northeastern University. Past President of Massachusetts Society of Certified Public Accountants and of American Institute of Accountants. Chairman of Task Force on Budget and Accounting.

Stilwell, Charles J., Shaker Heights, Ohio. Denison University. Starting in 1910, entire business career with Warner & Swasey Company, machine tools, Cleveland, Ohio; now President. Member, Army Ordnance Association, National Machine Tool Builders Association (former President). Member of the Task Force on Procurement.

Stockton, Charles H., Boston, Mass. Harvard College and Harvard Law School. During World War II served in office of General Counsel, Navy Department, and became Assistant Counsel for the Bureau of Ships. Member of Advisory Committee to Task Force on Procurement.

Stouffer, Gordon A., Cleveland, Ohio. Chairman of the Board, the Stouffer Corporation. Also President, the Portersville Stainless Equipment Corp. Member of the Task Force on Subsistence Services.

Suits, C. Guy, Schenectady, N.Y. University of Wisconsin. Presently Vice President and Director of Research with General Electric Company. Member of Subcommittee on Research Activities in the Department of Defense.

Tangeman, Walter W., Cincinnati, Ohio. University of Cincinnati. President of University of Cincinnati Research Foundation; member of the Executive Committee of Machinery and Allied Products Institute. Executive Vice President, the Cincinnati Milling Machine Co. Member of Task Force on Use and Disposal of Surplus Property.

Tiffany, Kenneth C., Royal Oak, Mich. University of Detroit. Served in Finance and Procurement in War Department during World War II.

Vice President, Burroughs Adding Machine Company. Member of Task Force on Budget and Accounting.

Tipton, Royce J., Denver, Colo. University of Colorado. Formerly connected with the Rio Grande Compact negotiations on behalf of Colorado; Consulting Engineer to U.S. Bureau of Reclamation; Colorado Water Conservation Board; Colorado Planning Commission. Adviser to foreign governments on water resources. Chief Engineer, San Luis Valley Land & Mining Company. Member of Task Force on Water Resources and Power.

Tuck, William Hallam, Upper Marlboro, Md. Princeton University. Member of Hoover Relief Organizations during and after World War I and after World War II. War Department Mission on Supplies for Japan and Korea; Director General, U.N. International Refugee Organization. Served with British Expeditionary Forces and U.S. Army, World War I; Captain U.S.N.R., World War II. Director, Allied Chemical & Dye Corporation. Vice President, Belgian American Educational Foundation. Member Task Force on Personnel and Civil Service.

Tuttle, Elbert Parr, Atlanta, Ga. Cornell University. Formerly General Counsel for the Treasury Department. Now Judge of the U.S. Court of Appeals, Fifth Circuit. Member of Task Force on Legal Services and Procedure.

Vanderbilt, Arthur T., Newark, N.J. Wesleyan, Columbia and Tulane universities. Formerly Dean, New York University Law School; Judge, Circuit Court, New Jersey. Now Chief Justice of the Supreme Court of New Jersey. Consultant to Task Force on Legal Services and Procedure.

Van Steenwyk, Elmer A., Ambler, Pa. Mankato Teachers College and University of Minnesota. Executive Vice President of the Associated Hospital Service of Philadelphia and the Hospital Service Plan of the Lehigh Valley. Present Chairman, Government Relations Committee of the Blue Cross Commission. Member, Medical Services Task Force Subcommittee on Health Insurance.

White, Leonard D., Chicago, Ill. Dartmouth, Clark, and Harvard and Chicago universities. Taught at Clark College, Dartmouth College, and the University of Chicago. Formely Member, U.S. Civil Service Commission and President's Committee on Civil Service Improvement. Member, U.S. Civil Service Commission Loyalty Review Board, 1950–1952. Now Professor of Public Administration, University of Chicago. Member of Task Force on Personnel and Civil Service.

Wilbur, Dwight L., San Francisco, Calif. University of Pennsylvania. Assistant Chief and Chief, Medical Service, U.S. Naval Hospital, Oakland, Calif., during World War II. Associated with the Medical Services of the Veterans' Administration and the Department of the Army; connected with a number of hospital staffs, medical organizations and publications. Now member of faculty, Stanford University School of Medicine. Member of Task Force on Medical Services.

Williams, Clyde E., Columbus, Ohio. University of Utah. President of Battelle Institute since 1929. Member of Advisory Committee, Atomic

Energy Commission. President and member of Board of Trustees of American Allergy Foundation. Member of Subcommittee on Research Activities in the Department of Defense.

Winternitz, Milton C., New Haven, Conn. Johns Hopkins and Yale universities. Formerly Dean of Yale University Medical School, Professor of Pathology, and Associate Director, Institute of Human Relations, Yale University. Now Chairman, Division of Medical Sciences, National Research Council; also Director, Board of Science Advisers, Jane Coffin Childs Memorial Fund for Cancer Research. Member of Task Force on Medical Services.

Wolcott, Robert Wilson, Paoli, Pa. Lehigh University. President, Lukens Steel Company, 1925–1949. Now Chairman of the Board. Chairman of Task Force on Procurement and member of Committee on Business Organization of the Department of Defense.

Wood, Robert E., Chicago, Ill. United States Military Academy. Director of Panama Railway and Chief Quartermaster General of the Army in construction of the Panama Canal, 1905–1915; Acting Quartermaster General, U.S.A., during World War I. Entered business life in 1919 and was until recently Chairman of the Board of Sears, Roebuck & Company. Chairman of Task Force on Use and Disposal of Surplus Property and Member of Committee on Business Organization of the Department of Defense.

Wooten, Benjamin Harrison, Dallas, Tex. North Texas State College. Formerly President and Chairman of Board, Federal Home Loan Bank of Little Rock. Now President, First National Bank in Dallas; Chairman of Board, North Texas State College; Vice President, United Defense Fund, Inc. Member of Task Force on Real Property.

Wright, Edward Ledwidge, Little Rock, Ark. Little Rock College and Georgetown University. Served on National Conference of Commissioners on Uniform State Laws. Now in active law practice. Member of Task Force on Legal Services and Procedure.

Wright, J. David, Cleveland, Ohio. Adelbert College and Western Reserve Law School. President, Thompson Products, Inc. Member of Task Force on Budget and Accounting.

Index

35637

REMOTE JK 643 .C53 M3 1956 / The Hoover report, 1953-1955